Frommer's®

# Best Day Trips from London

5th Edition

by Christi Daugherty



WILEY

John Wiley & Sons, Inc.

Published by:
**John Wiley & Sons, Inc.**

Telephone (+44) 1243 779777
Email (for orders and customer service enquiries): cs-books@wiley.co.uk. Visit our Home Page on www.wiley.com



Editorial Director: Kelly Regan
Production Manager: Daniel Mersey
Commissioning Editor: Jill Emeny
Development Editor: Jill Emeny
Project Editor: Hannah Clement
Photo Research: Cherie Cincilla, Richard H. Fox, Jill Emeny
Cartography: Andrew Murphy
Further contributors: Stephen Brewer & Donald Olson; Norman Emeny for 'Walking Around Woodbridge' box p. 48; Bobby Jack for 'Play up Pompey' box p. 171

Wiley also publishes its books in a variety of electronic formats and by print-on-demand. Some content that appears in standard print versions of this book may not be available in other formats. For more information about Wiley products, visit us at www.wiley.com.
British Library Cataloguing in Publication Data

A catalogue record for this book is available from the British Library
ISBN 978-1-119-97056-9 (pbk), ISBN 978-1-119-97130-6 (ebk), ISBN 978-1-119-97131-3 (ebk), ISBN 978-1-119-97132-0 (ebk)

Typeset by Wiley Indianapolis Composition Services

Printed and bound in China by RR Donnelley

5 4 3 2 1

# CONTENTS

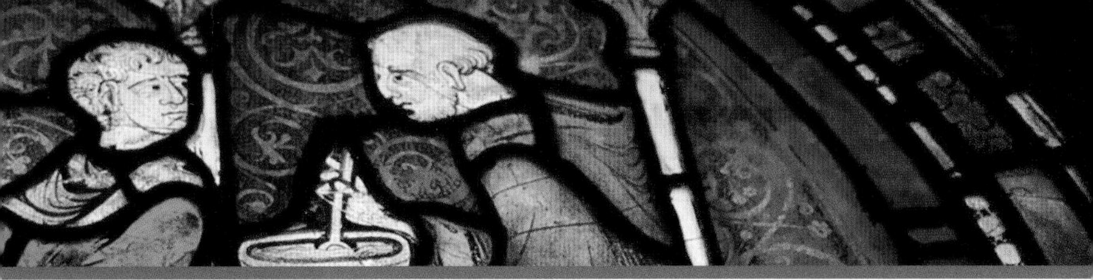

## 9 PLANNING YOUR DAY TRIP 206

# LIST OF MAPS

# ABOUT THE AUTHOR

A writer and editor, **Christi Daugherty** has written for Reuters, the Dallas Morning News and the New York Times. She's also written and contributed to several Frommer's guides, and her articles have appeared in newspapers and magazines around the world. Now settled in the U.K, she now often co-writes books with her husband, the writer and filmmaker Jack Jewers. They co-wrote the book, Ireland Day-by-Day, which published in 2010 as well as several editions of Frommer's Ireland.

## HOW TO CONTACT US

In researching this book, we discovered many wonderful places—hotels, restaurants, shops, and more. We're sure you'll find others. Please tell us about them, so we can share the information with your fellow travelers in upcoming editions. If you were disappointed with a recommendation, we'd love to know that, too. Please write to:

*Frommer's Best Day Trips from London,* 5th Edition
John Wiley & Sons, Inc. • 111 River St. • Hoboken, NJ 07030-5774
frommersfeedback@wiley.com

## ADVISORY & DISCLAIMER

## FROMMER'S STAR RATINGS, ICONS & ABBREVIATIONS

Every hotel, restaurant, and attraction listing in this guide has been ranked for quality, value, service, amenities, and special features using a star-rating system. In country, state, and regional guides, we also rate towns and regions to help you narrow down your choices and budget your time accordingly. Hotels and restaurants are rated on a scale of zero (recommended) to three stars (exceptional). Attractions, shopping, nightlife, towns, and regions are rated according to the following scale: zero stars (recommended), one star (highly recommended), two stars (very highly recommended), and three stars (must-see).

In addition to the star-rating system, we also use seven feature icons that point you to the great deals, in-the-know advice, and unique experiences that separate travelers from tourists. Throughout the book, look for:

**special finds**—those places only insiders know about

**fun facts**—details that make travelers more informed and their trips more fun

**kids**—best bets for kids and advice for the whole family

**special moments**—those experiences that memories are made of

**overrated**—places or experiences not worth your time or money

**insider tips**—great ways to save time and money

**great values**—where to get the best deals

The following abbreviations are used for credit cards:

| | | | | | |
|---|---|---|---|---|---|
| **AE** | American Express | **DISC** | Discover | **V** | Visa |
| **DC** | Diners Club | **MC** | MasterCard | | |

## TRAVEL RESOURCES AT FROMMERS.COM

Frommer's travel resources don't end with this guide. Frommer's website, **www.frommers.com**, has travel information on more than 4,000 destinations. We update features regularly, giving you access to the most current trip-planning information and the best airfare, lodging, and car-rental bargains. You can also listen to podcasts, connect with other Frommers.com members through our active-reader forums, share your travel photos, read blogs from guidebook editors and fellow travelers, and much more.

# 1

# THE BEST DAY-TRIP EXPERIENCES

Whether it's boating on a lazy river in Cambridge, listening to a choir sing in Canterbury Cathedral, or walking along the pebbly beach in Whitstable, you can have memorable experiences within just a few hours of London's hustle and bustle.

---

You may be surprised to discover just how much of England you can explore using London as a base. We've rounded up our favorite day trip destinations, all of which can be reached by train, bus, or car from the city, allowing you to be back in time for dinner. Some of our trips are less than an hour from central London so could be enjoyed within an afternoon, whilst the farthest, York, is 195 miles (314km) to the north, but you can get there in 2 hours on a fast intercity train and still have plenty of time to discover the destination.

## Day Trips Made Easy

For each day-trip destination, we provide you with all the useful information you need, including the practicalities of getting there, opening hours and admission fees. We also suggest a day's itinerary featuring the top attractions, along with suggestions for walks, cycle routes or boat trips in the surrounding area. In addition, we give you tips on dining and shopping and other places you can visit. We want to make sure that you don't miss the Tiepolo painting in Leeds Castle, that you visit Sissinghurst Castle Garden at a time when you can enjoy it without a crowd, and that you follow the best walking route when exploring the ancient town of Rye.

In "Planning Your Day Trips" (Chapter 10), you'll find general information on traveling in and out of London, including special passes that will bring down the cost of your trips.

There are a lot of trips to choose from, and each one is intriguing in its own way. What are your interests? Would you like to visit Monk's House, Virginia Woolf's country retreat near the Sussex Downs? Walk down the time-hallowed nave of 800-year-old Canterbury Cathedral? Stroll along the medieval walls that still encircle York? Explore enormous Windsor Castle, the queen's favorite royal residence?

There are trips for every interest in this book. To help you narrow down your options, here are some of our favorites, organized by category.

# THE best CHURCHES

- **Church of St. Mary, East Bergholt ★★** This 16th-century church is packed with extraordinary curios, including carvings that were a secret code for Catholics during the Reformation. The walls are lined with memorial stones carved with poetic and exquisitely morbid sayings. The church bells are in a cage outside and ring at ground level. See p. 25.

PREVIOUS PAGE: **Dover cliffs.**

Bells of the Church of St. Mary, East Bergholt.

The ancient church in Bradford on Avon.

- **King's College Chapel, Cambridge ★★★** This fine Gothic chapel dates back to the Middle Ages. Inside, Rubens's Adoration of the Magi is nearly as striking as the stained-glass windows, paid for by Henry VIII. Carols are broadcast worldwide from the chapel every Christmas Eve and there are concerts and organ recitals throughout the year. See p. 135.
- **St. Thomas Church, Salisbury ★** Although it may be slightly overshadowed by Salisbury's famous cathedral, this 700-year-old church is quite extraordinary, particularly for the medieval murals inside. The terrifying wall painting Doom shows people rising from their graves and marching toward heaven or hell. See p. 66.
- **Saxon Church of St. Laurence, Bradford on Avon ★★** So old that nobody knows quite how old it really is, this church was considered ancient in 1120, and was converted into a cottage for hundreds of years until its original function was re-established in the 19th century. Tall and narrow in characteristic Anglo-Saxon style, it is still used for services. See p. 19.

## THE best FOR BOOK LOVERS

- **Lewes** Both Virginia Woolf and her sister Vanessa Bell lived in this small town outside Brighton, and other members of the Bloomsbury Group regularly stayed here. **Charleston,** Bell's farmhouse, is an extraordinary place. Bell and her partner and friends painted the walls, floors, furniture—in fact anything that stood still—in fanciful designs.
- **Oxford** So many famous writers lived in Oxford that we don't have the space to list them all. The dreaming spires and ivory towers of this historic town were home to Oscar Wilde, C. S. Lewis, John Donne, and J. R. R. Tolkien, as well as many others. Today you can visit their colleges, drink in their pubs, and walk in their footsteps. See p. 139.

Best Day Trips From London
NORTH SEA
Yorkshire Dales National Park
Pennines
NORTH YORKSHIRE
EAST RIDING OF YORKSHIRE
WEST YORKSHIRE
SOUTH YORKSHIRE
LANCASHIRE
GREATER MANCHESTER
CHESHIRE
DERBYSHIRE
NOTTINGHAMSHIRE
LINCOLNSHIRE
STAFFORDSHIRE
SHROPSHIRE
WEST MIDLANDS
LEICESTERSHIRE
RUTLAND
NORTHAMPTONSHIRE
CAMBRIDGESHIRE
NORFOLK
ENGLAND
Peak District National Park
The Broads National Park
The Wash
Humber
Spurn Pt.
Witham
Trent
Bridlington
Hornsea
Driffield
Stamford Bridge
York
York Minster
Beverley
Kingston upon Hull (Hull)
Barton upon Humber
Selby
Goole
Grimsby
Cleethorpes
Scunthorpe
Harrogate
Skipton
Keighley
Haworth
Leeds/Bradford
Leeds
Bradford
Halifax
Huddersfield
Wakefield
Castleford
Pontefract
Tadcaster
Barnsley
Doncaster
Rotherham
Sheffield
Clitheroe
Burnley
Accrington
Preston
Blackburn
Bolton
Bury
Rochdale
Oldham
Manchester
Wigan
Leigh
St. Helens
Warrington
Widnes
Stockport
Wilmslow
Macclesfield
Northwich
Glossop
Buxton
Bakewell
Chesterfield
Matlock
Leek
Stoke-on-Trent
Crewe
Nantwich
Whitchurch
Market Drayton
Uttoxeter
Stafford
Derby
Burton upon Trent
Ashby-de-la-Zouch
Loughborough
Nottingham
West Bridgford
East Midlands
Mansfield
Worksop
Gainsborough
Market Rasen
Lincoln
Newark-on-Trent
Grantham
Louth
Mablethorpe
Horncastle
Skegness
Boston
Spalding
Stamford
Melton Mowbary
Oakham
Leicester
Glenfield
Market Harborough
Kettering
Corby
Peterborough
Chatteris
March
Wisbech
Ely
King's Lynn
Sandringham
Hunstanton
Wells-next-the-Sea
Fakenham
Swaffham
Cromer
North Walsham
Norwich
Great Yarmouth
Lowestoft
Beccles
Attleborough
Thetford
Diss
Shrewsbury
Telford
Much Wenlock
Wolverhampton
Dudley
Walsall
West Bromwich
Birmingham
Solihull
Lichfield
Tamworth
Nuneaton
Coventry
Rugby
Kidderminster
Ludlow
M1
M6
M62
M180
M53
A1(M)

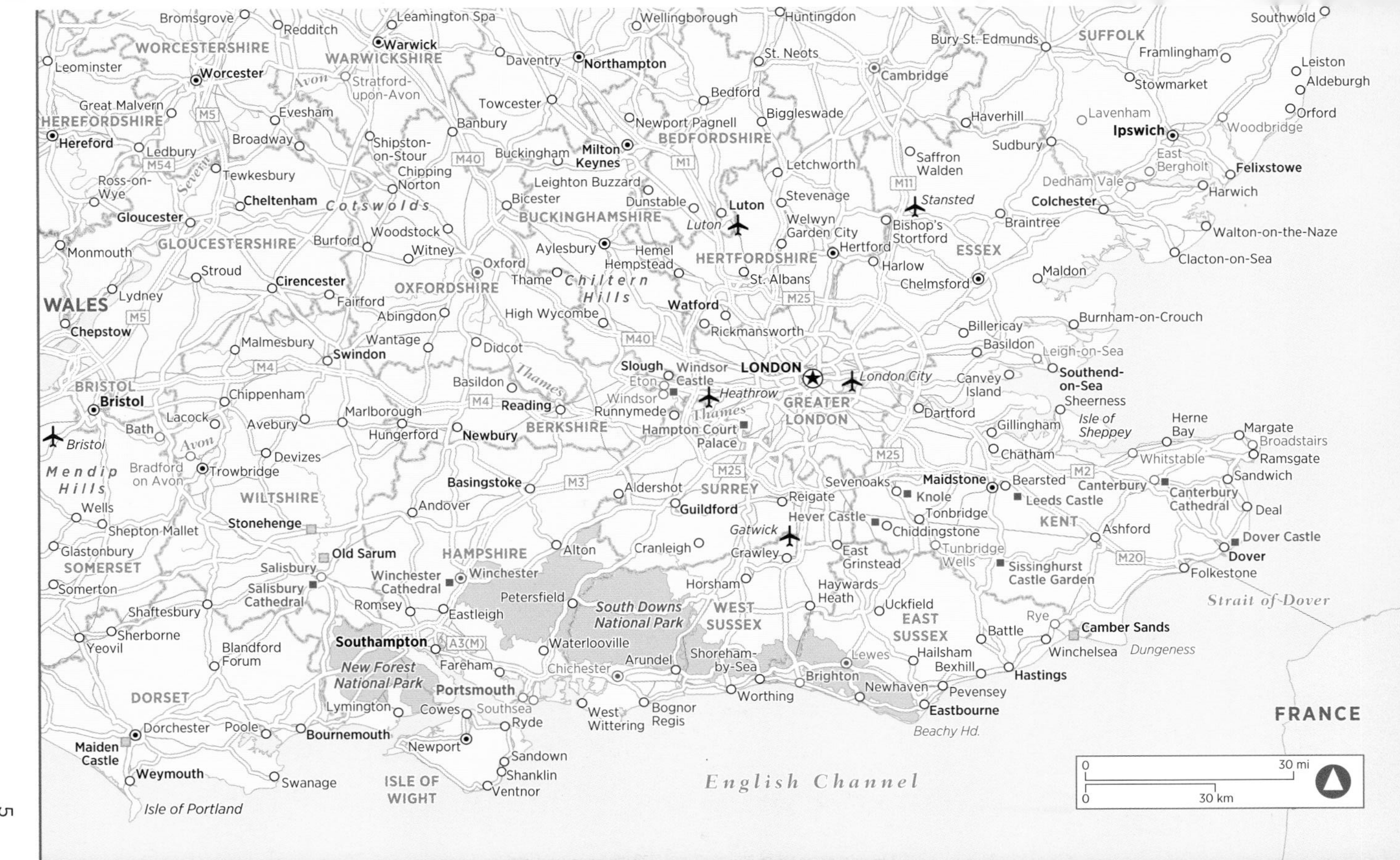

FRANCE
30 mi
30 km
0
Strait of Dover
English Channel
SUFFOLK
ESSEX
KENT
GREATER LONDON
EAST SUSSEX
WEST SUSSEX
SURREY
HAMPSHIRE
BERKSHIRE
OXFORDSHIRE
BUCKINGHAMSHIRE
HERTFORDSHIRE
BEDFORDSHIRE
WARWICKSHIRE
WORCESTERSHIRE
HEREFORDSHIRE
GLOUCESTERSHIRE
WILTSHIRE
SOMERSET
DORSET
BRISTOL
WALES
ISLE OF WIGHT
South Downs National Park
New Forest National Park
Chiltern Hills
Cotswolds
Mendip Hills
Isle of Sheppey
Isle of Portland
Thames
Severn
Avon
Southwold
Leiston
Aldeburgh
Orford
Woodbridge
Felixstowe
Harwich
Walton-on-the-Naze
Clacton-on-Sea
Framlingham
Stowmarket
Ipswich
East Bergholt
Dedham Vale
Lavenham
Colchester
Bury St. Edmunds
Haverhill
Sudbury
Braintree
Maldon
Burnham-on-Crouch
Leigh-on-Sea
Southend-on-Sea
Sheerness
Cambridge
Saffron Walden
Stansted
Bishop's Stortford
Harlow
Chelmsford
Billericay
Basildon
Canvey Island
London City
Dartford
Gillingham
Chatham
Margate
Broadstairs
Ramsgate
Sandwich
Deal
Herne Bay
Whitstable
Canterbury
Canterbury Cathedral
Dover Castle
Dover
Folkestone
Ashford
M20
M2
Leeds Castle
Bearsted
Maidstone
Sissinghurst Castle Garden
Camber Sands
Dungeness
Rye
Winchelsea
Hastings
Battle
Bexhill
Pevensey
Eastbourne
Beachy Hd.
Hailsham
Newhaven
Lewes
Brighton
Uckfield
Tunbridge Wells
Tonbridge
Knole
Sevenoaks
Chiddingstone
Hever Castle
East Grinstead
Haywards Heath
Reigate
Crawley
Gatwick
Horsham
Worthing
Shoreham-by-Sea
Arundel
Bognor Regis
Chichester
West Wittering
Huntingdon
St. Neots
Biggleswade
Letchworth
Stevenage
Welwyn Garden City
Hertford
St. Albans
M25
M11
Luton
Bedford
Newport Pagnell
Dunstable
Hemel Hempstead
Watford
Rickmansworth
LONDON
Heathrow
Windsor Castle
Eton
Windsor
Slough
Runnymede
Hampton Court Palace
Guildford
Aldershot
Cranleigh
M40
M1
M3
M4
Wellingborough
Northampton
Milton Keynes
Leighton Buzzard
Aylesbury
High Wycombe
Thame
Bicester
Buckingham
Daventry
Towcester
Banbury
Reading
Newbury
Basildon
Didcot
Oxford
Abingdon
Wantage
Basingstoke
Alton
Petersfield
Waterlooville
Winchester
Winchester Cathedral
Eastleigh
A3(M)
Fareham
Portsmouth
Southsea
Ryde
Sandown
Shanklin
Ventnor
Newport
Cowes
Southampton
Romsey
Andover
Lymington
Bournemouth
Swanage
Poole
Leamington Spa
Warwick
Stratford-upon-Avon
Shipston-on-Stour
Chipping Norton
Woodstock
Witney
Burford
Fairford
Swindon
Marlborough
Hungerford
Old Sarum
Salisbury
Salisbury Cathedral
Stonehenge
Devizes
Avebury
Redditch
Evesham
Broadway
Cheltenham
Cirencester
Malmesbury
Chippenham
Trowbridge
Bromsgrove
Worcester
Tewkesbury
Gloucester
Stroud
Lacock
Bradford on Avon
Bath
Bristol
M5
M54
Great Malvern
Ledbury
Ross-on-Wye
Lydney
Leominster
Hereford
Monmouth
Chepstow
Wells
Shepton Mallet
Glastonbury
Somerton
Yeovil
Sherborne
Shaftesbury
Blandford Forum
Dorchester
Maiden Castle
Weymouth

- **Rye** With its ancient cobbled streets and 900-year-old church, Rye has long been a popular getaway for writers including the Anglo-American novelist Henry James, humorist E. F. Benson, and novelist Radclyffe Hall. See p. 36.
- **Stratford-upon-Avon** England's greatest playwright was born, lived much of his life, and died in this Warwickshire town. William Shakespeare is a hot commodity in Stratford, but even the commercialization doesn't diminish the awe of visiting the places where he and his family lived. See p. 188.
- **Winchester** The ever-popular author Jane Austen is buried in **Winchester Cathedral.** Her home, in the nearby village of Chawton, 17 miles (27km) from Winchester, is perfectly maintained and filled with Austen memorabilia. See p. 72.

## THE best FOR FAMILIES

- **Brighton** What's more fun for kids than a day at the seaside? Brighton can be as laid-back as you want it to be, a place where you can stroll along the beach, swim (if you dare) in the chilly English Channel, and visit the carnival attractions of **Palace Pier.** There's plenty for everyone to see and do. See p. 154.
- **Dover Castle** This fortress has just about anything a connoisseur of castles can dream of—a ring of walkable walls, a huge keep (complete with multimedia shows), dank dungeons, miles of secret tunnels, even a Roman lighthouse to climb. See p. 99.
- **Hampton Court** Hampton Court is huge, and the littlest visitors won't be much interested, but older children (ages 10 and up) may get a kick out of the costumed guides who lead tours of the staterooms. They'll also love running through the maze, trying to find the way out. See p. 80.

Brighton's popular fairground rides.

The maze at Hampton Court Palace.

- **Leeds Castle** An incredible maze of 2,400 yew trees, a creepy grotto, a well-stocked aviary, beautiful grounds and gardens, and, oh yes, a castle to tour will make Leeds a big hit with all members of the family. Plus there's an adventure playground. See p. 111.
- **York** There's something magical about York, with its medieval walls and ancient streets and tiny lanes. The **Jorvik Viking Centre** is a must-see experience for families, where you sit in "time capsules" and ride back to the Viking age, strange smells and all. Another hit with children is the **National Railway Museum ★,** filled with working historic trains and climb-aboard old locomotives. See p. 196.

## THE best PUBS

- **Haunch of Venison, Salisbury ★★★** Salisbury's oldest pub, this lovely old hostelry has been an inn since at least 1320. It's believed to have once held a brothel popular with clergy from the Cathedral, with tunnels below providing secret ways in and out. Today, good pub food and real ale are served in a warren of rooms and snugs. See p. 72.
- **The Crooked Billet, Leigh-on-Sea ★★** In an 18th-century building on the waterfront in **Old Leigh,** this comfortable pub is cozy, with fires burning in the winter, and with doors and windows open in the summer to let in the sea breeze. Try some of the local seafood, fresh from the boats, with a pint of ale. See p. 165.
- **The Dirty Duck, Stratford-upon-Avon ★★** The wood-paneled rooms in this historic pub have long been popular with actors from the nearby Royal Shakespeare Theatre. It was originally called The Black Swan, but was dubbed The Dirty Duck by US soldiers stationed nearby during WWII. See p. 196.

The Crooked Billet, Leigh-on-Sea.

- **The Marlborough Head, Dedham ★★** This friendly, low-beamed real-ale-serving pub dates to the 17th century, and has all the warming fireplaces and creaky floors your heart could desire. See p. 27.
- **The Old White Swan, York ★★★** A much-loved York institution, the Old White Swan has been an inn since the 16th century, and is actually made up of nine interconnected buildings, with those at the rear being the oldest. The maze of rooms is believed to be extraordinarily haunted. See p. 204.

Brighton seafront and pier.

## THE best BEACHES

- **Brighton Beach** A lively, busy pebble beach smack-dab in the middle of bohemian Brighton, this beach reaches the length of the town and has walkways above and below, with seafood venders, colorful stalls renting beach equipment, busking musicians, and a laid-back holiday feel. See p. 154.
- **Camber Sands, near Rye ★★** This beach is a sprawling, uncrowded expanse of pebble and sand beach backed by high dunes. It stretches for 7 miles (11km) and is ideal for kite flying, surfing, or just lounging. See p. 40.
- **Holkham Beach, near Sandringham ★★** You walk down a path through a forest and across tumbling dunes to reach this picturesque, flat, sandy beach: A vast, uncrowded coastline, stretching as far as the eye can see. See p. 93.
- **Isle of Wight, near Portsmouth ★★** Just a few miles offshore from Portsmouth, this little island is loved for its sandy, family-friendly beaches and marinas favored by the yachting set. Lovely old Victorian streets make it a wonderfully old-fashioned place to explore when you get tired of the sea and sand. See p. 172.
- **Orford Ness, Woodbridge ★★★** This extraordinary coastal reserve contains marked walking trails that lead you across a wild and beautiful 5-mile (8km) shingle spit, home only to seabirds and abandoned buildings once used by the military—tremendously isolated and gorgeous. See p. 47.

Camber Sands.

# THE best MUSEUMS

- **Ashmolean Museum, Oxford ★★** An extraordinary collection fills this historic building with casts of ancient Greek art—including the Parthenon frieze—Eastern antiquities, and ancient coins and jewelry. Its art collection includes such masterpieces as Paolo Uccello's Hunt in the Forest. See p. 144.
- **Fitzwilliam Museum, Cambridge ★★** This important art collection includes stunning antiquities, medieval illuminated manuscripts, medieval armor, and masterworks by artists including Van Dyck and Picasso. See p. 136.
- **Pallant House Gallery, Chichester ★★★** This small but vital gallery has an outstanding collection of modern art, with works by artists including Henry Moore, Graham Sutherland, and Peter Blake. It also holds the studio and archive of the German artist Hans Feibusch. See p. 60.
- **Roman Baths Museum, Bath ★★★** In A.D. 75, Romans channeled the thermal waters bubbling underground into a luxurious bathing complex. The Victorians built the classical museum that now surrounds it. A terrace overlooks the pool where legionnaires once soaked in the steaming waters, and elaborate stonework and Roman saunas still remain. See p. 127.
- **Sainsbury Centre for Visual Arts, Norwich ★★** Esteemed architect Norman Foster designed this modern structure filled with paintings by artists including Francis Bacon, Henry Moore, Alberto Giacometti,

RIGHT: Roman Baths Museum, Bath; BOTTOM: Pallant House Gallery, Chichester.

and others. There's a strong collection of Art Nouveau paintings, as well as pottery and other artifacts from the ancient Mediterranean. See p. 186.

## THE best RESTAURANTS

- **Ale & Porter, Bradford on Avon ★** This unassuming cafe in a grand, stone building, punches above its weight. Everything is freshly made in the sunny dining room—the coffee is roasted in-house, the chocolate is handmade, as are the pastries, cakes, and quiches. See p. 22.
- **Old Brewery Tavern, Canterbury ★★** Respected chef Michael Caines runs the kitchen in this gastro-pub, where the white-washed walls and polished wood floors let you know that this is no ordinary boozer. The menu is filled with beautifully made pub standards: Crisp fish, smoky grilled steaks, and thick burgers. See p. 57.
- **Simply Seafood, Leigh-on-Sea ★★** Literally housed inside a cockle-shed on the seafront in Leigh-on-Sea, this casual restaurant sells seafood so fresh that if it were any fresher it would flop on your plate. The food is simply prepared here—it's all about fresh, briny goodness. See p. 165.
- **The Real Eating Company, Lewes ★** In a laid-back restaurant with big windows overlooking the busy street, this place pumps out astonishingly good food: For breakfast, the poached eggs with hollandaise are creamy and perfectly cooked; for lunch, hearty grilled steaks, juicy burgers, and freshly made soups lead the way. See p. 36.
- **Woods Restaurant, Bar and Produce Store, Tunbridge Wells ★★** In the historic Pantiles, this warm, bright eatery with wood floors and big windows uses seasonal, sustainable, local meats and produce to make stellar meals. Its brunches are legendary—try the eggs Benedict with smoked salmon. You can also buy local jams and honey in its shop. See p. 152.

## THE best MARKETS

- **Charter Market, Salisbury ★** This historic market has been running virtually without interruption since the 13th century—although the wares on offer have undoubtedly changed over the years. Nowadays venders sell everything from locally raised meats and produce to jewelry, clothing, and art. See p. 70.
- **Green Park Arts and Crafts Market, Bath ★** This busy market runs Tuesdays through Sundays every week with experienced venders selling everything from antiques and art to handmade crafts and locally produced honey. See p. 131.

Market Square, Cambridge.

- **Lavenham Market, Lavenham ★** In the tiny town of Lavenham, this market on the fourth Sunday of every month at the village hall is a proper local market with home-baked pies and cakes, locally raised meats and produce, and plants and flowers from local gardens. See p. 30.
- **Market Square, Cambridge ★** In the center of Cambridge, this lively open-air market runs every day of the week—Monday to Saturday it's a general market with local farm produce, clothes, and books, while Sundays its emphasis switches to arts and crafts, along with homemade cakes, fresh-baked bread, and organic foods. See p. 134.

## THE best PICNIC SPOTS

- **By the River Cam, Cambridge** The river is bounded by banks covered in soft green grass that lead off into nearby meadows and are overlooked by the jagged rooftops of the colleges. Watch novice punters splash into the water while you nibble a sandwich. See p. 136.
- **Christ Church Meadow, Oxford** This green, wildflower- strewn meadow is traversed by walking paths. After making your way through the tall grass, find a smooth spot to spread out a blanket and relax with a view of Oxford's spires. See p. 146.
- **Hever Castle** Hever's grounds, with acres of smooth green grass dotted with whimsical topiary and ancient trees, is ideal for a picnic. In the summer you can watch jousters fight it out as you dine. See p. 105.
- **Leeds Castle** The grounds at Leeds Castle go on for miles: You can choose to sit on a bench in the formal gardens or in the shade of a tree where the grounds become wilder. If you're lucky you'll witness hot-air balloons taking off into the blue. See p. 111.
- **Stonehenge** Miles of land around this ancient stone site are part of the property of the conservation group English Heritage, and visitors are welcome to spread out a blanket and picnic while taking in the extraordinary view of Stonehenge's sturdy pillars and tables. See p. 63.

LEFT: Hever Castle's gardens; RIGHT: Choose a good spot for a picnic beside the River Cam.

## THE best FOR A SUNNY DAY

- **Brighton** With its long pebble beach lined with ice-cream sellers and mini carousels, bars, and shellfish stalls, Brighton was made for bright and breezy days. The elaborate, Victorian pier, with carnival rides and games, will keep you amused for hours. See p. 154.
- **Cambridge** Although you can come here any time, in summer the students are away and so you can explore all the colleges. And half the fun in Cambridge is renting a boat to punt down the river, followed by a leisurely lunch on the shore—a perfect way to spend a sunny afternoon. See p. 132.
- **Hever Castle** It would be a shame not to spend time in the beautiful grounds here—the formal Italian garden and yew maze, not to mention all the outdoor activities, are such a pleasure. Come on a sunny day and bring a picnic. See p. 105.
- **Leeds Castle** The grounds at this historic castle are at least half the reason to come. On a rainy day you might miss out on hot-air balloon flights, falconry, treetop climbing, and the adventure play land, not to mention the lovely gardens. See p. 111.
- **Whitstable** This charming seafront town is fine in the rain, when everything takes on delicate watercolor shades, but on a sunny day you can spend an afternoon strolling its frozen-in-time streets, exploring the shops on Harbour Street, and wandering down the beach to nearby villages. See p. 172.

## THE best FOR A RAINY DAY

- **Bath** Packed with enough museums and galleries to keep you inside and dry no matter how long the rain lashes down, Bath is a perfect refuge on one of those days when it just won't stop pouring. See p. 124.

The harbor at Whitstable.

TOP: The breathtaking interior of York Minster; RIGHT: Guided tour at Hampton Court.

- **Hampton Court** This royal palace is so vast that exploring it can take hours. On a day when the rain pounds outside, its sturdy, 16th-century walls make you feel snug and protected. See p. 80.
- **Windsor Castle** The queen's favorite castle has enough to see inside to keep you warm and dry for the better part of a day. Make your way to the tea shop and watch the rain pelt down while you sip a hot cup of tea and munch on a scone. See p. 118.
- **York** Like Bath, this historic cathedral city is filled with shops to duck into, tea shops in which you can seek cover from a storm, and then there's the enormous and extraordinary **York Minster ★★★,** where you can while away hours. See p. 196.

## THE best FOR SHOPPING

- **Brighton** This town offers one of the most unique and varied shopping experiences outside of London—explore the narrow winding **Lanes ★★★,** filled with small creative shops, jewelry stores, and boutiques. The **North Laine ★★** is similarly charming and jam-packed with funky shops, and all with a view of the sea. See p. 154.

The North Laine in Brighton.

Peruse the many antique shops in Lewes.

- **Leigh-on-Sea** This unassuming small seaside town isn't a flashy shopping mecca like Brighton, but its streets are lined with creative, locally owned, small boutiques, pottery shops, and art galleries filled with works by local artists. See p. 161.
- **Lewes** With its hilly, historic streets filled with antiques stores, art galleries, and craft shops, Lewes is ideal for an afternoon of browsing, coffee drinking, and relaxing. See p. 31.
- **Oxford** The streets of Oxford are filled with creative independent shops selling art, books, and clothing, as well as a covered market with an eclectic array of jewelry, handmade crafts, and music—so everybody will find something to buy here. See p. 139.
- **York** This historic city's narrow winding lanes make shopping an act of discovery. From **Stonegate,** with its jewelry stores and clothing shops, to **The Shambles ★,** with its collectibles, crafts, and souvenirs, and down to Lendel Lane with antiques and art, shopping is a joy here. See p. 196.

## THE best FOR ART LOVERS

- **Cambridge** Many of Cambridge's beautiful colleges are packed with museum-quality art. The chapel at **King's College ★★** holds Rubens's *Adoration of the Magi.* Similarly, the chapel at **Jesus College** is enlivened with stained-glass windows designed by Edward Burne-Jones and a ceiling by William Morris. See p. 132.

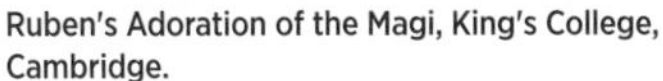
Ruben's Adoration of the Magi, King's College, Cambridge.

Old Leigh Studios, Leigh-on-Sea.

- **Dedham Vale** In the heart of Constable Country on the border of Essex and Suffolk, this area inspired the English landscape painter John Constable (1776–1837), who was born in **Flatford.** You can visit the scene of his most famous works. See p. 23.
- **Lavenham** This crooked little medieval town has inspired artists for centuries, and today its streets are lined with art galleries. Painters can often be found working in the street, trying to capture Lavenham's unusual light. See p. 27.
- **Leigh-on-Sea** This busy fishing village and commuter town has become an artists' enclave with dozens of galleries scattered around the town and in **Old Leigh** by the seafront. You can buy works by talented, contemporary artists at reasonable prices. See p. 161.
- **Windsor Castle** Not only is the building itself a work of art, but the magnificent **State Apartments** ★★★ are furnished with classical art from the Royal Collection, including works by Rembrandt, Rubens, and Gainsborough. See p. 118.

# 2

# A TASTE OF THE ENGLISH COUNTRYSIDE

Just a few miles from central London, the crowded urban landscape transforms into green hills, beckoning city-dwellers craving fresh air and the opportunity of an amble along canals and riversides, or through ancient woodlands. Amid this bucolic scenery lie historic towns with half-timbered buildings lining market squares and quiet harbors, most of which are easily traversed on foot. Many are steeped in history and a casual day can be spent strolling around antique emporiums or local museums followed by lingering pub lunches, or afternoon tea and cake.

---

Just a short walk out of East Bergholt in Dedham Vale will lead you through the countryside that inspired some of Constable's most famous paintings, and a quiet corner of Rye reveals a stained-glass window by pre-Raphaelite artist Sir Edward Burne-Jones. In Lewes enter the elegant study belonging to Virginia Woolf, or step back even further to the charming, simple home belonging to Anne of Cleves, given to her by Henry VIII after their divorce.

## BRADFORD ON AVON

Bradford on Avon, a small Wiltshire town originally known as "Broad Ford" before the 11th century (due to the wide river moving languidly through the middle of it), hasn't changed much in the last few centuries. Cottages and townhouses

**The town bridge dates to Norman times.** PREVIOUS PAGE: **Canal boats at Bradford on Avon.**

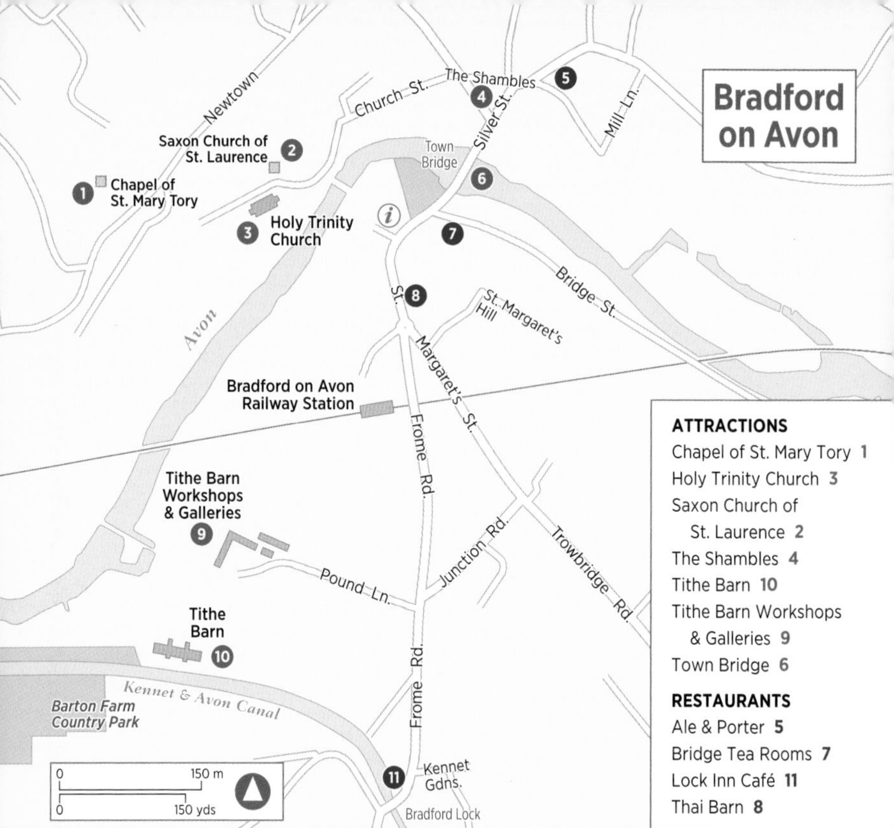


built with local Bath limestone stand sturdily on a steep hill up winding lanes, while the stone bridge in the center of town, built in Norman times to replace the ford, is still in use today.

Bradford has been settled for millennia. The remains of a large Roman villa were uncovered here, and the town flourished in the wool and cloth trade until the industry faded in the late 19th century and shifted northward to Yorkshire. These days Bradford's popular with weekend visitors wanting a retreat in the countryside, and it's only a short hop by bus or car to the nearby spa town of Bath.

There isn't a huge amount to see here, but take a stroll along the Kennet canal and Bradford's a calming place to spend at least half a day. Alternatively, you could combine it with a trip to the nearby spa town of Bath (p. 124).

## Essentials

### VISITOR INFORMATION

The **Tourist Information Centre** is in Westbury Gardens next to the bridge (✆ **01225/865-797;** www.bradfordonavon.co.uk). It's tiny but helpful, with maps, brochures, and a Lilliputian gift shop.

## GETTING THERE

### By Train

There are no direct trains to Bradford on Avon from London, so you'll need to change at Bath. Trains to Bath depart every 30 minutes from London Paddington and the entire journey takes under 2 hours. The standard same-day, round-trip fare from London, if purchased on the day of travel, is about £48.

### By Bus

There's no direct bus service from London to Bradford on Avon. However, you can take a National Express bus to Bath and then change to a local **First Group** bus to Bradford (✆ **08712/002-233;** www.firstgroup.com). The whole journey costs you around £17.

### By Car

Bradford is 109 miles (175km) west of London on the A363. From London take the M4, turn off before Bath at Chippenham, and follow signs to A363. The journey takes about 2¼ hours. Street parking is time-limited to 2 hours or less and the five public carparks in the town, marked with a blue P, can often fill up quickly on Saturdays. Parking costs from £5 a day.

## GETTING AROUND

Bradford on Avon is compact and you can traverse the entire town in 20 minutes on foot. A good place to start your tour is the bridge, where the river divides the town in half.

## A Day in Bradford on Avon

The upstream half of the town bridge dates from Norman times, and the downstream half dates to the 16th century when it was widened to allow more traffic to pass. The domed building in the middle of the river was probably first built as a **toll house** in the 17th century, but was later used as the community's lock-up, where drunks and troublemakers were kept overnight. Looking out from the bridge, notice the old weaver's cottages climbing up the hillsides, and also along the river, the 19th-century cloth mill buildings, now homes and offices.

The 17th century toll house.

On Church Street, the grand **Holy Trinity Church** is primarily Tudor, built in the early 1500s on the site of a Norman church (open 9am–3pm daily). Still, it's young compared to the humble **Saxon Church of St. Laurence ★★**, which is so old that nobody knows for sure when it was actually constructed—the notes of the 12th-century historian William of Malmesbury show that the church was considered ancient in 1120 although he believed that it dated to the late 6th century. Tall and narrow in characteristic Anglo-Saxon style, the church is bare inside, with no pews or furniture, but some elements have been found and restored, including carved stones used as an altar and a round Saxon cross. The church was only recognized as a Saxon building in 1857, having been used, in part, as a home. Today, it still holds services and is open for general visitors from 9am to 6pm daily.





It's a steep climb up the hill to **Tory Street**—you can either go up busy Wine Street or wind your way up the stone paths past the weaver's cottages. These cottages, now sought-after residences, were considered poor humble dwellings in the 17th century. At the peak of the hill perches the little **Chapel of St. Mary Tory ★** (open daily 9am–4pm), built in 1480. The word Tory is a corruption of the Anglo-Saxon word 'tor' (meaning 'steep hill') and they're not kidding about that—the church perches right at the very top of the town, but you're rewarded for your efforts by the view: From the churchyard you can see for miles.

Back down by the river, **The Shambles,** an area of narrow streets dotted with coffee shops and boutiques, has been a market street since Saxon times.

Cross the river on the pedestrian bridge by Holy Trinity Church, and follow signs up to the **Tithe Barn** off Frome Road. The grade II listed structure is quite rare: only a few barns of this kind still exist. Built in the 14th century, this was essentially a tax office for the wealthy and powerful **Shaftesbury Abbey,** 24 miles (38km) away. The fact that the barn is bigger than any of the churches in the area is an indication of just how successful the abbey was. People were expected to give a small percentage of their harvest, wealth, or labor every year. Everything collected here would be sent back to the abbey, with a small amount going to the town churches. The barn is open daily 10am to 5pm. Nearby, the **Tithe Barn Workshops & Galleries** in Pound Lane (www.tithebarnartscrafts.co.uk) house a tearoom and plenty of antiques, arts, and other crafty goods to browse. Open all year Wednesday through Sunday 11am to 5pm.

Saxon Church of St. Lawrence.

A rare example of a 14th century Tithe Barn.

### OUTDOOR ACTIVITIES

You can rent bicycles and canoes from **Towpath Trail** on Frome Rd. (✆ **01225/867-187;** www.towpathtrail.co.uk). Canoes hold four people, and cost £10 an hour; bikes cost from £15 a day. If you want somebody else to do the work, you can cruise on the narrowboat **MV Barbara McLellan** (✆ **0800/121-4679**), which departs weekends from the Wharf Cottage in Bradford on Avon and travels to Widbrook and Avoncliff. Tickets (£7 round-trip) can be purchased at the Wharf Cottage's cafe. The Wharf Cottage is on the canal off Frome Road. Sailing season is April to October.

## Shopping

The Shambles and the streets around it make up the small shopping center of Bradford, with pricey antiques stores and gift shops. **Best Laid Plans,** 31 Market St. (✆ **01225/863-069**), sells gifts, home decor, and stationery. **Artemis Gallery,** 32 Market St. (✆ **01225/863-087**), sells fine antiques. Up by the Tithe Barn, **Granary Trading Company,** Pound Lane (✆ **01225/867-782**), sells gifts, shabby-chic accessories, and refurbished vintage furniture.

## Where to Eat

Near the station, the **Bridge Tea Rooms,** 24a Bridge St. (✆ **01225/865-537;** www.thebridgeatbradford.co.uk), serves breakfast, lunch, and tea in a 17th-century building. The decor is rather twee, with Victorian paintings and waitresses wearing period maid costumes, but the tea itself is exemplary. The full afternoon tea comes with finger sandwiches, cakes, and scones with clotted cream (£16).

Stroll along the Kennet Canal.

For a pub lunch on the water, head to the **Lock Inn Café,** Frome Rd. (✆ **01225/868-068**; www.thelockinn.co.uk), overlooking the canal and famed for the over-the-top Boatman's Grill (steak, pork, lamb, bacon, and sausage), priced at £12. The more reasonably sized beef and ale stew is comfortingly warming on a chilly day. The delightful **Ale & Porter** ★, 25 Silver St. (✆ **01225/868-135;** www.aleandporter.co.uk), serves up coffee, roasted in-house, and a selection of handmade chocolates, pastries, cakes, and quiches. **Thai Barn,** 9–10 St. Margaret's St. (✆ **01225/866-443;** www.thaibarn.co.uk), is a modern restaurant with slick, white tablecloths, wicker seats, and an attractive garden area in summer. Opt for one of the many aromatic curries, or for vegetarians the Pad Thai can be spiced up with an extra chili kick (mains from £7).

## Walking: The Kennet Canal

There are two waterways in Bradford: The **River Avon,** which runs through the town center, and the Kennet Canal, which runs nearby. You'll find the canal just past **Pound Lane,** about five minutes' walk from the train station. Start your walk there near the Towpath Trail. If feeling ambitious, you can walk all the way to Bath, but a stroll to the **Cross Guns** pub (**01225/862-335;** www.crossguns.net), a real ale pub in nearby Avoncliff, in good time for lunch is highly recommended.

## Nearby

The beautiful, Georgian city of **Bath** is 8 miles (13km) away with its steaming Roman baths and streets lined with historic buildings. Trains and local buses run to Bath from Bradford on Avon throughout the day. See p. 17.

Just 8 miles (13km) northeast of Bradford on Avon, off the A350, the tiny village of **Lacock** ★ is wonderfully preserved. The whole town is overseen by the National Trust (www.nationaltrust.org.uk), and it's filled with enchanting medieval and 16th-century homes and churches. **Lacock Abbey** (image right) on High Street is a whimsical manor house built on the foundations of a 13th-century convent.

# EAST BERGHOLT & DEDHAM VALE

Known as 'Constable Country,' this stretch of countryside on the border of Essex and Suffolk inspired the English landscape painter John Constable (1776–1837) to produce some of his most famous work. Dedham Vale is as idyllic as its name suggests; gentle green hills swathed in woods, bisected by the glittering fingers of the River Stour. Its most feted section—the area around the charming country villages of East Bergholt, Flatford, and Dedham—can easily be seen in a single afternoon if traveling by car.

You really do need a car to fully explore this area, as most of the sights are out in the countryside, or in the three scattered towns, all of which are fairly poorly serviced by public transportation.

## Essentials

### VISITOR INFORMATION

There's a small **Visitor Information Centre** at Bridge Cottage, Flatford Lane, Flatford (✆ **01206/299-460**). It's open daily 10am to 5pm over the summer months (weekends only 11am–4:30pm in winter).

### SCHEDULING CONSIDERATIONS

The area is full of beauty spots that are popular with locals, and so the crowds will always be at their highest on sunny, summer weekends.

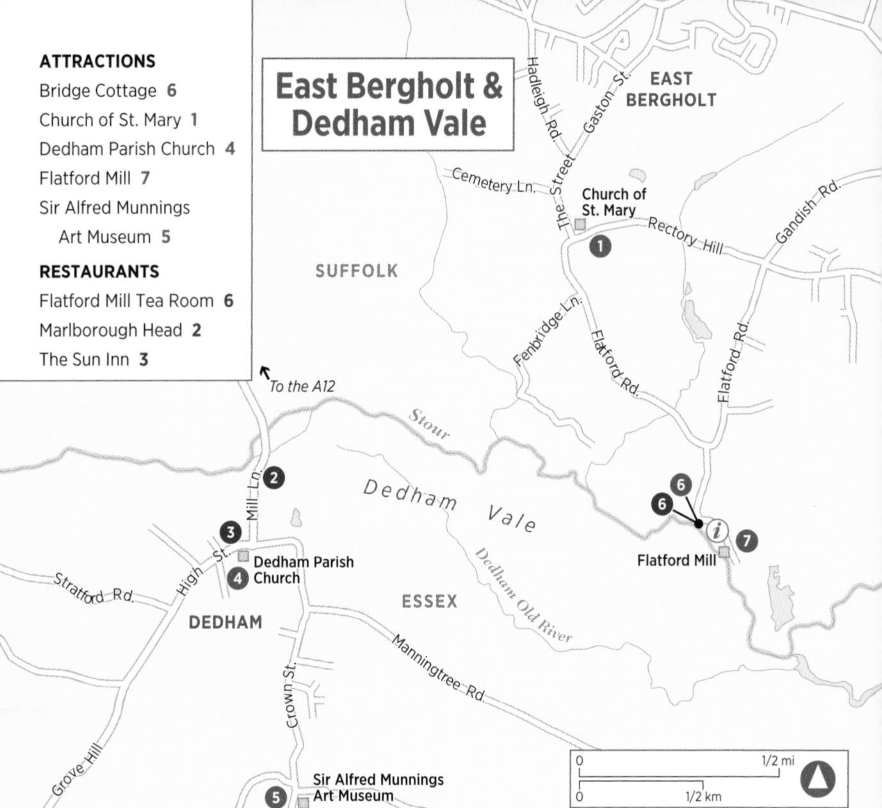


## GETTING THERE

### By Train

Trains leave every 20 minutes from London Liverpool St. to Colchester, the nearest major town. The journey takes just under 1 hour and a round-trip ticket costs £15. Colchester is 10 miles (16km) from East Bergholt and Dedham Vale, so you need to catch a bus or taxi to reach the final destination. **Carters Coaches** (✆ **01473/313-188;** www.carterscoachservices.co.uk) runs a service from Colchester to East Bergholt twice a day (tickets £7.50), alternatively, taxis are available at Colchester station—the fare costing around £20.

### By Bus

**National Express** buses run to Colchester (most changing at Stansted) throughout the day but the journey takes between 3 to 4 hours, starting from London Victoria (fares start from £10.50). See **By Train** (above) for information about how to get from Colchester to East Bergholt.

### By Car

From London take the A12 past Colchester and turn off at Dedham; from there follow signs to East Bergholt and Flatford. The journey should take under 2 hours.

## GETTING AROUND

The three villages form a triangle, with East Bergholt and Flatford about 1 mile (1.6km) apart and Dedham around 2 to 3 miles (3–5km) from both. You can walk, but the route between East Bergholt and Flatford is a tiny road with no pathway, and rather hazardous on foot. So the most reasonable way to explore the area is by car. However, by far the prettiest way to travel between Flatford and Dedham is by rowboat; for details contact **Flatford Boats,** The Granary, Flatford (✆ **01206/298-111;** www.flatfordboats.com).

# A Day in Dedham Vale

Peaceful **East Bergholt's** chief attraction is the older, Tudor-era part of town, with its breath-catching, pretty, old lanes and stone cottages with manicured lawns. The 16th-century **Church of St. Mary ★★** (✆ **01206/298-932**) is packed with extraordinary curios—look for the section of stone wall beside the entrance, carved with symbols that were used as secret code by Catholics during the Reformation in the 16th century. The interior is lit by pools of blue and purple light from tinted-glass windows. To the rear of the nave a small room holds artifacts from the church's early history and the memorial stones on the wall nearby, marked with poetic dedications, are also worth a moment's pause. In the churchyard, the original bells are kept in a cage-like hut (they're rung at ground level), an odd arrangement, built as temporary storage over 500 years ago.

A few miles away in tiny blink-and-you'll-miss-it **Flatford,** look out for the 16th-century **Bridge Cottage** (✆ **01206/298-260;** www.nationaltrust.org.uk) signposted off the B1070. The cottage houses an exhibition of John Constable's life and work, and you can also take tours of the building (11:30am, 1:30, and 2:30pm; £2.50). It's open year-round, summer daily from 10:30am to 5pm,

East Bergholt's 16th century Church of St. Mary.

Flatford Mill and pond.

although winter hours vary and so it's wise to check the website before visiting. Admission is free.

There is no public access to the adjoining **Flatford Mill ★**, but you can walk around the idyllic pond and along grassy footpaths by the river, perhaps stopping for a picnic lunch. This is the setting for Constable's most famous work, The Hay Wain, and you'll notice that the view he reproduced is almost entirely unchanged after 200 years.

Five miles (8km) from the mill the small but elegant Georgian town of **Dedham ★** was the birthplace of John Constable. The main street, lined with elegant red-brick houses and whitewashed shops selling local arts and crafts, is an attraction in itself; a lovely place to wander for an hour, soaking up the atmosphere. Take a quick look inside **Dedham Parish Church** (✆ **01206/322-136;** www.dedham-parishchurch.org.uk), built in 1492, and one of the birthplaces of the Puritan movement. The dream-like painting of The Ascension in the nave is an original Constable.

A quarter mile or so down a marked footpath from High Street, the **Sir Alfred Munnings Art Museum** (✆ **01206/322-127;** www.siralfredmunnings.co.uk) is devoted to the work of a lesser-known artistic son of the town. Munnings (1878–1959) painted scenes of vanishing rural East Anglian life but is best-known for his equestrian paintings. The gallery is open April to October Wednesday, Thursday, and weekends 2 to 5pm. Admission is £5 for adults, and £1 for children.

## Shopping

Dedham has a handful of craft and antiques stores; **Shakespeare House Gallery,** High St. (✆ **01206/322-552**), stands out for its selection of art and jewelry while the **Dedham Arts and Craft Centre,** High St. (✆ **01206/322-666;**

www.dedhamartandcraftcentre.co.uk), is an indoor market where local creatives sell their work. Both are usually open daily from 10am to 5pm.

## Where to Eat

The **Flatford Mill Tea Room,** (✆ **01206/298-260**), at Bridge Cottage, has snacks, sandwiches, and light meals and benefits from an attractive view over the River Stour. In Dedham, the **Marlborough Head ★★**, High St. (✆ **01206/323-250**), is a friendly, low-beamed pub serving fish and chips, burgers, and the like—with decent vegetarian options, most at £10 and under. Also in Dedham, **The Sun Inn ★**, High St. (✆ **01206/323-351**), is an old coaching inn that makes good use of locally sourced produce in its Italian menu.

# LAVENHAM

Like a piece of history preserved in amber, the medieval town of Lavenham in Suffolk has hardly changed since the 16th century. The narrow streets are lined with ancient half-timber buildings listing with age that once housed the weavers and merchants who thrived in this wool market town in medieval times. Today, it is a charming, if touristy, place popular with day-trippers and history buffs.

Expect to spend half a day here and consider heading onto the larger market town of Bury St. Edmunds in the afternoon.

## Essentials

### VISITOR INFORMATION

The tiny **Lavenham Tourist Information Centre,** Lady St. (✆ **01787/248-207;** www.southandheartofsuffolk.org), is open from Easter to October, daily 10am to 4:45pm and weekends from November to March.

The Market Cross, Lavenham.

## SCHEDULING CONSIDERATIONS

Lavenham is very popular and can be uncomfortably crowded on summer weekends, and so it's worth coming on a weekday or out of season. A farmers' market is held in Lavenham on the fourth Sunday of every month at the village hall on Church Street. It fills the hall with a swell of local produce, home-baked pies, and meats. The market runs from 10am to 1:30pm and admission is free.

## GETTING THERE

### By Train

Trains run from London Liverpool St. to Sudbury, requiring one change at Marks Tey. The journey takes 1⅓ hours and you can expect to pay around £26 for the round-trip. Sudbury is 7 miles (11km) from Lavenham, so you can either take a taxi the rest of the way (at a cost of about £15) or use the local bus no. 753, which provides an hourly service to Lavenham. Taxis are usually waiting at Sudbury station, or you can try **Elite Taxis** (✆ **01787/881-212**).

### By Car

Lavenham is 76 miles (122km) northeast of London. From London, take the M11 to the A131, and then turn onto either the A1141 or B1071. If you have the time, the slower B1071 route makes for a prettier journey. The journey should take just over 2 hours. You can park on the street at the edge of the town (it's free and legal), although there are also two free public carparks—one off Church Street and the other off Prentice Street near Market Place.

## GETTING AROUND

Lavenham is easy to navigate and you can walk from one end of town to the other in 20 minutes but, because of the hills and occasional cobbles, it's definitely worth wearing flat shoes.

# A Day in Lavenham

With more than 300 timber-framed medieval buildings, half the joy of visiting Lavenham is to be found in simply wandering the narrow streets. Many of the houses are painted in a bright pink hue—this is known as "Suffolk pink," and was once the result of minerals in the chalk, sand, and clay used to coat the houses, although these days the pink wash is maintained for the sake of tradition. Follow the historic **Shilling Street** ★ up-hill to Market Place, where a half-timbered building holds **Little Hall** ★ (✆ **01787/247-019;** www.littlehallorg.uk), a 14th-century house filled with artifacts and antiques. It's open April to October Wednesday through Sunday 2 to 5:30pm, Mondays 11am to 5:30pm. Admission is £3 for adults, and children under 15 are admitted free.

Across the rectangular Market Place Square, the timber-framed **Guildhall** (✆ **01787/247-646;** www.nationaltrust.org.uk) is slightly younger than Little Hall (it was built in 1529) but is much bigger, sprawling along one edge of the square. Inside, a display explains in great detail all you'll ever need to know about Lavenham's wool trade, but the character of the old building on its own is well worth the price of admission. It's open April through October daily from 11am to 5pm and November weekends from 11am to 4pm. Admission is £4.30 adults and £1.90 for children.

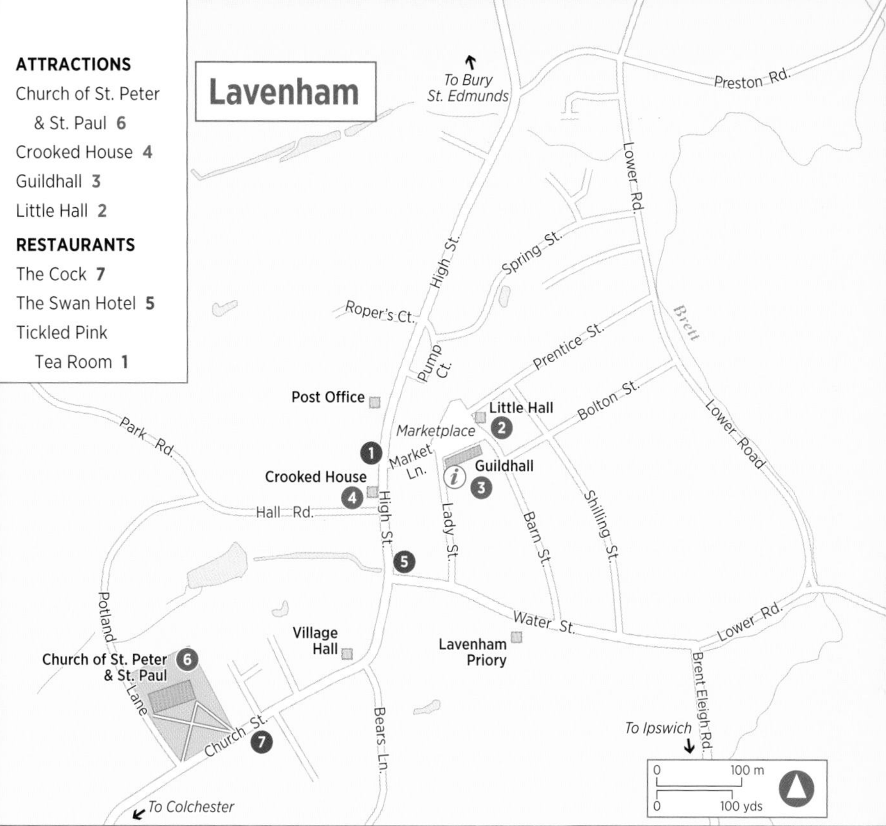


High Street is lined with amazing historic houses, including the spectacular **Crooked House ★**, now home to an excellent art gallery (see p. 30). At the foot of High Street, **The Swan Hotel ★★** (**01787/247-477;** www.theswanatlavenham.co.uk) has been welcoming visitors since the 1400s. A favorite of American and British airmen from nearby bases during WWII, the walls are covered in messages from that era, written by pilots about to fly missions over Germany.

If you continue to follow High Street down, you'll reach the stern gray stone walls of the **Church of St. Peter & St. Paul ★**. Completed in 1520, it's a big church for such a tiny town (its tower was built 141 feet (44m) tall, specifically to be taller than any in surrounding towns), and this is mainly due to the funding from John de Vere, Earl of Oxford, and Thomas Spring, a wealthy local wool merchant. The stone masons made sure they were remembered—de Vere's family star is carved on every side of the tower and Spring's coat of arms is chiseled on the parapet in 32 places. Inside, the wood carvings are exceptional.

## ORGANIZED TOURS

The visitor's center offers guided walking tours through the town from Easter to October, on Saturdays at 2:30pm and Sundays at 11am. Tickets are £3 for adults, under-14s are free—booking ahead is recommended.

### Nearby

Lavenham is 10 miles (16km) from **Bury St. Edmunds** (www.visit-burystedmunds.co.uk), a busy modern city with an historic heart. The town holds the remains of an 11th-century abbey, the **Theatre Royal** (✆ **01284/755-127;** www.theatreroyal.org), the country's only surviving Regency theater, the impressive **Ickworth House** (✆ **01284/735-270;** www.nationaltrust.org.uk) manor house and gardens, and the **West Stow Country Park** (✆ **01284/728-718;** www.stedmundsbury.gov.uk/weststow), with its reconstructed Anglo-Saxon village.

## Shopping

At 17 Market Place, the **Angel Gallery** (✆ **01787/248-417**), housed in a 15th-century building, offers paintings, pottery, and sculpture. Nearby at 36 Market Place, **Elizabeth Gash Knitwear** (✆ **01787/248-561**) sells colorful hand-knitted clothing for all ages. In the 14th-century Crooked House, 7 High St., the **Crooked House Gallery** (✆ **01787/247-865**) is another arty highlight with a wide-ranging collection of works by British artists. **Lavenham Market** ★ takes place in the village hall on the last Sunday of the month. Come here for all kinds of locally produced produce and home-baked goods.

## Where to Eat

**Tickled Pink Tea Room,** 17 High St. (✆ **01787/248-438**) offers steaming pots of tea and fresh cakes, scones, and sandwiches in a wondrously girly environment. At the foot of High Street, **The Swan Hotel** ★★ (see p. 29) serves hearty dishes such as shepherd's pie and trout fillet—perfect for a chilly day.

The Crooked House Gallery on High Street.

Church of St. Peter and St. Paul.

The Swan Hotel.



It isn't the cheapest option generally, but you can indulge in a well-cooked, two-course meal for £17. **The Cock** (✆ **01787/247-407;** www.thecockatlavenham.co.uk) on Church Street, serves up traditional pub favorites such as scampi or sausages and mash.

# LEWES

A charming, historic town built around a castle on a precipitous hill, Lewes has always attracted revolutionaries and artists. In the 18th century it was home to Thomas Paine, the rebel whose writings helped spark the American Revolution, and in the early 20th century it was the country getaway of Virginia Woolf and the writers and artists that made up the Bloomsbury Group.

Peaceable as this country town seems, Lewes has a fiery past. When "Bloody" Queen Mary I (reigned 1553–58) tried to reinstate Catholicism to England after her father, Henry VIII, broke from the Church, Protestants in Lewes were persecuted and 17 of them were burned at the stake.

There is enough to see in Lewes and the surrounding area to take up a full day if taken at a leisurely pace.

## Essentials

### VISITOR INFORMATION

The Lewes tourism information office is at 187 High St. (✆ **01273/483-448;** www.lewes.gov.uk).

### SCHEDULING CONSIDERATIONS

Lewes is famed for its all-consuming celebrations on **Guy Fawkes Night** (November 5), when the townspeople and a host of visitors join in a massive and often energetic torchlight parade, and huge fireworks displays take place.





### GETTING THERE

#### By Train

Southern trains run direct to Lewes from London Victoria every 30 minutes on the Brighton line; however, it can be faster to take a train to Brighton and change there to a more frequent regional train for Lewes. A round-trip ticket costs about £30.

#### By Car

If you're driving to Lewes from London, take the M23 south and follow signs. The 57 mile (91km) journey takes around 1¾ hours. Most on-street parking is limited to residents, but there are public carparks near the train station, on South Street, and at the bottom of the hill on Harvey's Way. Expect to pay £4 a day.

> **Walking the "Twittens"**
>
> **Lewes still has many historic touches, including narrow footpaths called "twittens," winding through the town around the ruins of its castle. Locals use these to shortcut from one part of town to another.**

### GETTING AROUND

Lewes is easily walkable from the train station, which is in the middle of the historic town center. The town is built on a very steep hill—so you'll thank yourself for wearing good walking shoes. The more historic buildings are scattered and so expect to do a good bit of walking—the castle is at the top of the hill, the Anne of Cleves House is on the side of the hill, and there's good shopping on the steep High Street and at the base of the hill.

## A Day in Lewes

Built on a steep hillside, Lewes's streets are precipitous but if you start at the highest point—at least it's all downhill from there. **Lewes Castle ★**, perched on the crest of the hill at the center of town, dates to the days of **William the Conqueror** (approximately 1028–87) in the 11th century. Now largely in ruin, there's still enough of it left to show how formidable it must once have been and amazing views to be had over the **Sussex Downs** from the ramparts. In the adjoining **Barbican House Museum** (**✆ 01273/486-290**), you can learn more about the local history—open hours are Tuesday through Saturday from 10am to 5:30pm and Sunday, Monday from 11am to 5pm. Admission is £6.40 adults, £5.70 students and seniors, and £3.20 for children.

Thomas Paine, who may have helped spark the American Revolution with his pamphlet "Common Sense," lived in the half-timbered **Bull House** on High Street. The building is currently being restored and is only rarely open to the public. However, you can go into the **White Hart Hotel** (**✆ 01273/476-694;** www.whitehartlewes.co.uk) nearby at 55 High St., where he regularly went with friends to debate politics (although much of it has been heavily modernized).

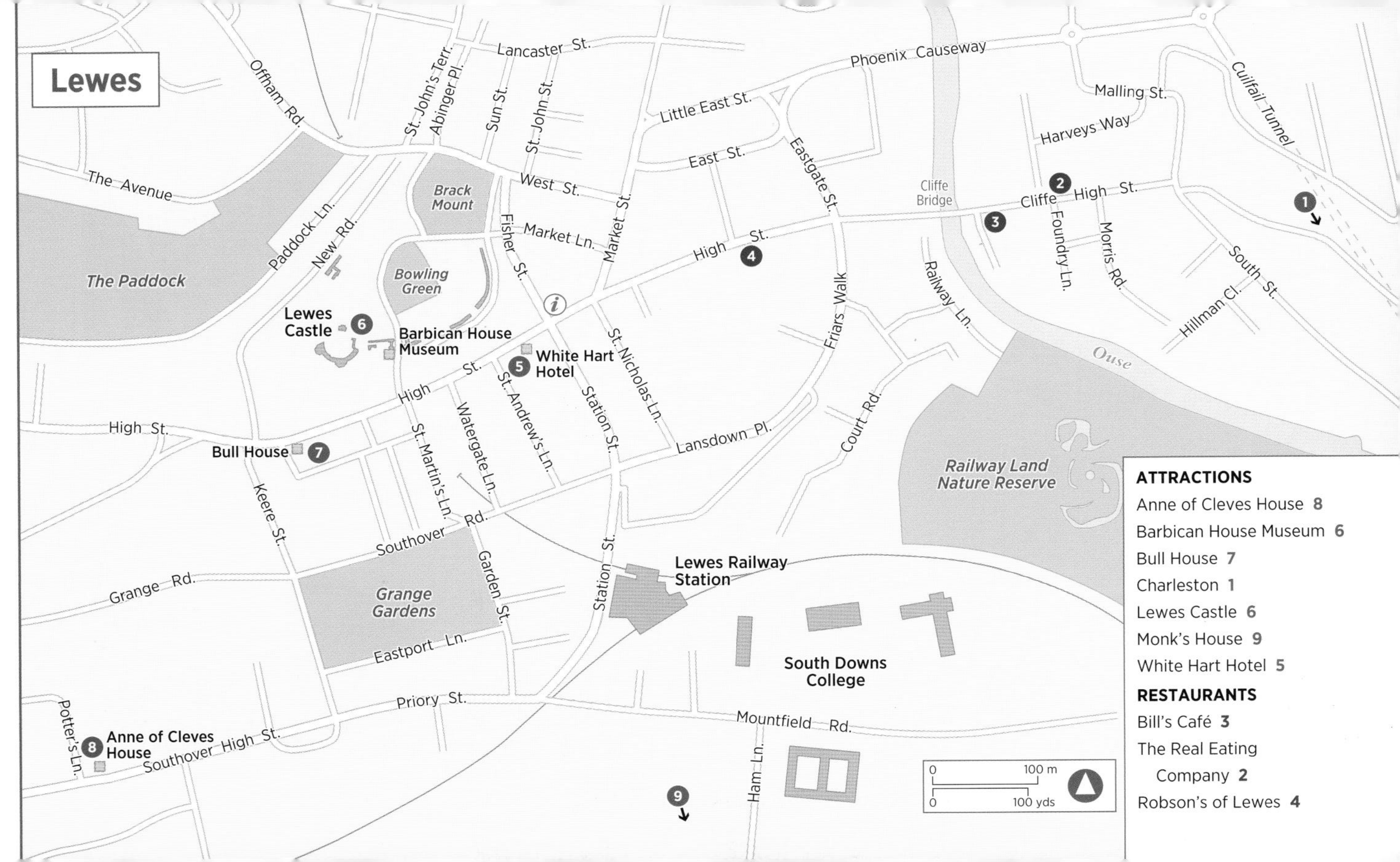

Lewes
ATTRACTIONS
Anne of Cleves House 8
Barbican House Museum 6
Bull House 7
Charleston 1
Lewes Castle 6
Monk's House 9
White Hart Hotel 5
RESTAURANTS
Bill's Café 3
The Real Eating Company 2
Robson's of Lewes 4
0
100 m
0
100 yds
Offham Rd.
St. John's Terr.
Abinger Pl.
Sun St.
St. John St.
Lancaster St.
Phoenix Causeway
Little East St.
Malling St.
Harveys Way
Cuilfail Tunnel
East St.
Eastgate St.
West St.
The Avenue
Brack Mount
Cliffe Bridge
Cliffe High St.
Market Ln.
Market St.
Fisher St.
Foundry Ln.
Morris Rd.
Paddock Ln.
New Rd.
Bowling Green
The Paddock
High St.
South St.
Hillman Cl.
Railway Ln.
Friars Walk
Ouse
Lewes Castle
Barbican House Museum
White Hart Hotel
St. Nicholas Ln.
St. Andrew's Ln.
Station St.
Court Rd.
Lansdown Pl.
Bull House
St. Martin's Ln.
Watergate Ln.
Railway Land Nature Reserve
Keere St.
Southover Rd.
Garden St.
Lewes Railway Station
Grange Rd.
Grange Gardens
Eastport Ln.
South Downs College
Priory St.
Mountfield Rd.
Potter's Ln.
Anne of Cleves House
Southover High St.
Ham Ln.

From there, a steep downhill walk brings you to the charmingly humble **Anne of Cleves House ★**, Southover St. (✆ **01273/474-610;** www.sussexpast.co.uk), which Henry VIII presented to his fourth wife after he divorced her in 1541. The kitchen and bedroom have rough-hewn floors and rustic furnishings, and there's a small, fragrant garden filled with herbs. Open Tuesday through Saturday 10am to 5pm, and Sunday and Monday 11am to 5pm. Admission is £4.40 for adults, £3.90 students and seniors, and £2.20 for children.

The kitchen inside Anne of Cleves House.

Three miles (5km) out of central Lewes, **Monk's House ★★**, off the A27 in Rodmell (✆ **01323/870-001;** www.nationaltrust.org.uk), was the home of novelist Virginia Woolf and her husband, the biographer Leonard Woolf. Only four rooms in the small, unassuming white clapboard house are open to visitors, including Virginia's study and bedroom. The decor is kept much as it was during Virginia's life, simple but elegant in muted colors with the art she collected during her life still on the walls. Her sister Vanessa Bell and the artist Duncan Grant

Shopping in Lewes High Street.

Bill's Café.

provided some of the unique decorations. It's open from April to October on Wednesdays and Saturdays 2 to 5:30pm. Admission costs £4.20 for adults and £2.10 for children.

Slightly farther out of Lewes, **Charleston ★★★** is off the A27 in the village of **Firle** (✆ **01323/811-265;** www.charleston.org.uk). Once the home of Vanessa Bell, it could well be called an art house, as she and Duncan Grant (who lived here until 1978) covered the walls, doors, and furniture in elaborate and beautiful paintings and murals. Their collections of art by Picasso and Renoir can be found tucked away in unexpected spaces. Entry by guided tour (lasts 1 hour, 1–6pm) is available Wednesday through Saturday and there's free-flow timed entry on Sunday and national holidays only. During July and August, the doors open early at noon and the ticket office always opens 30 minutes before the house, and so it's advisable to head here early to assure your place. Admission is £9 for adults and £5 for children 6 to 16.

## Shopping

Art and craft enthusiasts should aim for High Street. **Adamczewski ★**, 88 High St. (✆ **01273/470-105**), is a charming establishment, where everything is handmade—from the shelves to the soap and perfume. Near the station, lose yourself for an hour or so in the **Church Hill Antiques Centre ★** at 6 Station St. (✆ **01273/474-842**), where 60 dealers sell jewelry, linens, glass, and clothes. **Charleston** has an excellent gift shop (✆ **01323/811-265**), brimming with fabrics, ceramics, and prints based on designs created by Vanessa Bell and Duncan Grant.

### Nearby

The bustling, lively, arty city of **Brighton** is 8 miles (13km) south of Lewes on the coast. The two are connected by a short 10 minute train journey. With great shops, museums, and restaurants Brighton will keep you busy. Or you could just sit on the pebble beach and soak up some rays. See p. 154.

Just outside of Lewes is **Glyndebourne (✆ 01273/813-813; www.glyndebourne.com)**, a world-famous opera house tucked away in the Sussex countryside. Catching a performance here is a coveted experience among opera fans, but if you're one of them book in advance—tickets sell out early.

## Where to Eat

**The Real Eating Company ★**, 18 Cliff High St. (✆ **01273/402-650;** www.real-eating.co.uk), is a casual restaurant with big windows overlooking the busy street. The menu changes regularly but for lunch there are usually steaks, hamburgers, and freshly made soups. Not far away, **Bill's Café ★**, 56 Cliffe High St. (✆ **01273/476-918;** www.bills-website.co.uk), is a sunny, laid-back deli-cum-restaurant, with fresh, hot, daily specials as well as quiches, salads, sandwiches, and sinful desserts. **Robson's of Lewes,** 22 High St. (✆ **01273/480-654**), is a light-filled space, where you can pause for a cup of tea or light lunch, or order a picnic to go.

# RYE

"Rye is like an old beautifully jeweled brooch worn at South-England's throat." So wrote Patric Dickinson, one of the many writers who have fallen under the spell of this remarkably beautiful coastal town in East Sussex, 62 miles (100km) southeast of London. Once upon a time, the sea lapped at the footsteps of this medieval town, and it thrived as both a powerful seaport and a hub for smugglers. Gradually the harbor began to silt in the 18th century and the sea receded, leaving the coastline 2 miles (3km) away from Rye—a seaport without a sea. The historic town center has steep streets that wander down to a long-dry harbor, while the 900-year-old stone church and even older castle towers are perfectly preserved. Cars seem out of place on the narrow cobblestone lanes, and the pub at the foot of the hill still carries an 18th-century warning about smugglers and George Washington's revolution.

Rye claims to have more historic buildings than any other town in England, and is jam-packed with half-timbered Tudor and Elizabethan houses, a 14th-century entrance gate (Land Gate), a 12th-century defensive tower (Ypres Tower), handsome Georgian town houses, secret passageways, quaint corners, cobbled lanes, windy viewpoints, enticing shops, and wonderful restaurants.

All this charm made the town a popular getaway for writers including Henry James, E. F. Benson, and Radclyffe Hall. Until fairly recently, the town's streets were full of bookshops; sadly only a few remain today, but those that closed have at least been replaced by independent boutiques and shops, which are a pleasure to visit.

Rye is small enough to explore in a few hours, so you have time to head out to nearby towns such as Winchelsea, which once looked out at Rye across a bay

Rye
ATTRACTIONS
Lamb House 5
Landgate 11
Mermaid Inn 4
Rye Heritage Centre 2
St. Mary's Church 6
Strand Quay 1
Town Hall 9
Ypres Tower 8
RESTAURANTS
The Fish Café 10
The Ship Inn 3
Simon the Pieman 7
0 100 m
0 100 yds
Rye Railway Station
Landgate
Eagle Rd.
Rope Walk
New Rd.
Tower St.
East Cliff
Fishmarket Rd.
Cinque Ports St.
Conduit Hill
Ferry Rd.
Jarretts Cl.
Market Rd.
High St.
East St.
Cyprus Pl.
Lion St.
The Mint
Wish St.
Wish Ward
West St.
Town Hall
Mermaid Inn
Mermaid St.
St. Mary's Church
Rye Heritage Centre
Lamb House
Ypres Tower
The Deals
Church Square
Strand Quay
Tillingham
Strand
Watchbell Ln.
Watchbell St.
Winchelsea Rd.
South Undercliff
Rock Channel
Rother
Brede

and now can be seen across a sea of marsh grass, and Battle where the Battle of Hastings took place in 1066.

## Essentials

### VISITOR INFORMATION

At the **Tourist Information Centre,** 4–5 Lion St. (✆ **01797/226-696;** www.visitrye.co.uk), you can obtain a free town map. The center is open daily from April to September 10am to 5pm, and October to March 10am to 4pm. The **Rye Heritage Centre** on Strand Quay (✆ **01797/226-696;** www.ryeheritage.co.uk) also has ample information.

### SCHEDULING CONSIDERATIONS

In summer months, Rye can be packed on weekends and holidays, and because it's a tiny town it can feel overrun, and so you could opt to visit on a quieter weekday instead. In September, the **Rye Arts Festival** (✆ **01797/224-442;** www.ryefestival.co.uk) lights up the town with concerts, lectures, and performances. Every autumn **Rye Bonfire Weekend** (held the nearest weekend to November 5), and Guy Fawkes Night is marked with a dramatic torchlight procession and bonfire.

### GETTING THERE

#### By Train

There are no direct trains to Rye from London. Trains to Ashford International depart every 30 minutes from London St. Pancras—the journey takes around 40 minutes. From Ashford, trains depart for Rye every hour—that journey takes 25 minutes. The standard, same-day, round-trip fare from London is about £30. It's an easy 10 minute walk from Rye train station on Cinque Ports Street to Strand Quay, a good place to start your explorations.

Mermaid Street.

#### By Car

Rye is 10 miles (16km) northeast of Hastings on the A259. From London, take the A21 to Flimwell and then turn onto the A268 and follow signs for Rye. The trip usually takes just over an hour. Rye has no free street parking, and so park in one of the many carparks at the foot of the hill (the one behind the train station charges £1.50 a day).

Stained glass window, St. Mary's Church.

The 12th century Ypres Tower.

## GETTING AROUND

Rye is compact enough for you to traverse the entire town in 15 minutes at a pace. Decent walking shoes come in handy here: It's on a hill and the streets are steep.

## A Day in Rye

Start on the old waterfront at the foot of the hill on **Strand Quay.** The gloomy, black, wood-framed buildings are actually former sail lofts, where fishermen once repaired their sails. Most of these now house eclectic antiques stores, restaurants, and ice-cream shops, but one holds the **Rye Heritage Centre** (**✆ 01797/226-696;** www.ryeheritage.co.uk), which offers extensive information about the history of the town. It opens from 10am to 3pm, with admission at £3.

Right behind the sail lofts, the steep, cobbled **Mermaid Street** comprises a line of quaint cottages with names like "The House with Two Front Doors." At the top, the **Mermaid Inn ★** (**✆ 01787/223-065;** www.mermaidinn.com) is a half-timbered Tudor building that once hosted the cut-throat "Hawkhurst Gang" of smugglers, and is believed to be haunted by some of them.

Where Mermaid Street curves into West Street you'll see **Lamb House** (**✆ 01892/890-651;** www.nationaltrust.org.uk), a dignified, redbrick Georgian house that served as the last residence of American writer Henry James, who became a British citizen and lived here from 1898 to 1916. Some rooms are open to the public mid-March through October Thursdays and Saturdays 2 to 6pm: Admission is £3.80 for adults, £2 for children 5 to 15.

Follow West Street to the shady churchyard where **St. Mary's Church ★★** has stood at the highest point in Rye for 900 years. Inside, the colonnaded nave

LEFT: The only remaining 14th century gate in Rye; RIGHT: Rye Harbour Nature Reserve.

is surprisingly airy and graceful, and the long pendulum of the 16th-century clock swings steadily above your head. The beautiful stained-glass window by Sir Edward Burne-Jones, the pre-Raphaelite painter, dates from 1891. Climb the church tower (£2.50) for a magnificent view over the rooftops of Rye to the marshes below.

## Nearby

**Winchelsea** ★ (www.winchelsea.net), the smallest town in England, stands 2 miles (3km) west of Rye on the A259 and is also a pleasant bike ride or walk. In 1277, a charter fortified Winchelsea against French invaders and resulted in the town being rebuilt and laid out in grid form, the first such example of town planning in England (it was reputedly used as a model for New York City's grid street system). At that time, Winchelsea had a harbor and, like Rye, was one of the "Ancient Towns" affiliated with the Cinque Ports defense network. Today Winchelsea is a quiet town with some fine old buildings and great views toward the coast. Four miles (6km) south of Rye on the Camber Road, **Camber Sands** ★★ is a sprawling expanse of sandy beach surrounded by dunes. It stretches for 7 miles (11km) and is well-signposted, just outside the tiny town of **Camber** (www.camber-sussex.co.uk). The historic town of **Battle** ★ (www.battle-sussex.co.uk), 15 miles (24km) from Rye, is the site of the 1066 Battle of Hastings, where the Norman Conquest began, and you can explore the picturesque abbey that now sits on the old battlefield.

Just south of the church, on **Pump Street,** you'll find the 12th-century **Ypres Tower** (✆ **01797/226-728**). Built by King Henry III as a guard tower, it now houses a small local history museum displaying an 18th-century fire engine, local pottery, ironwork, and items relating to smuggling and town life. Standing on the terrace, where cannons point toward France, you're looking out at what was once the sea.

From Ypres Tower, take Pump Street north to **Market Street** passing the arcaded **Town Hall,** dating from 1742 (not open to the public), and then continue north on East Street, turning right on East Cliffe. At the end of it you'll see the formidable **Landgate ★**, one of three such gates erected in the 14th century and the only one remaining. You can still see the murder holes at the top through which boiling oil could be poured on raiding parties. Returning along East Cliffe brings you back to High Street, lined with shops and galleries, which winds its way down to the Heritage Centre.

## ORGANIZED TOURS

The Heritage Centre (p. 38) offers recorded audio tours (£4) that guide you on a walking tour of the town. You can move at your own pace, and the information about Rye and its history is thorough and interesting.

## OUTDOOR ACTIVITIES

The **Rye Harbour Nature Preserve** can easily be reached on foot or bicycle by taking Harbour Road, a small road off the A259 on the Hastings side of the town. The distance is about 2 miles (3km). The road leads to the 209-acre (84-hectare)

Plenty of opputunities for antique shopping in Rye.

preserve, a tract of shingle ridges formed over hundreds of years as the sea receded. The varied habitat of grazing marsh, arable fields, and intertidal salt marsh is known for its bird life, particularly for its 50 or so breeding species of terns, oystercatchers, and plovers.



## Shopping

At the foot of the hill just beyond the station, **Glass Etc ★**, 18–22 Rope Walk (✆ **01797/226-600**), is a glittering gem filled with beautiful antique pieces to suit most budgets. Near the Heritage Centre **Black Sheep Antiques ★**, 72 The Mint (✆ **01797/224-508**), has a good mix of British and French antiques, some quite affordable. Rye pottery has a distinctive country cottage style, and **David Sharp Pottery,** 55 The Mint (✆ **01797/222-620**), is filled with colorful handmade creations. The Rye **Farmers' Market** (www.ryemarket.org.uk), held on Wednesday from 10am to 1pm on Strand Quay, has stalls selling fish and local organic produce, plus cakes and breads. On Friday, the **Rye Country Market** is held in the Rye Community Centre, Conduit Hill, starting at 10am; here you'll find more local products, including crafts.

## Where to Eat

**The Fish Café ★★**, 17 Tower St. (✆ **01797/222-226**), is an elegant eatery at the foot of the hill specializing in fresh, local seafood. Mains range in price from £13 to £15 and dishes of particular note include the grilled sole and the shellfish

The long sandy expanse of Camber Sands.

Simon the Pieman near St. Mary's Church.

platter. A charming, old tearoom in the shadow of St. Mary's Church, **Simon the Pieman,** 3 Lion St. (✆ **01797/222-207**), serves lunches, or an afternoon tea with cake and scones, all for less than £10. At the bottom of the hill, **The Ship Inn ★**, The Strand (✆ **01797/222-233;** www.theshipinrye.co.uk), dates to 1592, and its low beams and open fireplaces attest to its heritage. A big, sprawling pub, it dishes-up satisfying, seasonal food using fresh, local produce—try the grilled mackerel with chips or the local lamb chop with stuffed tomato. It's open for breakfast, too, and its Sunday roast lunches are legendary.

# WOODBRIDGE

Approach this sleepy corner of Suffolk by car from a certain direction and you'd be forgiven for thinking you were by the sea, as the road leads you past a bustling marina filled with yachts and fishing boats. In fact Woodbridge overlooks a tidal estuary of the River Deben, but it still has the feel of a coastal town, with sloping, narrow streets, quaint shops, and cozy old pubs.

Woodbridge was briefly catapulted to global fame in the 1930s when archaeologists working at Sutton Hoo (a stretch of land on the outskirts of the town) unearthed one of the greatest archaeological finds of the 20th century. In A.D. 625 an Anglo-Saxon king had been buried there, together with his longboat and a massive hoard of treasure. In addition, if you've got time to explore a little further afield, the atmospheric remains of Framlingham Castle and the pretty seaside town of Aldeburgh are within a short drive.

A morning could be easily spent seeing the sights of the town and having lunch, before heading onto the excellent museum at Sutton Hoo and the somber burial mounds in the afternoon.

## Essentials

### VISITOR INFORMATION

The **Tourist Information Centre,** Station Buildings (✆ **01394/382-240;** www.visit-suffolk.co.uk), is at the station, not far from the riverside. In summer the opening hours are Monday through Saturday, from 9am to 5:30pm, and Sunday 10am to 4pm.

## SCHEDULING CONSIDERATIONS

Woodbridge is a popular destination in summer. Coming midweek will avoid the biggest crowds, but do check that everything you want to see will be open—some attractions are not. Try to arrive before noon if you're driving, as the few parking spaces quickly fill.

The Shire Hall on Market Hill.

## GETTING THERE

### By Train

There are no direct trains from London to Woodbridge; take a train from London Liverpool St. to Ipswich and change there for one of the smaller local trains. The total journey takes about 1½ hours and costs £35. It's highly advisable to book in advance for cheaper fares.

### By Car

Woodbridge is 87 miles (140km) northeast of London; the A12 goes directly there from northeast London.

The Tide Mill overlooking the River Deben.

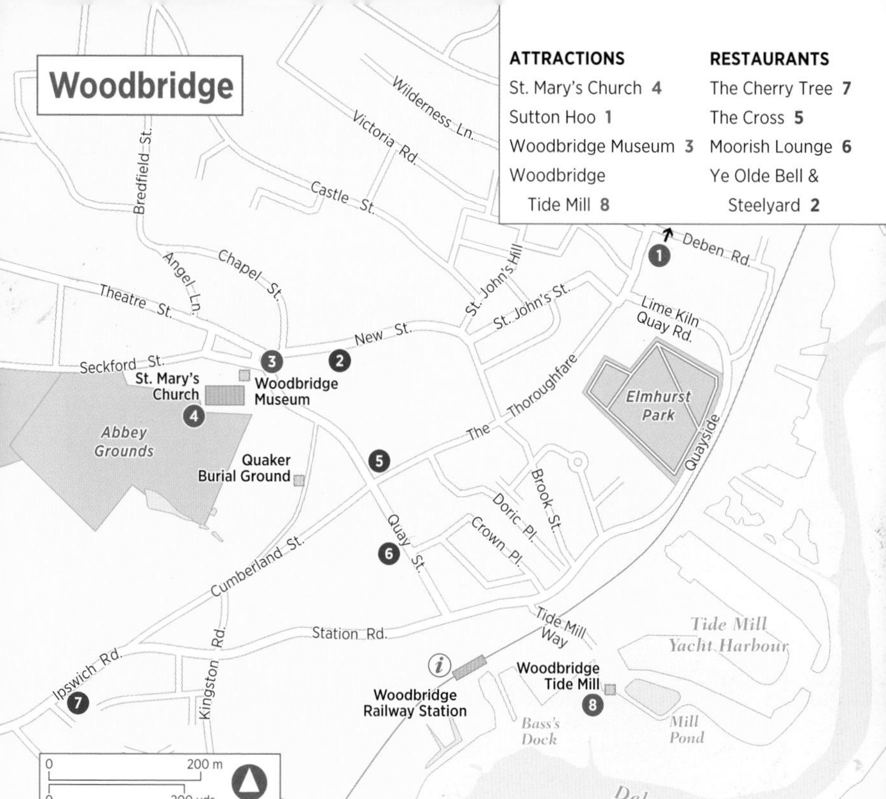


## GETTING AROUND

Woodbridge is a small town and very easy to navigate. If you arrive by train you'll have an ideal starting point because the station's well-situated for both the tide mill and the river Deben, and only a short walk to The Thoroughfare.

## A Day in Woodbridge

A short walk from the railway station on Tide Mill Way, the **Woodbridge Tide Mill** ★ is a picturesque, white stone building overlooking the River Deben. There's been a mill here since the 12th century, although the current building only dates from the 1700s. At the time of writing a major refurbishment was underway that should see the mill re-open in early 2012 with a new visitor center and improved access. It's expected to be open to visitors daily in summer from 11am to 4:30pm, with entry around £3.

The small but informative **Woodbridge Museum** (✆ **01394/380-502**) on Market Hill gives a neat overview of the town's history. There are also exhibits on Sutton Hoo (see below) and Burrow Hill, a large Saxon cemetery excavated in the 1980s. The museum is open from Easter to October, Thursday through Sunday, from 10am to 4pm (daily July–Aug). Admission is only £1 for adults and

30p for children. On Market Hill, the 15th century **St. Mary's Church** houses tombs and an elaborately carved font. You can also climb the tower for sweeping views of the town.

The most important haul of Anglo-Saxon treasure in history was found at **Sutton Hoo** ★ ☺ (**01394/389-700;** www.nationaltrust.org.uk). Disappointingly, the treasures themselves are kept at the British Museum (www.britishmuseum.org) in London, but there are replicas on display here, and the purpose-built museum is informative and well-maintained, with a short film, walk-through reconstruction of the burial ship, and dressing-up box. The grounds contain a trail that takes you past several burial mounds, with information boards along the route. There's also a family-friendly cafe with a terrace overlooking the mounds. Sutton Hoo is signposted off the A1152 between Woodbridge and Sutton. It's open April to October, daily from 10:30am to 5pm, and weekends 11am to 4pm for the rest of the year (with some extra days in Mar).

St. Mary's Church.

## Shopping

There are plenty of independent retailers in Woodbridge and you'll find many reasons to stop and browse, not only on the main thoroughfare but also on the side streets, particularly Market Hill. There are a number of book outlets, but **Browsers Bookshop** ★, 60 The Thoroughfare (✆ **01394/388-890;** www.browsersbookshop.com), is the most modern and inviting of them all, stocking a good number of books on the local area, and with a small cafe. **Darcy B's Little Mermaid,** 20 Market Hill (✆ **01394/388-811;** www.darcy-b.com), sells Scandinavian-influenced designer homewares and accessories. Woodbridge, as with many country towns, enjoys a table sale and there's plenty going on throughout the year from vintage and antiques fairs to local farmers' markets—so before you set-off, check the useful, local website to see if anything is going on (www.choosewoodbridge.co.uk/whats-on).

## Nearby

Housed in a once-top-secret USAF base 6 miles (9.5km) southwest of Woodbridge, is the **Bentwaters Cold War Museum ★★ (✆ 07588/877-020;** www.bentwaters-as.org.uk). The base has been preserved as it was when it closed in 1993, including the war rooms, command center, and nuclear decontamination areas. It opens April through October on Sundays only 10am to 4pm, plus a handful of extra days in May and August. Admission is £5 for adults and £4 for children.

The last refuge of Mary Tudor ("Bloody Mary") before she marched to London to claim her crown, **Framlingham Castle ★ (✆ 01728/724-189;** www.english-heritage.org.uk), is a reasonably intact 12th-century ruin, 12 miles (19km) north of Woodbridge. Open hours vary depending on the time of year, so check the website for accurate timings. Admission is £6.30 for adults and £3.80 for children. The no. 63 bus passes through Woodbridge on the way to the castle.

Fifteen miles (24km) northeast of Woodbridge, **Aldeburgh ★★** (www.visit-suffolkcoast.co.uk) is a very pretty seaside town with a charming, old-fashioned beach promenade and a distinctive steel sculpture on the beach called *The Scallop* (image right) by local artist Maggi Hambling. The ridiculously popular **Fish & Chip Shop** (www.aldeburghfishandchips.co.uk) on High Street is certainly one of the best in the area and should not be missed, but be prepared to queue at weekends. Thirteen miles (21km) west of Woodbridge is the extraordinary coastal reserve at **Orford Ness ★★★ (✆ 01728/648-024;**

www.nationaltrust.org.uk). Marked walking trails take you across the wild and beautiful five-mile (8-km) shingle spit, home only to seabirds—although there are abandoned buildings here and there, a remnant of its past as a military testing zone (radar was developed here in the 1930s). Orford Ness can only be reached by ferry from **Orford Quay** (£7.50 adults, £3.75 children). Crossings run late June to September Tuesday through Saturday from 10am to 2pm; also Saturdays only, late April to mid-June and October. Orford Quay is 13 miles (21km) along Orford Rd. (the B1084).

### Walking Around Woodbridge

For a short walk that takes you around the main sights of the town, start at the Community Centre car park. Toward the rear right-hand corner, follow a grass-edged footpath to Kingston Road, turn left, cross the railway level crossing, and then turn left on to River Walk. Continue past the railway footbridge to Ferry Quay walking toward the **Tide Mill** (p. 45). Turn left onto Tide Mill Way, crossing the railway level crossing, and then left again into Quayside. Walk over the pedestrian crossing at the Riverside Cinema, and walk up Quay Street for a few minutes, continuing over Cross Corner and onto Church Street, which leads to the steeper Market Hill. At the top, you'll find the **Shire Hall** and the **Woodbridge Museum** (p. 45). Continue down New Street to **The Thoroughfare,** turn right toward Cross Corner, and continue straight up Cumberland Street with its 16th- and 17th-century buildings. End the walk at the **Cherry Tree Pub** (below).

## Where to Eat

The 16th-century **Ye Olde Bell & Steelyard ★★**, 103 New St. (✆ **01394/382-933;** www.yeoldebellandsteelyard.co.uk), is about as satisfyingly old-looking a pub as you're likely to find. A respectable choice of real ales and ciders is served alongside homemade Thai seafood laksa or steak and kidney pie. Baguettes and a children's menu is available at lunchtime, priced from £4. There are some old-fashioned games too, such as bar skittles and shove-halfpenny. Another old oak-beamed pub serving superb meals is **The King's Head Inn,** 17 Market Hill (✆ **01394 383117;** www.kingsheadwoodbridge.co.uk), the appetizing menu often includes some excellent vegetarian and fish options. **The Cherry Tree,** 73 Cumberland St. (✆ **01394/384-627;** www.thecherrytreepub.co.uk), is a cozy, low-ceilinged pub with a pile of board games in the corner, serving above-average hot and cold bar food (starting from around £5 for a sandwich at lunchtime). **The Cross,** 2 Church St.

The Cherry Tree

(✆ **01394/389-076;** www.thecross1652.com), is an excellent and stylish vegetarian bistro-cum-wine-bar with occasional live music, serving pizzas and clever veggie twists on popular dishes (mains £11-£14). The **Moorish Lounge,** 3 Quay St. (✆ **01394/388-508;** www.moorish.me), is particularly inviting during the warmer months when you can bask out in the sunny courtyard with a glass of wine, tucking into meze. Homemade flatbread pizzas are £9, whilst meze dishes start from £2.50 for dips, up to £6.50.

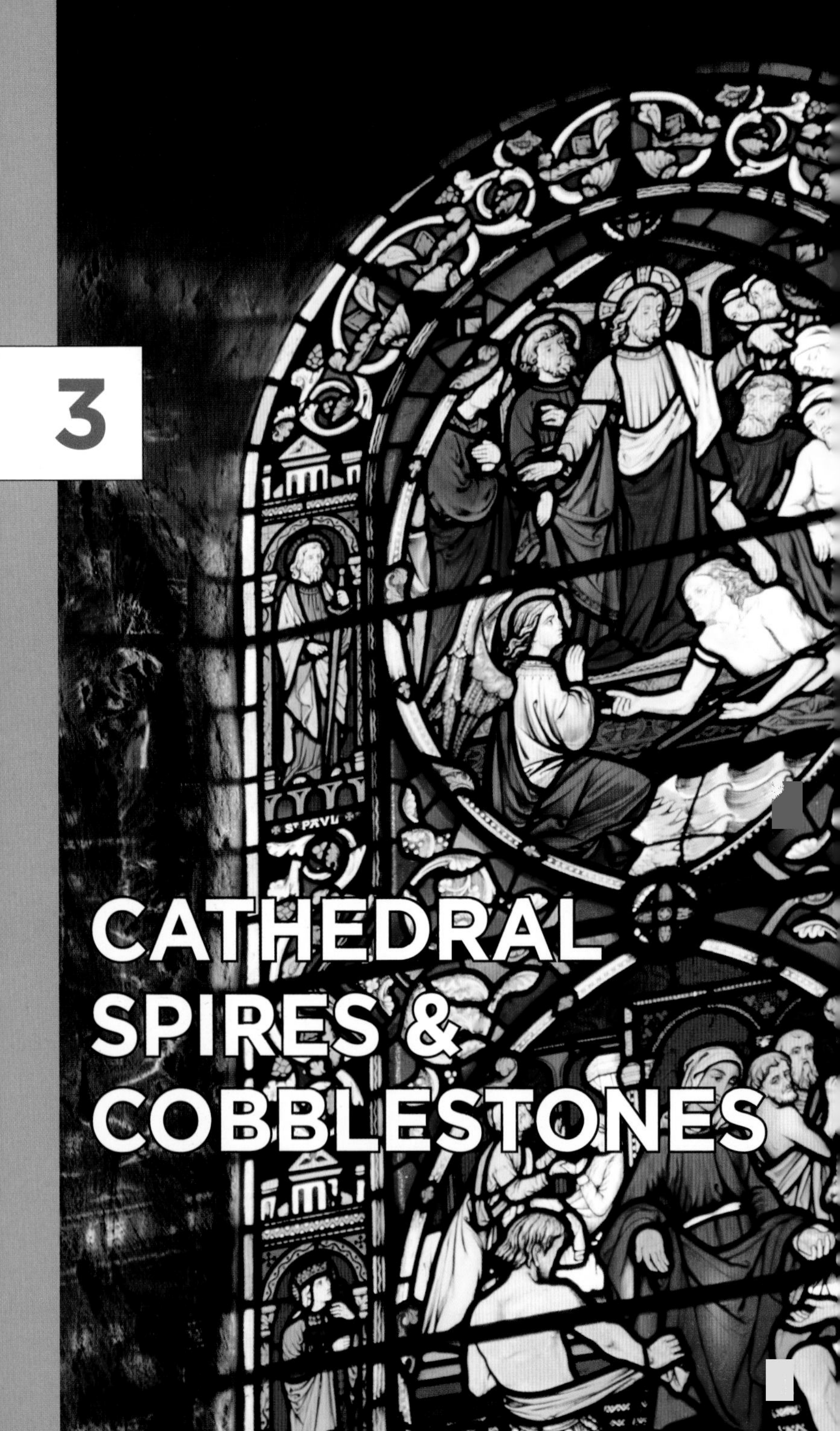


# 3

# CATHEDRAL SPIRES & COBBLESTONES

The magnificent cathedrals of England that long ago represented the power, wealth, and stature of sovereigns, can today be appreciated for their architectural beauty, breathtaking views, and sheer craftsmanship. Through the centuries many churches were subjected to dramatic changes and have become places of sanctuary. Today, the marks left at St. Thomas à Becket's shrine by medieval pilgrims in Canterbury can still be touched, and many great works of art and literature have been inspired by Salisbury: Thomas Hardy and Anthony Trollope both set novels here and Turner and Constable captured the cathedral on canvas.

---

The streets and buildings that surround these monuments often reflect the long and colorful history of the cities, from winding lanes and tiny alleyways to cobblestoned-streets lined with gabled shop-fronts. Often, only a short walk away, are peaceful pathways leading into the surrounding countryside: head off on the Crab and Winkle way on a disused railway line in Canterbury or see the marshlands of Salterns Way, on a ramble from Chichester.

## CANTERBURY

Immortalized by Chaucer in The Canterbury Tales, this city 60 miles (96km) southeast of London has been a religious epicenter for centuries—first for the Catholic Church and then for the Church of England. The city's most famous feature, the soaring cathedral, began to rise in 1070. There, in a corner of the northwest transept, knights of Henry II murdered Thomas à Becket, then Archbishop of Canterbury, in 1170. Becket was canonized as a saint just 3 years later, at which point Canterbury became one of Europe's most popular pilgrimage centers. For nearly 400 years, until Henry VIII had the shrine destroyed in 1538, pilgrims from throughout England and Europe flocked to this medieval spiritual center in search of miracles and a bit of adventure. Bell Harry, the graceful cathedral bell tower that guided the pilgrims across the fields and orchards of the Kent countryside, will lead you to this appealing city, too. Canterbury Cathedral remains one of England's greatest and most venerable glories—its social and spiritual impact over the centuries has been profound.

However, this city on the banks of the River Stour was a prominent religious site long before Chaucer wove his 13th-century tales. In A.D. 595, a Benedictine monk known as Augustine of Canterbury was sent by Rome to convert the then-pagan English. He founded an abbey here in 597 that became one of Europe's great centers of learning. Its evocative remains now spread across a grassy field

FACING PAGE: **Chichester Cathedral.**

Stained glass window depicting Thomas à Becket, Canterbury Cathedral.

not far from the cathedral; both the cathedral and the abbey are UNESCO World Heritage Sites.

Plan to spend the whole day in Canterbury because there's plenty to do to fill the time. Alternatively, you can spend the afternoon taking in Kent's sea breezes in the nearby coastal town of Whitstable, just a short train ride away.

## Essentials

### VISITOR INFORMATION

The **Tourist Information Centre,** 12–13 Sun St. (✆ **01227/378-100;** www.canterbury.co.uk), opposite Christchurch Gate near the cathedral, is open Monday through Saturday, 9:30am to 5pm, and Sunday, 9:30am to 4:30pm. There you can pick up a Canterbury Attractions Passport (£20 adults, £17 children), which admits you to the cathedral and abbey and two other sights of your choice.

### SCHEDULING CONSIDERATIONS

Canterbury is popular year-round, but crowds swell in summer. If you want to visit the cathedral in relative peace, choose a weekday and arrive early. Alternatively, come late in the day and you might even catch Evensong, an atmospheric experience.

### GETTING THERE

#### By Train

Canterbury has two train stations, both within easy walking distance of the city center. Trains run to Canterbury from London Victoria every 30 minutes, and from Charing Cross around once an hour. The journey takes 1½ hours and a round-trip ticket costs about £20.

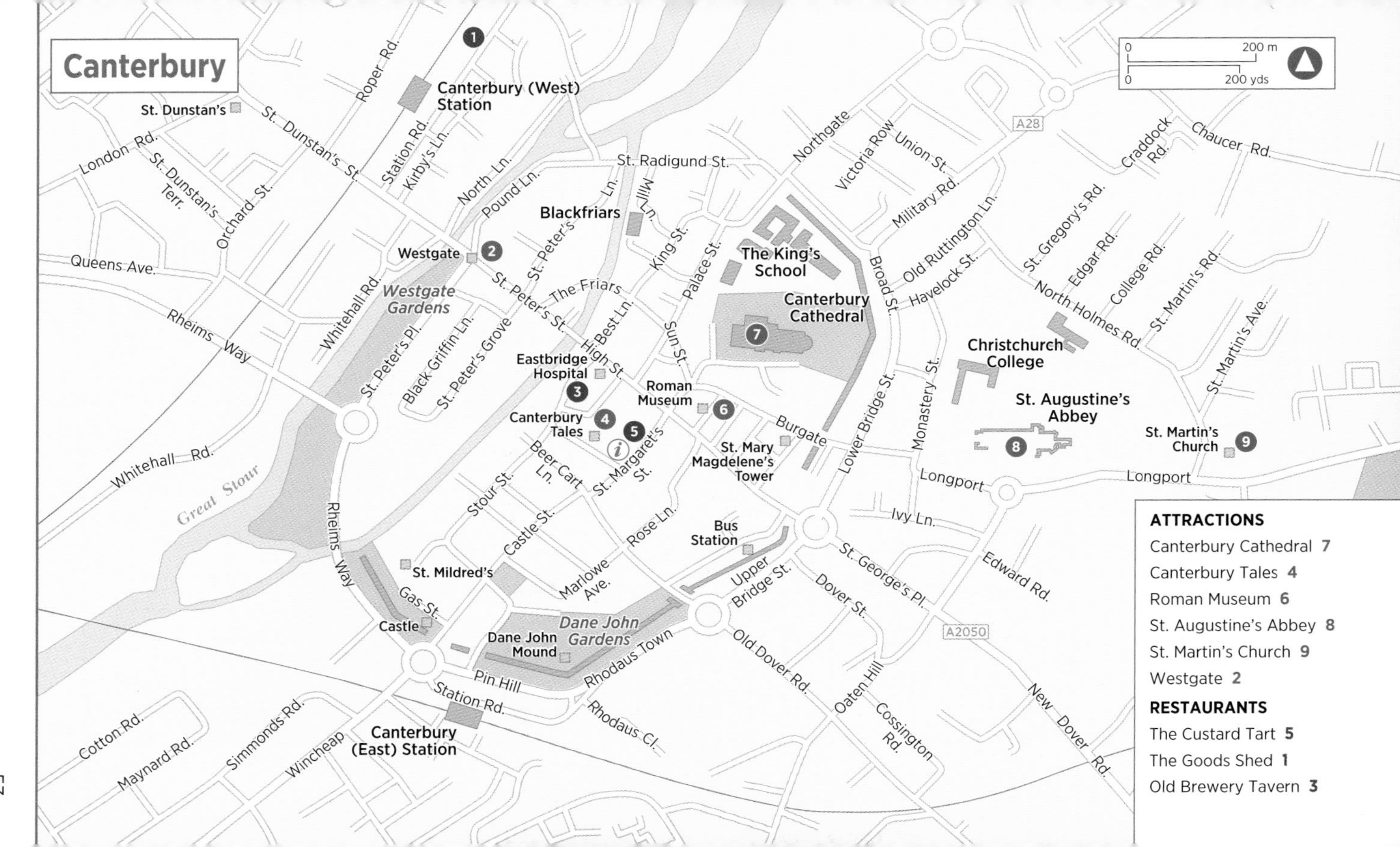

Canterbury
0 200 m
0 200 yds
Canterbury (West) Station
St. Dunstan's
Westgate
Westgate Gardens
Blackfriars
The King's School
Canterbury Cathedral
Eastbridge Hospital
Roman Museum
Canterbury Tales
St. Mary Magdelene's Tower
Christchurch College
St. Augustine's Abbey
St. Martin's Church
Bus Station
St. Mildred's
Castle
Dane John Gardens
Dane John Mound
Canterbury (East) Station
Great Stour
Roper Rd.
St. Dunstan's St.
London Rd.
St. Dunstan's Terr.
Orchard St.
Station Rd.
Kirby's Ln.
North Ln.
Pound Ln.
St. Radigund St.
Mill Ln.
Ln.
Queens Ave.
Whitehall Rd.
Rheims Way
St. Peter's Pl.
Black Griffin Ln.
St. Peter's Grove
St. Peter's St.
St. Peter's Ln.
The Friars
Best Ln.
High St.
King St.
Palace St.
Sun St.
Burgate
Northgate
Victoria Row
Union St.
Military Rd.
Old Ruttington Ln.
Havelock St.
Broad St.
Lower Bridge St.
Monastery St.
Longport
Ivy Ln.
St. Gregory's Rd.
Edgar Rd.
College Rd.
North Holmes Rd.
St. Martin's Rd.
St. Martin's Ave.
Craddock Rd.
Chaucer Rd.
A28
A2050
Beer Cart Ln.
St. Margaret's St.
Stour St.
Castle St.
Rose Ln.
Marlowe Ave.
Gas St.
Upper Bridge St.
St. George's Pl.
Edward Rd.
Dover St.
Old Dover Rd.
Oaten Hill
Cossington Rd.
New Dover Rd.
Rhodaus Town
Rhodaus Cl.
Pin Hill
Cotton Rd.
Maynard Rd.
Simmonds Rd.
Wincheap
ATTRACTIONS
Canterbury Cathedral 7
Canterbury Tales 4
Roman Museum 6
St. Augustine's Abbey 8
St. Martin's Church 9
Westgate 2
RESTAURANTS
The Custard Tart 5
The Goods Shed 1
Old Brewery Tavern 3

### By Bus

**National Express** (✆ **08717/818-178;** www.nationalexpress.com) offers a frequent, direct bus service from London's Victoria bus station to Canterbury's bus station on St. George's Lane, a few minutes' walk from the cathedral. The trip takes 1 hour and 50 minutes; round-trip tickets cost £9 to £14.

### By Car

From London, take the A2 and then the M2. The trip takes about 2 hours. Much of the city center is pedestrian only, and so park in one of the public carparks at the edge of the city center, on Sturry Road, Wincheap, or New Dover Road.



### GETTING AROUND

Canterbury city center is easily walkable, but if you need to travel beyond the center taxis are usually available outside the train stations; or you can order a taxi by calling **Lynx** (✆ **01227/464-232**) or **Cabwise** (✆ **01227/712-929**).



## A Day in Canterbury

For a pilgrim's tour of Canterbury, enter the city through the **Westgate,** where St. Peter's Street crosses the River Stour. The gate has stood guard over the road to and from London for some 600 years, and hundreds of thousands of medieval pilgrims, on their way to visit St. Thomas à Becket's shrine, passed through this gateway into the city. A spiral access stairway leads up to the battlements for a panoramic view of the city and its cathedral.

Turn north onto Mercery Lane and follow it to Christ Church Gate, dominated by **Canterbury Cathedral** ★★★ (✆ **01227/762-862;** www.canterbury-cathedral.org). The soaring edifice, begun in 1070, was the first in England erected in the Gothic style. The cathedral houses the medieval royal tombs of Henry IV

The ruins of St. Augustine's Abbey.

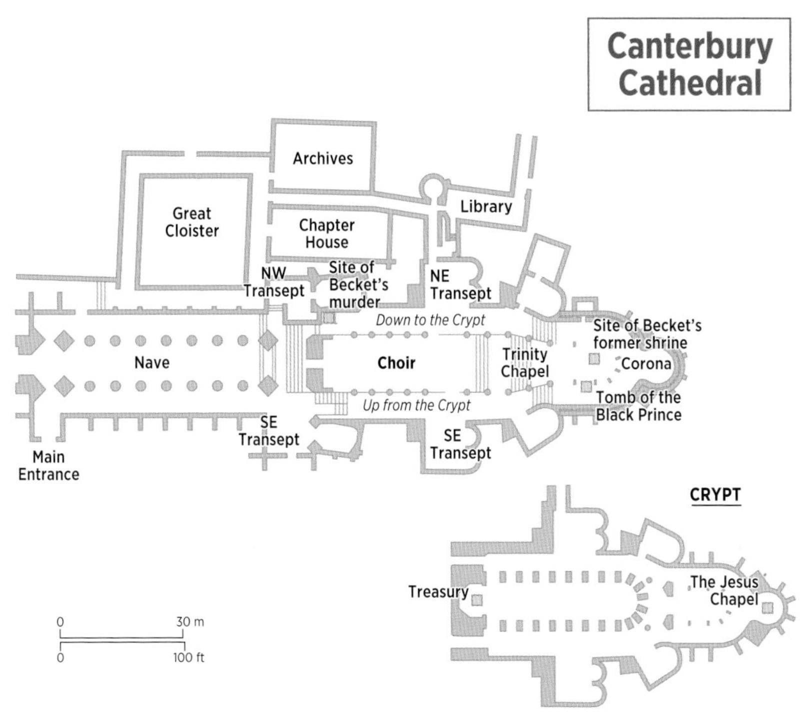


and Edward the Black Prince, but more stirring are the grooves that legions of pilgrims wore into the stone floor as they crawled on their knees past Thomas à Becket's shrine in the **Trinity Chapel.** Puritans ransacked the church during the English Civil War in the 1640s—the marauders spared much, except for the vibrant paintings that once covered the walls. You can still make out a fragment, depicting St. Paul and the viper, in the northeast corner. The cathedral is open daily 9am to 5pm (Nov–Feb until 4:30pm). Admission is £9 for adults, £8 for seniors, students, and children.

Follow Burgate east, crossing Lower Bridge Street and Monastery Street, to Longport, (the walk takes about 15 minutes) to the atmospheric ruins of **St. Augustine's Abbey ★★** (✆ **01227/767-345**). St. Augustine founded a monastic community here in A.D. 597, when he came to England from Rome to spread Christianity. The community flourished, and by 1500 the abbey was a center of learning, with a 2,000-volume library. Devastatingly, it was destroyed along with most of the country's abbeys by Henry VIII, who later had a palace built on the grounds to house Anne of Cleves (their marriage was short-lived, and Anne later moved to Hever Castle; see p. 105). The ruins of the abbey and the palace are open April to June Wednesday through Sunday 10am to 5pm, July and August daily 10am to 6pm, and September through March Sunday 11am to 5pm. Admission is £4.50 for adults, £3.80 for seniors and students.

## HENRY II VERSUS THOMAS À BECKET: A MEDIEVAL power STRUGGLE

Thomas à Becket was born in 1118, the son of a prosperous merchant. As a young man he worked for the Archbishop of Canterbury who introduced him to the newly crowned king, Henry II. The two became great friends, and Henry later named Becket his chancellor. When the archbishop died, Henry saw the opportunity to increase his influence over the Church by naming his friend to the highest religious post in the land. Becket was quickly invested as a priest, ordained a bishop, and made archbishop. But responsibility changed Becket, and the two men clashed. When Becket refused to absolve two English bishops whom he'd excommunicated, Henry flew into a rage shouting, "Who will rid me of this meddlesome priest?" Four knights who heard him say those words arrived at Canterbury a few days later. Fearing arrest, Becket fled to the cathedral where the knights found him at the altar and killed him messily—hacking at him as he crawled away from them.

The brutal act shocked Europe. Soon miracles were reported at Becket's tomb and pilgrims descended on the cathedral. To show penance, the king donned sackcloth and walked barefoot through the streets while 80 monks flogged him, and then spent the night alone in Becket's tomb.

Another 5 minutes east from St. Augustine's Abbey on North Holmes Road is the oldest parish church in England and another UNESCO World Heritage Site **St. Martin's Church** (✆ **01227/459-482**). St. Martin's was already more than a century old when Augustine arrived in A.D. 597, and parts of the structure date to Roman times, although much of it was rebuilt in the 17th century. It's open daily from 9am to 5pm and admission is free.

Backtrack to Christ Church Gate on Burgate, and follow Butchery Lane to the **Roman Museum** ★ (✆ **01227/785-575**). The period is chronicled through reconstructions, video presentations, and hands-on displays in this small but fascinating museum in the excavated Roman levels of the city between the cathedral and High Street. It's open Monday through Saturday from 10am to 4pm year-round, and on Sunday (June–Oct only) from 1:30 to 4pm. Admission is £6 for adults, £5 for seniors and students; children 15 and under get in free (when entering with an adult).

Take St. George's Street north to St. Margaret's Street and turn left. The **Canterbury Tales** ☺, 23 St. Margaret's St., in St. Margaret's Church (✆ **01227/454-888**; www.canterburytales.org.uk), re-creates scenes from Geoffrey Chaucer's spirited and sometimes bawdy stories about medieval pilgrims on their way to the city. Open daily 10am to 5pm (Nov–Feb until 4:30pm and July–Aug from 9:30am). Admission is £8 for adults, £7 for seniors and students, and £6 for children.

### ORGANIZED TOURS

**Historic walks** led by well-informed guides leave from the Tourist Information Centre on Sun Street daily at 2pm. Additional walks are held daily in July and August at 11:30am. The cost is £5 for adults, £4.50 students, and £3.50 children 11 and under.

The River Stour runs through Canterbury.

The **Canterbury River Navigation Company,** Westgate Gardens (✆ **07816/760-869;** www.crnc.co.uk), offers boat trips along the River Stour from Easter until late September or early October from the slipway at West Gate. Trips start at £8 for adults, £4 for children.

## Shopping

There are a few independent arts and crafts shops on **The King's Mile,** down Palace Street from the cathedral. Other places you might want to visit include **The Goods Shed** (see 'Where to Eat' below), a Victorian market outside Canterbury West train station, filled with produce sold by local farmers. Antique collectors will want to pop into **Burgate Antiques,** 23 Palace St. (✆ **01227/456-500**), which is filled with objects from the 18th and 19th centuries.

## Where to Eat

In the market next to Canterbury West train station, **The Goods Shed ★** (bookings only ✆ **01227/459-153;** www.thegoodsshed.co.uk) serves the freshest meat and produce available, and so the menu changes twice daily. Expect tender steaks and grilled seafood with seasonal vegetables, with mains priced around £12. On High Street adjacent to the Abode Canterbury Hotel, the **Old Brewery Tavern ★★** (✆ **01227/826-682**) is a gastro-pub with respected chef Michael Caines in the kitchen (his namesake five-star restaurant is in the hotel as well) and thus the crisp fish, grilled steaks, and thick burgers are the best in town (main courses £7–£15). **The Custard Tart,** 35 St. Margaret's St. (✆ **01227/765-178**), is a tiny teashop a short stroll from the cathedral, with sublime, freshly made tarts and cakes.

### The Crab & Winkle Way

This rural 7-mile (11-km) walking and cycling route starts at Canterbury West station and follows an abandoned railway line through forests, past lakes, and under Victorian bridges. Pick up a free detailed map covering the route and attractions at the **Canterbury Tourist Information Centre** (p. 52) or look on the website for the **Crab & Winkle Line Trust** (www.crabandwinkle.org). **Downland Cycles** (✆ **01227/479-643;** www.downlandcycles.co.uk), located on St. Stephen's Rd. just outside Canterbury West train station, rents bikes for £15 per day, plus £5 extra for helmets (Mon–Sat 9:30am–5:30pm).

### Nearby

Canterbury is just 7 miles (11km) from the historic seaside town of **Whitstable** (see p. 172), with its narrow medieval lanes and lovely ocean views. The seaside town of **Broadstairs** is 16 miles (26km) away and can be reached easily by train from Canterbury (p. 51). The white cliffs of Dover are 18 miles (29km) away, where you can visit the extraordinary **Dover Castle.** See p. 99.

# CHICHESTER

Chichester, about 70 miles (113km) south of London near the Sussex coast, is a handsome cathedral city of medieval and 18th-century houses on beautiful lanes and streets. And despite the quiet, country air that prevails, Chichester also boasts four attractions, any one of which would draw visitors: a beautiful Norman cathedral, with a graceful steeple that can be seen from far out at sea; Pallant House, one of Britain's finest galleries of modern art; the Chichester Festival Theatre, one of the country's most acclaimed stages, regularly hosting England's leading actors; and Fishbourne Roman Palace, a massive, 2,000-year-old domestic complex, graced with exquisite mosaics.

You can visit these sights while soaking in the pleasant atmosphere of Chichester, enjoying its lively streets and lanes that are still largely surrounded by Roman and medieval walls. Many of these byways, including the city's four major thoroughfares, follow the grid the Romans laid out for their city of Noviomagus Reginorum, which later became the major city of the Kingdom of Sussex.

You can spend a pleasant full day in Chichester, but you may want to linger long enough to enjoy Evensong in the cathedral or even a performance at the Festival Theatre before returning to London. You could also combine a trip to Chichester with a visit to Brighton (see p. 154), and if you have a car you can easily drive to Lewes, with nearby Monk's House and Charleston (see p. 34 and 35).

## Essentials

### VISITOR INFORMATION

The **Tourist Information Centre,** 29a South St. (✆ **01243/775-888;** www.visitchichester.org), is open most of the year Tuesday to Saturday from 9:15am to 5:15pm, with a slightly later opening of 10:15am on Mondays. Throughout April to September, it's also open on Sundays from 10:30am to 3pm.

### SCHEDULING CONSIDERATIONS

The Chichester Festival—one of the country's leading arts festivals—takes place over three weeks from late June to early July, filling the city with musicians, artists, and theatrical performances (✆ **01243/795-718;** www.chifest.org.uk).

### GETTING THERE

#### By Train

From London Victoria, **Southern trains** (✆ **08451/272-920;** www.southernrailway.com) depart every 30 minutes throughout the day for Chichester. The trip

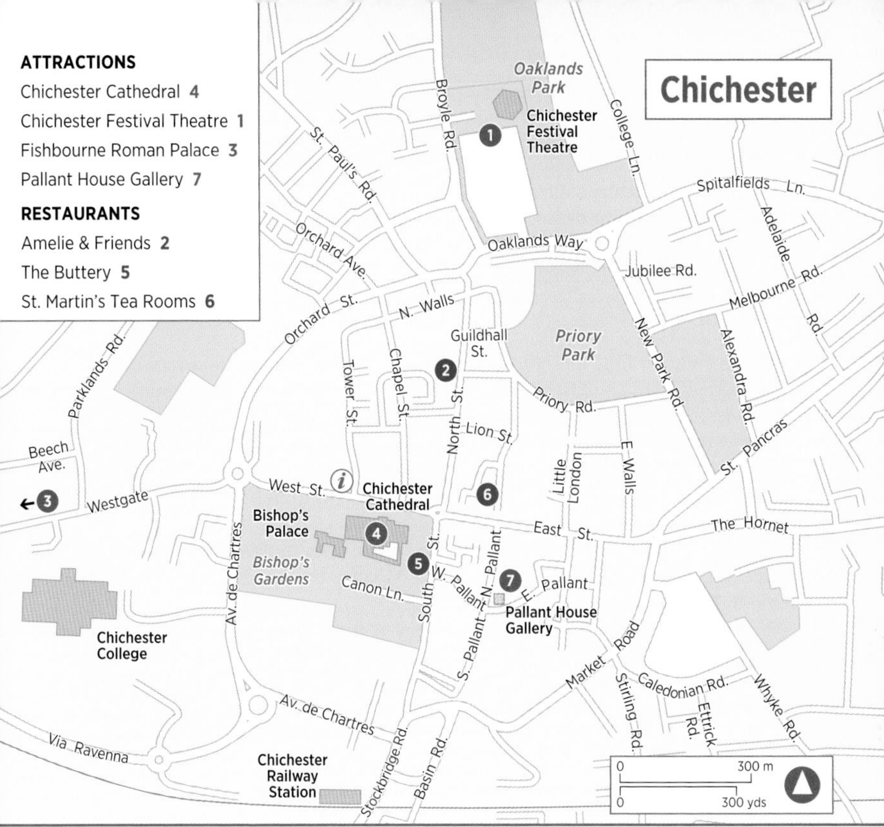


takes 1½ hours, and the round-trip fare is around £27. Chichester train station is on the edge of the city center, a short walk from the cathedral and most other sights.

### By Car

The drive from London takes about 2 hours, depending on traffic. Follow the A3 south to Hindhead, and from there a well-marked route on the A287 and A286 into Chichester.

## GETTING AROUND

Most of the center of Chichester is closed to traffic, making it a pleasure to stroll around. Fishbourne Roman Palace is about 1 mile (1.6km) west of the center. If you're relying on public transportation you can take a train from Chichester, or bus no. 56 or 700.

## A Day in Chichester

Chichester's four main streets (appropriately named South, North, East, and West) bisect the city at right angles to one another and meet at the medieval Market Cross. From there, it's a short walk down West Street to **Chichester Cathedral** ★★★ (✆ **01243/782-595;** www.chichestercathedral.co.uk).

### Salterns Way

**Salterns Way is a cycle-and-walking route from the center of Chichester to Chichester Harbour, a distance of about 11 miles (18km). The picturesque route passes through fields, woods, and marshlands, before reaching the Sussex coast. Pick up maps at the tourist office, and ask about bike rentals if you'd rather ride than walk.**



Completed in 1123, the Norman cathedral is light and airy, and topped with a distinctive sharp spire, which was added 700 years later, after the first one collapsed. The art collection includes fine Romanesque sculptures, including a 12th-century relief of the raising of Lazarus and some exquisite 14th-century stained glass. A growing collection of modern art encompasses the abstract stained-glass window by the 20th-century artist Marc Chagall, and a stainless steel hand of Christ floating high in the nave, the work of Spanish artist Jaume Plensa. The cathedral is open daily from 7am to 6pm (until 7:15pm in summer). Free 45 minute guided tours are offered Monday through Saturday at 11:15am and 2:30pm.

Nearby, the **Pallant House Gallery ★★★**, 9 North Pallant (✆ **01243/774-557;** www.pallant.org.uk), houses a strong collection of modern art, with works by artists including Picasso, Henry Moore, Graham Sutherland, and Peter Blake. It also holds the studio and archive of the German artist Hans Feibusch. Open Tuesday through Saturday 10am to 5pm (until 8pm on Thurs), and Sunday 12:30 to 5pm. Admission is £9 for adults, £2.30 for children 6 to 15; admission is half-price on Tuesdays and free on Thursday after 5pm.

**The distinctive spire of Chichester Cathedral.**

LEFT: **The Pallant House Gallery;** RIGHT: **Sculpture outside the Chichester Festival Theatre.**



The stubby 1960s building at the end of North Street is the **Chichester Festival Theatre** (**✆ 01243/784-437;** www.cft.org.uk), one of the country's top regional venues. Sir Laurence Olivier was its first artistic director, and the theater's schedule is packed with performances by top British talent.

In a quiet suburban neighborhood about 1 mile (1.6km) west of the city center, **Fishbourne Roman Palace ★★★**, Salthill Rd. (**✆ 01243/785-859;** www.sussexpast.co.uk/fishbourne), holds remarkable remnants of a grand Roman house. Built around A.D. 75, it was discovered only in 1960 when a water mains crew uncovered it by chance. The largest domestic Roman building found in Britain, it contains 20 well-preserved mosaic floors; in the most exuberant, a cupid rides on the back of a dolphin. Open daily March through October 10am to 5pm; November through February 10am to 4pm. Admission is £7.90 for adults, £7 for seniors and students, £4.20 for children. Local buses no. 56 or 700 head to Fishbourne from the bus stop at the cathedral (alight at Salthill Road), or you can catch a train from Chichester station that takes only three minutes (one-way ticket costs £2.30). Walking to the palace takes about 15 minutes and you can pick up a map at the tourist office.

**A well-preserved mosaic at Fishbourne Roman Palace.**

## ORGANIZED TOURS

If you're in the city on a Saturday, the Chichester City Guide walks are an excellent way to see the city. The tour takes just over an hour and costs £3.50. They begin at the

**Tourist Information Centre,** 29a South St. (✆ **01243/775-888**), each Saturday at 2:30pm.

## Shopping

The area around Market Cross has most high-street stores and a handful of more unique boutiques and independent stores. For local gifts, both the **Cathedral** and **Pallant Gallery** have shops where you can buy jewelry, art, and cards, while **Art For All,** The Square, Eastgate (✆ **01243/781-532**), specializes in limited edition art prints. **Montezuma's,** 29 East St. (✆ **01243/537-385**; www.montezumas.co.uk), is a temple of ethical artisan chocolate, and they also cater brilliantly for vegans.

## Where to Eat

Stop for lunch in the grand, vaulted room of the 12th-century **The Buttery ★,** 12a South St. (✆ **01243/537-033;** www.thebuttery.org/chichester.htm): the sandwiches, baguettes, and filled potatoes start from £4.60. The pricier but atmospheric **St. Martin's Tea Rooms ★,** 3 St. Martin's St. (✆ **01243/786-715;** www.organictearooms.co.uk), uses only organic ingredients in its rustic, homemade food, served up in historic, beamed rooms, warmed by wood fires (lunch from £4.50 to £8.50). For a mid-morning caffeine-fix, pop into **Amelie & Friends ★★,** 31 North St. (✆ **01243/771-444;** www.amelieandfriends.com), and pick up one of the flavorsome salads (such as Chichester cucumber with poppy seed and red chili, or Jersey Royal potato salad with goat's cheese) to have in the park later (£6.50 for two options).

St. Martin's Tea Rooms.

## Nearby

Arundel is a small town 11 miles (18km) from Chichester dominated by the hulking walls of **Arundel Castle ★★**. First built in the 11th century, the castle is a stern fortress on the banks of the winding Arun River, first built to protect the country from invasion. Today it's filled with antiques and works by Old Masters such as Van Dyck and Gainsborough. The castle has 40 acres (16 hectares) of grounds, including a walled kitchen garden as well as lush, formal gardens, all surrounded by parkland. The town of Arundel is worth a wander too, with a mixture of historic and modern architecture, and the castle park is a great place for a picnic. If you're driving, the sandy "blue flag" beach of **West Wittering** (www.westwitteringbeach.co.uk) can be reached from Chichester on the A286 following the signs to The Witterings. There's a cafe here selling ice creams and beach goods. You could also combine a trip to Chichester with a visit to **Brighton** (see p. 154), just 30 miles (48km) east along the A27 and easily reached by trains along the coast, which run about every 30 minutes. Or, if you have a car, you can easily visit nearby **Lewes,** and **Monk's House** and **Charleston** (see p. 31).

# SALISBURY & STONEHENGE

Long before you enter the city, the spire of Salisbury Cathedral comes into view just as John Constable and J. M. W. Turner captured it on canvas long ago. This is one of England's most pleasant and unspoiled cities, and it's little wonder so many painters and writers were drawn to it. Along with Gainsborough and Turner, Thomas Hardy and Anthony Trollope both spent time in Salisbury and set novels here. The half-timbered inns and houses lining the medieval lanes surround a still-lively marketplace.

Salisbury is actually two cities: Old Sarum and New Sarum. Old Sarum was an Iron Age fortification that the Romans took over and that later flourished as a Saxon, Danish, and Norman town well into the Middle Ages, when New Sarum, the city we know as Salisbury, began to grow up around the huge cathedral. William the Conqueror disbanded his troops in Old Sarum in 1070, when the Norman invasion of England was finally complete; the remains of his castle can still be seen.

Walk the city's medieval streets and lanes, or mingle with the crowds in the marketplace. You may find yourself wishing you didn't have to rush away from Salisbury—you can spend a full day enjoying the city sights, including a walk through the Water Meadows.

Lying in the valley of South Wiltshire's River Avon, Salisbury's location makes it an excellent starting point for visits to the ancient stone circles at Stonehenge and Avebury.

## Essentials

### VISITOR INFORMATION

The **Salisbury Information Centre,** in the marketplace on Fish Row (**✆ 01722/334-956;** www.visitwiltshire.co.uk/salisbury), provides maps and information. Open September to May Monday through Saturday 9:30am to 5:30pm, and between June and August it's also open Sunday 11am to 3pm.

## SCHEDULING CONSIDERATIONS

**St. George's Day** in April is a traditional medieval celebration of the city's patron saint, where you can watch St. George slaying the dragon in the Wiltshire mummers play, and take in acrobats and fireworks. Note: The festival isn't always on St. George's Day itself (April 23); check ahead with the Tourist Information Centre.

During the annual **Salisbury International Arts Festival** (✆ **01722/332-977;** www.salisburyfestival.co.uk) the city drapes itself in banners, and street theater—traditional and unusual—is offered everywhere. There are also symphony and chamber music concerts in Salisbury Cathedral, children's events, and much more. It takes place from mid-May to the beginning of June.

## GETTING THERE

### By Train

Trains for Salisbury depart every 30 minutes from London Waterloo; the trip takes around 1½ hours, fares start at £35. Salisbury train station is at the western edge of the city center, off Fisherton Street, within easy walking distance of the city center.

### By Car

The quickest route from London is on the M3, and then the A30. The trip takes about 1½ hours. Convenient car parks near the city center are Central Car Park, north of the marketplace on the west side of the River Avon; and Culver Street Car Park, a few blocks northeast of the Cathedral Close. Fees at most carparks near the center are around £5 per day.

### By Bus

**National Express** buses (✆ **08717/818-178;** www.nationalexpress.com) leave London Victoria bus station for Salisbury every 2 to 3 hours. The bus ride takes at least 3 hours and sometimes requires a change at Southampton or Bristol: fares cost about £18 round-trip. The bus station is at the east end of the marketplace, which is within easy walking distance to the cathedral.

## GETTING AROUND

Salisbury is compact and easy to walk, all the more so because many of its main streets are pedestrianized. If you require a taxi, try **City Cabs** (✆ **01722/423-000**).

# A Day in Salisbury

The best place to begin an exploration of Salisbury is the heart of the city—the **marketplace** ★★, where venders have congregated since 1227 and continue to peddle their wares every Tuesday and Saturday. The medieval **Poultry Cross,** so called because it once marked the poultry section of the market, along with the narrow medieval lanes—Fish Street and Butcher Row—are markers of past trade here.

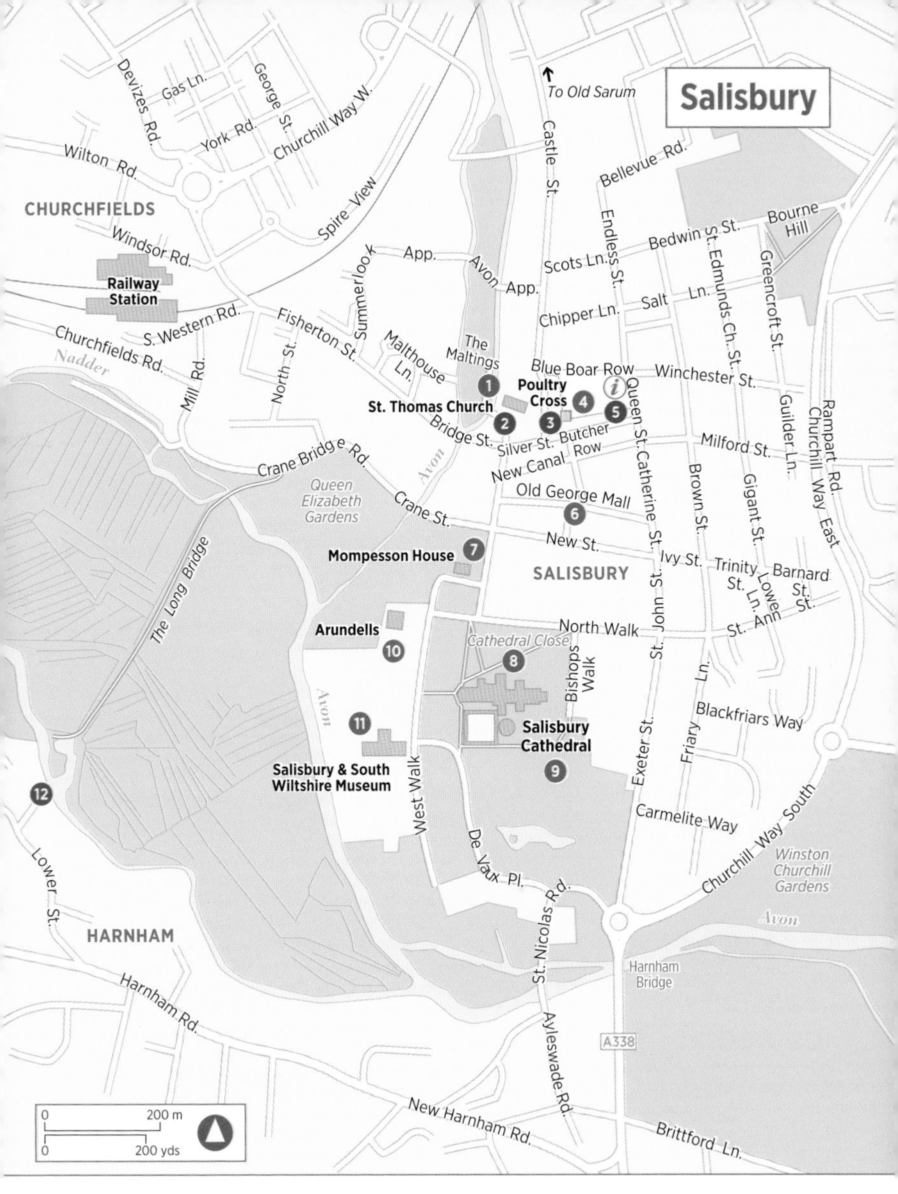


**ATTRACTIONS**

Arundells **10**

Cathedral Close **8**

Mompesson House **7**

Old George Mall **6**

Poultry Cross **4**

St. Thomas Church **1**

Salisbury & South Wiltshire Museum **11**

Salisbury Cathedral **9**

**RESTAURANTS**

Haunch of Venison **3**

The Old Mill **12**

Polly Tearooms **2**

Reeve the Baker **5**

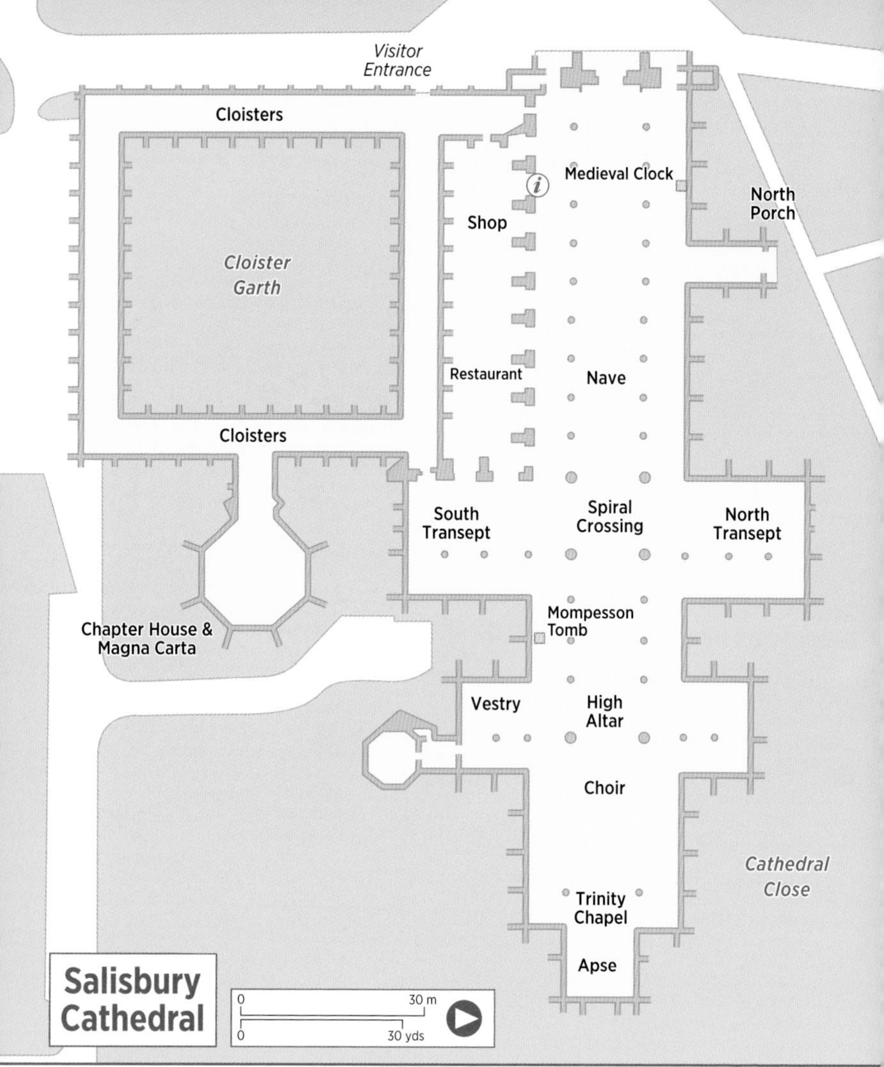


Just to the west of the marketplace, off Silver Street, is 700-year-old **St. Thomas Church ★**. Step inside to see the terrifying painting Doom, which was probably the gift of a medieval pilgrim to the cathedral. Dating to 1475, it hangs over the chancel arch and depicts ordinary folk rising from their graves and marching toward heaven or hell. Once common in English churches, such depictions of the Last Judgment were largely destroyed during the Reformation and are now quite rare.

Nearby, High Street leads south to the main cathedral, past half-timbered buildings. The **Old George Mall** (near the corner of New St.) is a former inn that was already 300 years old when the diarist Samuel Pepys stayed here in

1668. Nowadays it leads into an open-air shopping center with many popular highstreet stores (www.oldgeorgemall.co.uk).

As you near the Cathedral you'll see **Cathedral Close ★★** ahead of you, like a small city protected by stone walls and medieval gates. From High Street, you'll pass through **High Street Gate,** with elaborate stonework above its old archway. The entrance from Queen Street, to the east, is through **St. Anne's Gate,** where George Frederick Handel is said to have given his first recital in England in a room over the gatehouse. Inside the close, you can tour the perfectly preserved **Mompesson House ★★** (✆ **01722/335-659;** www.nationaltrust.org.uk). Built in 1701, it still has its original intricate plasterwork and furnishings, including a huge collection of 18th-century glassware. The house is open March through October Saturday to Wednesday from 11am to 5pm. Admission is £5.20 for adults and £2.60 for children.

TOP: **The medieval Poultry Cross;** BOTTOM: **High Street Gate.**

Near it is **Arundells,** a sturdy 18th-century stone building that served as the home of former Prime Minister Sir Edward Heath in the 1980s. Still filled with Sir Edward's many artworks, it's open for 45-minute guided tours April through October Saturday to Tuesday 11:30am to 5:30pm. Admission costs £8.

The thoroughly Gothic Salisbury Cathedral.

Not far from Arundells, the **Salisbury & South Wiltshire Museum,** 65 The Close (✆ **01722/332-151;** www.salisburymuseum.org.uk), occupies a magnificent 11th-century building with a slightly haphazard collection of artifacts and information about the city and Stonehenge. It's open Monday to Saturday from 10am to 5pm (July–Aug also Sun 2–5pm). Admission is £6 adults, £4 seniors and students, £2 children 5 to 16.

Built over 38 years, from 1220 to 1258, the thoroughly Gothic **Salisbury Cathedral ★★★** (✆ **01722/555-120;** www.salisburycathedral.org.uk), made of cream-colored limestone, is an impressive sight. The elegant spire is 404 feet (123m) high, the tallest in the land, and can be seen from miles away, while the mechanical clock in the north aisle is one of the oldest pieces of working machinery in the world—it's been telling time since 1386. The octagonal Chapter House holds a copy of the **Magna Carta** (see below) amid stone friezes from the 13th century that tell Old Testament stories. The cathedral is open daily from 9am to 5pm (to 5:30pm June–Aug). There's no admission but a donation is requested of £5 for adults. Free tours are offered throughout the day; the tower tour (£8.50) climbs 332 winding steps past medieval scaffolding for amazing city views.

## ORGANIZED TOURS

The highly informative 1½-hour **Salisbury City Walk** (✆ **01725/518-658;** £4) begins at the Tourist Information Centre in Fish Row at 11am daily from April to October (Nov–Mar Sat and Sun only). You'll get an earful of tidbits about commerce in the bustling medieval city, the building of the cathedral, and life within Cathedral Close.

### The Magna Carta

**Housed in the Chapter House at Salisbury Cathedral is one of England's most treasured documents. Written in 1215 by a group of feudal barons, and passed into law in 1225, Magna Carta was written to limit royal power and create new rights for "freemen." Among other things, it protects land rights and guarantees freedoms for the Church from arbitrary actions by the monarchy. The influential document is seen as a forefather of later modern democratic documents, such as the U.S. Constitution.**

## Stonehenge ★★★

The world's most renowned prehistoric site, a stone circle of pillars and lintels, has risen above the Salisbury Plain for almost 4,000 years. Why these stones are here is still unknown, but archaeologists believe it was a meeting place and a ceremonial center. Whatever the reason for the presence of these great slabs, getting them here wasn't easy. The stones in the Inner Circle, the oldest part of the monument, are from the Prescelly Mountains in southwestern Wales, 240 miles (385km) away, and theories hold that they were dragged overland on rollers and sledges and floated over the sea and down rivers.

These days the site is a victim of its own popularity and frequently overcrowded. As you pull into the carpark, you're greeted by cheap-looking concession stands and confusing signs. Matters improve as you turn your back on these and follow a walkway to the stones themselves. The walkway leads you in a large circle around the stones—you're kept back from the rocks by a metal fence, but you do get a decent view of them as you stroll around. If you're traveling by car or taxi, try to be at the site when the gates open or arrive an hour or so before closing—it's likely the tour groups, at least, will be gone, and you can enjoy the spectacle of soft light playing over the mysterious stones in relative peace and quiet.

There's no regular bus service to Stonehenge, but you can take a tour bus; **Stonehenge Tours** (**✆ 01983/827-005;** www.thestonehengetour.info) depart from the Salisbury train and bus station daily for Old Sarum and Stonehenge. Buses leave the train station from late May through August, every half-hour from 9:30am to 5pm; September to mid-October, every hour between 10am and 4pm; and mid-October to late May, every hour between 10am and 2pm. The cost is £18 with admission to Stonehenge; £9 for children.

8 miles (13km) north of Salisbury off the A360. **✆ 0870/333-1181.** www.english-heritage.org.uk. Mar 16–May daily 9:30am–6pm; June–Aug daily 9am–7pm; Sept–Oct 15 daily 9:30am–6pm; Oct 16–Mar 15 daily 9:30am–5pm. Admission £7.50 adults, £6.80 seniors and students, £4.50 children 5–15.

### Walking Around Salisbury

A well-maintained footpath traverses the **Water Meadows ★** between Mill Road and the old Harnham Mill, crossing the River Avon and affording wonderful views toward the cathedral. A walk through the meadows and back to the city center covers a little less than 2 miles (3km). For a longer excursion, rent a bike from **Hayball Cycles,** 26–30 Winchester St. (✆ **01722/411-378**), for a spin around the city and onto a series of public footpaths that wind through the countryside; bike hire is from £12 a day.



## Shopping

At the center of the city, the bustling **Charter Market ★** is flowing with fresh produce and general goods on Tuesday and Saturday, while the **Wiltshire Farmers' Market** is held fortnightly on Wednesdays (www.visitwiltshire.co.uk). The **National Trust Shop,** 41 High St. (✆ **01722/331-884**), housed within the cathedral, carries gifts, books, CDs, and children's toys. Local interest books and walking maps are available in the independent **Cross Keys Bookshop,** 2 Cross Keys Chequer (✆ **01722/326-131**).

## Where to Eat

You can equip yourself with picnic fodder and delicious pastries at **Reeve the Baker,** 2 Butcher Row

TOP RIGHT: Salisbury's oldest pub, the Haunch of Venison; BOTTOM: View of Salisbury Cathedral from the Water Meadows.

## Nearby

With a mysterious stone circle bigger—if less dramatic—than the one at Stonehenge, the town of **Avebury ★★** (image below) is on the A4361, 29 miles (46km) from Salisbury, 1 mile (1.6km) off the A4. You're likely to find a visit to Avebury is more personal than one to Stonehenge because you can walk right up to the stones; even touch them if you wish. No fences and fewer tourists are virtually guaranteed and there's no admission cost. Avebury sprawls over 28 acres (11 hectares), with more than 100 stones in a giant circle around the village. Inside this large circle are two smaller ones, each with about 30 stones standing upright. The stones are made of sarsen, a sandstone local to Wiltshire, and some weigh up to 50 tons. While in town, stop by the **Alexander Keiller Museum ★** (✆ **01672/539-250**), which houses one of Britain's most important archaeological collections, including material from excavations at Avebury, plus artifacts from other prehistoric digs. It's open April through October daily 10am to 6pm; 10am to 4:30pm otherwise. Admission costs £4.40 for adults, £2.20 children 5 to 14. You can also combine a visit with **Winchester**, below.

A few miles north from Salisbury, **Old Sarum** (✆ **0117/9750-700**; www.english-heritage.org.uk), off the A345, Castle Road, was once a bustling castle town until the 15th century when Salisbury grew up around the cathedral. Nowadays you can visit the moody ruins of the Norman castle, cathedral, and Bishop's Palace inside the sturdy fortifications. To get there you can walk on a well-marked footpath along the river, or take a bus (local bus nos. 5, 6, 7, 8, and 9 stop nearby; the fare is about £3). The site is open April to June and September daily 10am to 5pm; July and August daily 9am to 6pm; October and February to March daily 10am to 4pm; November to January daily 11am to 3pm. Admission costs £3.70 for adults, £3.30 for seniors and students, and £2.20 for children 5 to 15.

The home of the Earl and Duchess of Pembroke, **Wilton House** (✆ **01722/746-720**; www.wiltonhouse.com), is 3 miles (5km) northwest of Salisbury on the A30, in Wilton village. This is a well-maintained 17th-century house containing paintings by Anthony Van Dyck, Peter Paul Rubens, and Pieter Bruegel. The River Avon flows through the gardens (home to giant Lebanon cedars planted in 1630), and is spanned by a Palladian bridge: It's open May to August Sunday to Thursday 11:30am to 4:30pm (last admission at 3:45pm). Admission is £14 for adults, £11.25 seniors and students, and £7.50 for children 5 to15.

(✆ **01722/320-367**), while cheese, fruit, and other produce can be picked up from local producers at the **Charter Market** (see above). The **Polly Tearooms,** 8 St. Thomas Square (✆ **01722/336-037**), offers a bright and atmospheric spot for sandwiches and cakes, with tables outside for sunny days. For a pub lunch, the **Haunch of Venison** ★★★, 1 Minster St. (✆ **01722/411-313**), Salisbury's oldest pub dating from 1320, serves sandwiches and grilled fresh fish in a warren of wood-paneled rooms (mains are around £10). Pleasantly located about a 10 minute walk across the Water Meadows from the cathedral, **The Old Mill** ★, Town Path, Harnham (✆ **01722/327-517**), is a flint-and-stone building that was once England's first paper mill. Now a friendly hotel and inn, it dishes out home-style cooking, with a choice of focaccia rolls and ploughman's lunches at lunchtime (£5.25 to £8.95).



# WINCHESTER

A bustling, attractive cathedral city kept youthful by the presence of a major arts university, Winchester's venerable historic pedigree stretches back two millennia. An important Roman military headquarters, it became capital of the ancient kingdom of Wessex after the Romans withdrew from Britain, and remained the most important city in England up until the time of the Norman Conquest in 1066. Winchester Cathedral, a magnificent Gothic edifice, soars above the city's low roofs and makes a graceful focus to its appealing city center.

Jane Austen fans can visit the great novelist's home in the nearby village of Chawton, and her grave in Winchester Cathedral. You'll also enjoy walking the streets, strolling through the water meadows that extend behind the cathedral to the banks of the River Itchen, and just soaking in the atmosphere of a well-preserved English cathedral city.

If you're really ambitious and can't get your fill of cathedrals and medieval charm, you can spend the morning in Winchester and the afternoon in nearby Salisbury, only 20 miles (32km) west (see p. 63), or vice versa.

## Essentials

### VISITOR INFORMATION

Based in the huge neo-gothic Guildhall building, the **Tourist Information Centre,** High St. (✆ **01962/840-500;** www.visitwinchester.co.uk), is open Monday through Saturday 10am to 5pm, and Sunday 11am to 4pm (closed Sun Oct–Apr). It offers a handy bicycle hire service, and a shop selling local art and crafts.

### SCHEDULING CONSIDERATIONS

Winchester is a busy working city all year round. Crowds are at their highest in summer, but it rarely gets overrun with visitors.

### GETTING THERE

#### By Train

Trains go to Winchester from London Waterloo every 30 minutes. The journey takes 1 hour and a round-trip fare costs around £30. Winchester train station is about a 10 minute walk from the cathedral and other major sights. There's a park and ride system to and from the train station (£3; tickets valid all day) but take

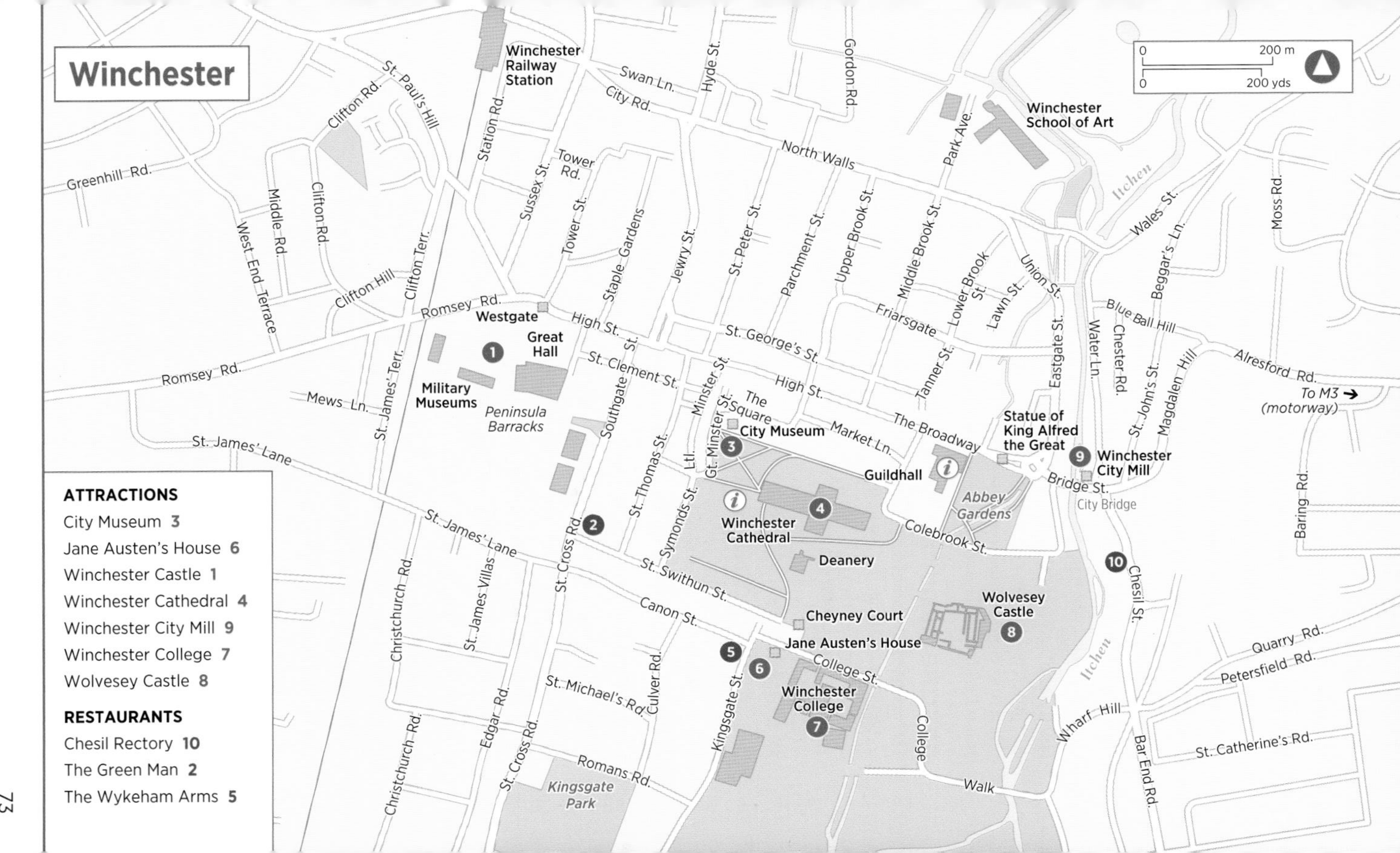
Winchester
0 200 m
0 200 yds
ATTRACTIONS
City Museum 3
Jane Austen's House 6
Winchester Castle 1
Winchester Cathedral 4
Winchester City Mill 9
Winchester College 7
Wolvesey Castle 8
RESTAURANTS
Chesil Rectory 10
The Green Man 2
The Wykeham Arms 5
Winchester Railway Station
Winchester School of Art
Westgate
Great Hall
Military Museums
Peninsula Barracks
The Square
City Museum
Guildhall
Statue of King Alfred the Great
Winchester City Mill
City Bridge
Abbey Gardens
Winchester Cathedral
Deanery
Cheyney Court
Jane Austen's House
Wolvesey Castle
Winchester College
Kingsgate Park
To M3 (motorway)
Itchen
Clifton Rd.
St. Paul's Hill
Swan Ln.
Hyde St.
Gordon Rd.
City Rd.
Park Ave.
Station Rd.
Greenhill Rd.
Tower Rd.
Sussex St.
North Walls
Moss Rd.
Wales St.
Middle Rd.
West End Terrace
Tower St.
Staple Gardens
Jewry St.
St. Peter St.
Parchment St.
Upper Brook St.
Middle Brook St.
Lower Brook St.
Lawn St.
Union St.
Beggar's Ln.
Clifton Hill
Clifton Terr.
Romsey Rd.
High St.
St. George's St.
Friarsgate
Eastgate St.
Water Ln.
Chester Rd.
Blue Ball Hill
St. Clement St.
Southgate St.
Minster St.
Tanner St.
St. John's St.
Magdalen Hill
Alresford Rd.
Mews Ln.
St. James' Terr.
Market Ln.
The Broadway
St. James' Lane
Gt. Minster St.
Ltl. Minster St.
St. Thomas St.
Bridge St.
Baring Rd.
Symonds St.
Colebrook St.
St. Cross Rd.
St. Swithun St.
Chesil St.
Christchurch Rd.
St. James Villas
Canon St.
College St.
Quarry Rd.
Petersfield Rd.
St. Michael's Rd.
Culver Rd.
Kingsgate St.
Wharf Hill
Edgar Rd.
College Walk
Bar End Rd.
St. Catherine's Rd.
Romans Rd.

care to get off at the city center stops (about 5 minutes from the station), or you could end up in the suburbs.

### By Bus

**National Express** (✆ **08717/818-178;** www.nationalexpress.com) runs direct buses from London Victoria bus station to Winchester about every 2 hours. The journey takes around 1½ hours and costs £5.50 to £16, depending on when you book.

### By Car

From London, the M3 goes directly to Winchester. The trip takes about 1½ hours. Don't even think about driving into the center—parking can be problematic. Look out for the two large pay carparks at the edge of the center on Tanner Street and Gordon Road and two on the east side of the cathedral (expect to pay around £5 a day). Parking is free on Sundays.

## GETTING AROUND

The center of Winchester is about a half-mile (0.8km) from the train station, and so you can easily walk. There are also taxis at the station and at ranks near the cathedral; or you can call **Winchester Taxis** (✆ **07919/181-403**) or **Steve's Taxis** (✆ **01962/849-953**).

# A Day in Winchester

Begin your tour at **Winchester Cathedral** ★★★ (✆ **01962/857-200;** www.winchester-cathedral.org.uk). The 900-year-old structure, begun in 1079, is graced with the longest nave of any church in Europe, and as befits a cathedral that was for so long a symbol of power and might, is the repository of many historic

Winchester Cathedral.

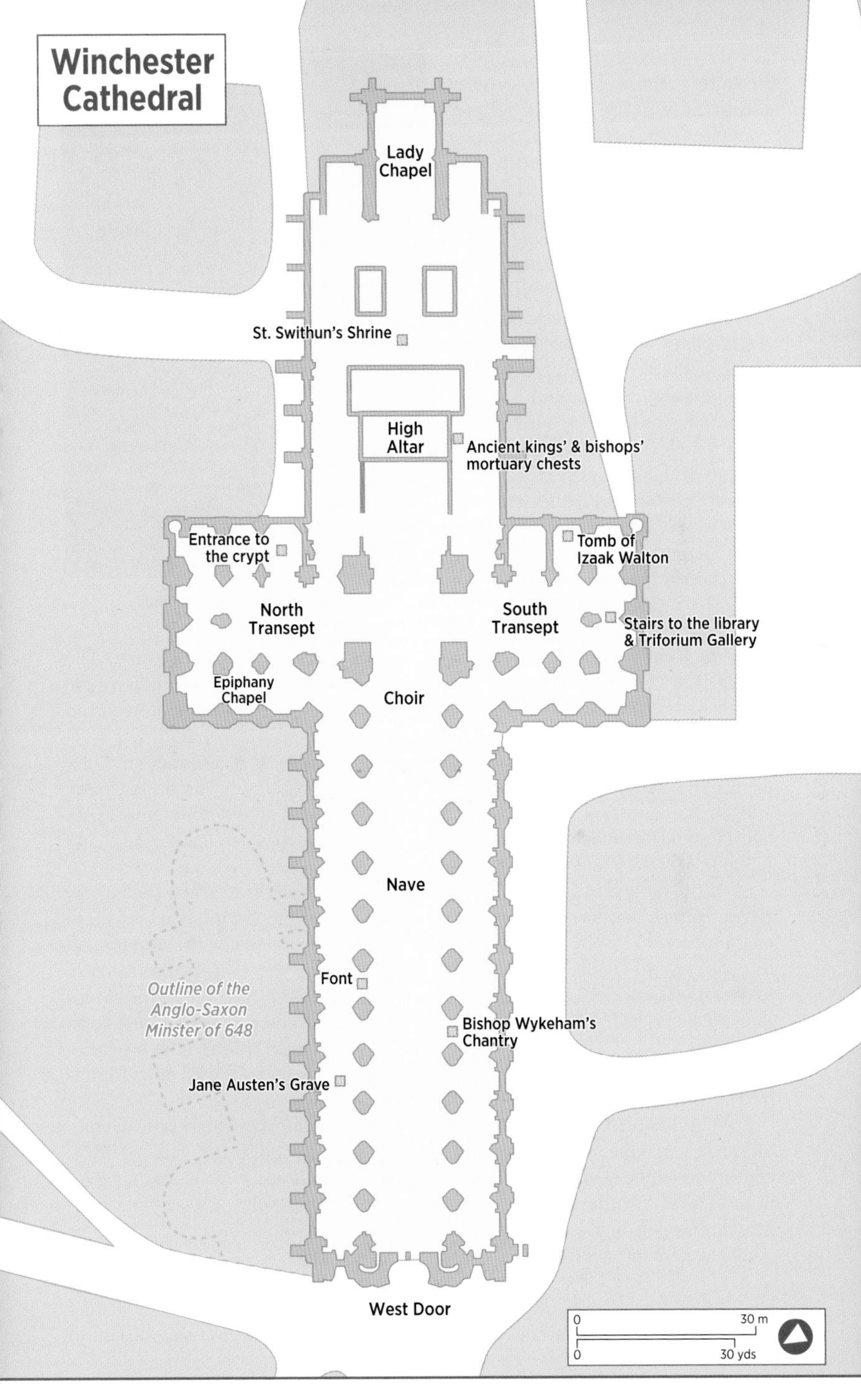
Winchester Cathedral
Lady Chapel
St. Swithun's Shrine
High Altar
Ancient kings' & bishops' mortuary chests
Entrance to the crypt
Tomb of Izaak Walton
North Transept
South Transept
Stairs to the library & Triforium Gallery
Epiphany Chapel
Choir
Nave
Font
Outline of the Anglo-Saxon Minster of 648
Bishop Wykeham's Chantry
Jane Austen's Grave
West Door
0
30 m
0
30 yds

treasures. Above the 15th-century **Great Screen** are mortuary chests containing the remains of a dozen Saxon kings. A more recent, but no less revered grave, is that of **Jane Austen**; look for the simple, stone marker laid into the floor in the north aisle. Nearby, a 12th-century font tells the story of **St. Nicholas** (270–343), the inspiration for Santa Claus, and on display in the library is the **Winchester Bible,** an extraordinary illuminated manuscript. The cathedral is open Monday through Saturday from 9:30am to 5pm and Sunday from 12:30 to 3pm. Admission is £6.50 for adults, £5 seniors, and free for under-16s. The price includes a 1-hour tour (hourly, Mon–Sat 10am–3pm; during winter months 10:15am, 12:15pm, and 2:15pm).

Jane Austen's gravestone in the cathedral.

On College Street, marked by a plaque, is **Jane Austen's House.** The writer lived in the tiny village of Chawton for most of her life, but moved here shortly before she died at the age of 42 in 1817. (You can't go inside, but you can visit her house in Chawton; see p. 78).

On nearby Kingsgate Street **Winchester College ★★**, founded in 1382, is the oldest public school in England. The chapel, cloister, scholars' dining room, and a 17th-century schoolroom are open by 45-minute guided tours only (Tues and Thurs 10:45am and noon; Mon, Wed, Fri, and Sat 10:45am, noon, 2:15, and 3:30pm; Sun 2:15 and 3:30pm.

At the far end of College Street, you can take a short walk along the narrow **River Itchen** and its water meadows. Ambles along the river and across these green meadows inspired the poet John Keats to write his poem *To Autumn,* and the path is aptly called "Keats' Walk." To the left are the evocative remains of **Wolvesey Castle ★**, where Queen Mary I and Philip of Spain held their wedding breakfast in 1554. Enough walls, arches, and foundations remain to give an idea of how grand it must once have been. You can roam through the evocative ruins from April through the end of September, daily 10am to 5pm; admission is free (www.english-heritage.org.uk).

**Winchester City Mill ★ ☺** (✆ **01962/870-057;** www.nationaltrust.org.uk) makes an appealing diversion for families; you can still see the original 18th-century machinery at work, plus there are interactive exhibitions and a pretty island garden, home to kingfishers, otters, and water voles. Open daily mid-March through late December 10:30am to 5pm. Admission costs £3.60 for adults and £2 for children.

The excellent **City Museum** (✆ **01962/863-064**) on the Square nearby, has a fine Roman mosaic as centerpiece and is dedicated to Winchester's history from the same period. It's open April to October Monday to Saturday 10am to

5pm, Sunday noon to 5pm (hours are slightly shorter in winter). Admission is free.

All that remains of once-mighty **Winchester Castle** is the **Great Hall ★** (✆ **01962/846-476**) on Castle Avenue. The first English parliament met here in 1246, but a more illustrious claim is made for the colorful, 13th-century painted table that hangs inside. Folklore once held it to be King Arthur's round table, though in reality it probably merely served as inspiration for the tale. The hall is open daily 10am to 5pm and admission is free.

### ORGANIZED TOURS

Every day during the summer, the Tourist Information Centre operates two useful walking tours: **Kings and Castles** at 11am and **Mitres and Mortarboards** at 2pm. Each tour takes from 1 to 1½ hours and costs £4.50 adults (children are free). You can find details at the center.

## Shopping

A day could easily be spent perusing the many shops of Winchester. For unique art, jewelry, and gifts, **Kingsgate Street** and **Parchment Street** are superb places to start. Elsewhere of note, the **Winchester Bookshop,** 10a St. George's St. (✆ **01962/855-630**), is a bibliophile's dream: three floors crammed with secondhand and antiquarian books, along with old prints. **Middle Brook Street** is the location of the **General Market** (Thursday to Saturday, 9am to 5pm) selling local food and crafts, and the **Taste of the South** (Wednesday 9am to 4pm) for specialty local foods.

Walkers beside the River Itchen.

### Nearby

Fifteen miles (24km) from Winchester, the charming house known as **Chawton Cottage** is where Jane Austen spent the last 7 years of her life. Here she wrote many books, including *Emma.* Now the **Jane Austen House Museum ★★** (✆ **01420/832-62;** www.jane-austens-house-museum.org.uk), the cottage is filled with antiques and memorabilia including Austen's needlework and jewelry. From Winchester, Chawton is on the A31. It's open daily from 10am to 5pm. Admission is £7 for adults, £6 seniors and students, and £2 for children.

Twelve miles (19km) from Winchester, **Mottisfont Abbey ★** (✆ **01794/340-757;** www.nationaltrust.org.uk/mottisfont), near the town of Romsey, started life in the 13th century as an Augustinian priory before being transformed (thanks to the Reformation) into a grand, riverside private home. The gardens are radiant in the height of summer, especially the **walled rose garden ★★**, where perfumes and colors are in full effect. It's open late February through October daily 10am to 5pm. Admission costs £7.60 adults and £3.80 children.

**Salisbury** is 20 miles (32km) west of the city and can be reached via train, in just over 1½ hours, with a change in Southampton. If you're driving, follow the A30 and A272 between the two cities; the trip by car takes only about 45 minutes. See p. 63.

## Where to Dine

Dating from 1450, the **Chesil Rectory ★**, 1 Chesil St. (✆ **01962/851-555;** www.chesilrectory.co.uk), is in a low-beamed, timber-framed building thought to be the oldest house in Winchester. Made with locally sourced ingredients, a two-course lunch is priced at £15.95. On Southgate St., **The Green Man ★** (✆ **01962/866-809**) is a relaxed, stylish Victorian pub serving substantial sandwiches and bar snacks at lunchtime, most £10 and under. **The Wykeham Arms ★★**, 75 Kingsgate St. (✆ **01962/853-834**), is a cozy 18th-century coaching inn with a very British menu of savory pies or seared scallops with cauliflower puree, with mains priced around £15.

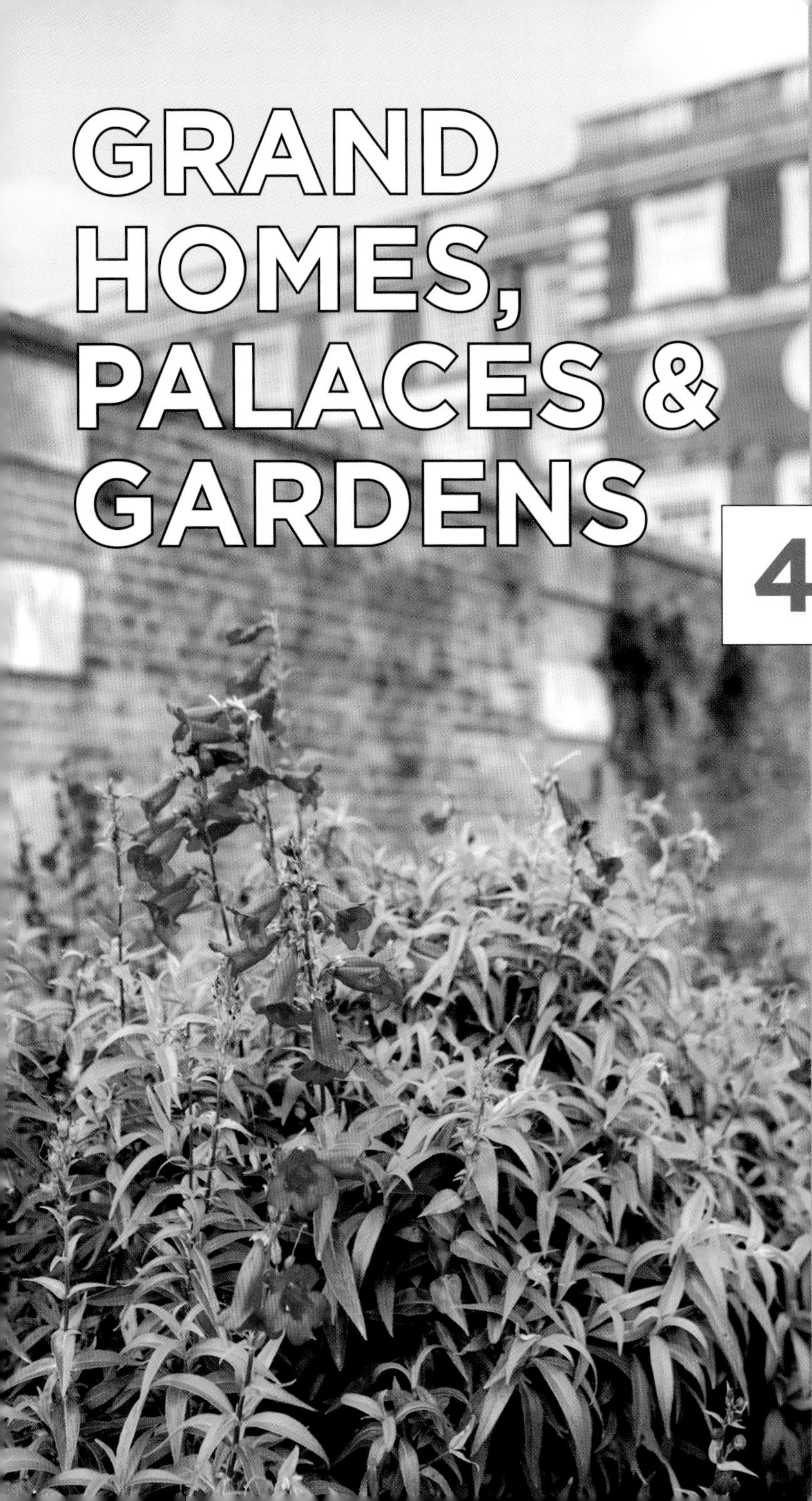

# GRAND HOMES, PALACES & GARDENS

4

The wealthy landowners who controlled much of England centuries ago may be long gone, but they left a grand heritage. Their enormous homes and vast estates are marvels of architectural and interior design, decked out with precious family heirlooms, antique furniture and gallery-worthy art. Some are just as popular for their grounds as for their residence, most notably Sissinghurst, purchased by the passionate horticulturist and author Vita Sackville-West in the 1930s. Inspired by forward-thinking, modern garden design of the times, it was transformed from a tumbling jungle of an estate into the exquisite place it remains today. Vita spent her childhood at Knole, a Tudor residence with sprawling grounds, which feature in Virginia Woolf's novel Orlando. The unmarked paths around the estate can lead you through miles of countryside.

---

The Royal family are still very much connected to both Sandringham and Hampton Court Palace, the latter reluctantly gifted to Henry VIII by Cardinal Thomas Wolsey in the 16th century to temporarily save his head. The maze is possibly the most famous attraction of Hampton Court but there is plenty to see within the palace, including the extensive Tudor kitchens which cover over 50 rooms.

# HAMPTON COURT

A sprawling redbrick palace on the banks of the Thames, just to the west of London, Hampton Court is one of many residences that once belonged to King Henry VIII. It was originally designed and built in 1514 by his friend and chancellor, Cardinal Thomas Wolsey, for himself, but when the two men fell out over Henry's divorce from Catherine of Aragon, Wolsey was convinced to handover the house to the king as a gift in order to keep his head firmly fixed to his shoulders.

Subsequent kings and queens altered and expanded the building to add more baroque frippery to the delicate perfection of the Tudor structure. Queen Mary II and William of Orange seriously considered demolishing the whole building to replace it with something that would match the splendor of Versailles. At present, the palace—while a mish-mash of architectural styles—is in excellent condition, complete with antique furniture and museum-quality art from the queen's extensive collection.

PREVIOUS PAGE: **Hampton Court Palace.**

## Hampton Court Palace

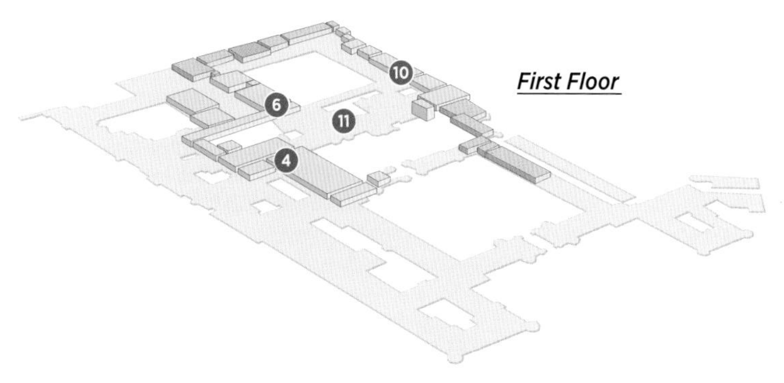


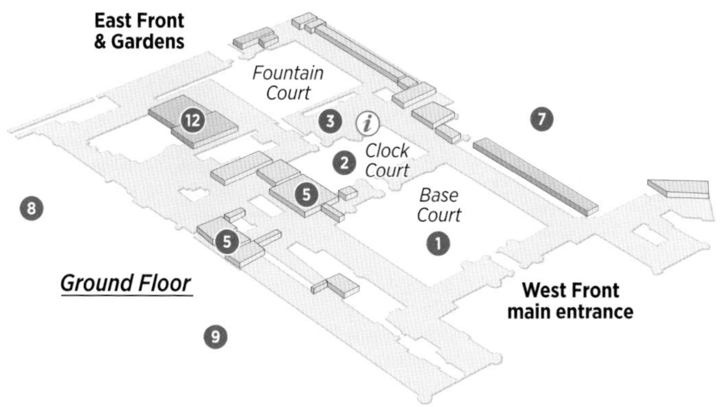


Base Court **1**
Chapel Royal **12**
Clock Court **2**
Georgian Private Apartments **11**
Henry VIII's Kitchens **5**
Henry VIII's Private Apartments **4**
Information Centre **3**
Mary II's Apartments **6**
The Northern Gardens **8**
The South Gardens **7**
Tiltyard Café **9**
William III's Apartments **10**

Aside from brief blips, Hampton Court has remained in the hands of Britain's royalty since Henry VIII, although no monarch has lived here since George II (reigned 1727–60). It was first opened to the public by Queen Victoria in 1838.

The building is enormous—the kitchens alone cover some 36,000 square feet (3,345 square meters)—and so exploring its many rooms (one supposedly haunted by the weeping ghost of Henry VIII's fifth wife Catherine Howard) can take half a day. The gardens are even bigger, and the maze will provide some amusement, especially to children.

Located in East Moseley, Surrey, 13 miles (21km) west of London on the north side of the River Thames, Hampton Court is one of the easiest and most rewarding day trips from London. You can visit Hampton Court as a half-day trip, if traveling by train or car, or make a visit a full day's outing, if you choose to reach the palace by boat (just as Henry VIII and Elizabeth I would have done).

## Essentials



### VISITOR INFORMATION

The **Information Centre** (✆ **0870/752-7777;** www.hrp.org.uk) in the Clock Court follows the palace's opening hours: April through October daily 10am to 6pm, November through March daily 10am to 4:30pm. Admission to the palace is £16 for adults, £13.20 for seniors and students, and £8 for children 5 to 15. You can get a discount by buying your tickets online in advance.



### SCHEDULING CONSIDERATIONS

Huge as the palace is, it can feel overrun on summer weekends and national holidays. To avoid crowds, come early on a weekday or start your visit after 2pm. The last admission to the palace each day is at 5:15pm in summer, 3:30pm in winter. On Sunday, visitors are welcome at choir services in the Chapel Royal at 11am and 3:30pm.

### GETTING THERE

#### By Train

The fastest, easiest, and most direct route is by train from London Waterloo to Hampton Court. Trains depart Waterloo at 12 and 42 minutes past each hour (some trains require a change at Surbiton). The journey takes 30 minutes; an on-the-day round-trip fare is £10.80. The palace entrance is well-signposted from the station, only a 5 minute walk away.

#### By Boat

If you have plenty of time, you can take a boat to Hampton Court from Westminster Pier, but bear in mind the journey takes 3 hours. From April to October, boats usually depart at noon and return at 4pm; contact **Westminster Passenger Service Association** (✆ **020/7930-2062;** www.wpsa.co.uk). One-way fares (you can return to London by train) are £15 for adults, £10 for seniors, and £7.50 for children 5 to 15.

#### By Car

The palace is located on the A308 and is well-signposted; follow the brown tourist attraction road signs. From the M25, take either exit 10 onto the A307 or exit

12 onto the A308. The palace is also accessible via the A3 and then the A309. The trip from central London takes only 30 to 60 minutes. Parking at Hampton Court costs £3.50 for 3 hours.

### GETTING AROUND

Hampton Court is a 5 minute walk from the train station; just follow the signs.

TOP: **Hampton Court Palace;** RIGHT: **The Astronomical Clock made for Henry VIII in 1540.**

## A Day in Hampton Court

From the time the palace was first built until the 1660s, **Hampton Court ★★★**, like most of the great houses near London, was approached by water. The impressive, Tudor **West Front** of the palace, where visitors enter today, was begun by Cardinal Wolsey (who lived around 1475–1530) and completed for Henry VIII.

In the **Base Court,** the first courtyard, the turrets surrounding the space sport the insignia of Henry VIII and Elizabeth I. On the far side of the court, you enter **Clock Court ★**, the principal Tudor courtyard and the heart of both Wolsey's and Henry VIII's palaces. Over the gateway, you can see Wolsey's coat of arms and the famous **Astronomical Clock** made for Henry VIII in 1540 on which the sun revolves around the earth.

Start your tour in the **Tudor Kitchens ★★**, a complex of some 50 rooms, set up as if in the process of preparing food for a great feast in 1542.

From there head to **Henry VIII's State Apartments ★★**, where the best rooms include the **Great Watching Chamber ★** with ceiling decorations including the arms and badges of Henry VIII and his third and favorite wife, Jane Seymour. Probably the most famous room in Hampton Court is the **Haunted Gallery ★**, so-called because it's allegedly haunted by Catherine Howard, who was said to have been dragged through the hall screaming when she tried to see her husband before her arrest and execution.

The **Chapel Royal ★★★**, built by Wolsey, has a Royal Pew where the monarch and his companions would sit, and a magnificent vaulted ceiling installed in 1536. Henry VIII married his final wife, Catherine Parr, here in 1543.

The **Wolsey Rooms ★★**, on the south side of the palace, were part of Cardinal Wolsey's private lodgings in the 1520s. These rooms, and the adjacent **Renaissance Picture Gallery ★★★**, are now used to display 16th- and early-17th-century paintings from the Royal Collection, including works by Lucas Cranach, Pieter Bruegel, Correggio, Agnolo Bronzino, Lorenzo Lotto, Parmigianino, and Titian.

The **King's Staircase ★★★** is the most spectacular in the palace and was decorated in about 1700 by the Italian painter Antonio Verrio. It leads to the **King's Apartments,** holding the **King's Privy Chamber ★** where ambassadors were received and court functions held, and the opulently furnished **Great Bedchamber.**

From the King's Apartments, make your way to the **Queen's State Apartments ★★★**. These rooms were begun by Sir Christopher Wren at the end of the 17th century. The **Queen's State Bedchamber ★★** is still furnished with its original state bed (complete with 18th-century mattresses). The magnificent **Queen's Gallery** was built as Queen Mary's private gallery.

Great feasts were once prepared in the Tudor Kitchens.

The famous yew tree maze.

The **Georgian Rooms ★★** are kept as they were during the last visit of the full court to the palace in 1737. The **Communication Gallery ★** linking the king's and queen's apartments is hung with portraits known as the Windsor Beauties, painted by Sir Peter Lely between 1662 and 1665 and representing the most beautiful women at the court of Charles II (reigned 1660–85).

The Hampton Court **gardens ★★★** are a delightful mix of 500 years of royal gardening history. The **Privy Garden,** the king's private plot on the south side of the palace facing the river, has been restored to the way it appeared when it was completed for William III in 1702. The **Great Vine ★**, planted in 1768 by landscape designer Lancelot "Capability" Brown, is the oldest known vine in the world and still produces 500 to 700 pounds (230–320 kilograms) of grapes each year. The grapes are harvested at the end of August and sold in the palace shops. The palace's famous **Maze ★★★** ☺ is nearby; formed of 1,000 yews planted in 1702, it covers a third of an acre (around a sixth of a hectare) and its paths wind for nearly half a mile.

Henry VIII conducts a tour of the palace.

## ORGANIZED TOURS

An **audio guide,** available free from the Information Centre, provides a wealth of information and anecdotes about the history and contents of the

### Nearby

**The Thames Path ★ runs 184 miles (296km) from the sea to the Cotswolds. Hampton Court is just by the river, and you can join the path behind the castle and either follow it out into the countryside, or back toward the city (through suburban Kingston, down to Teddington, and onto leafy Chiswick).**

building and the monarchs who lived there. Costumed guides also offer free tours of the State Apartments. These 30 minute tours must be booked in advance at the Information Centre in the Clock Court—they're popular, and so sign up as soon as you arrive.

#### OUTDOOR ACTIVITIES

Open from the first Saturday in December to mid-January, an ice-skating rink is set up near the West Front. Tickets for 1-hour sessions, including skate rental, cost (£12) for adults, £8 for children under 16, and can be reserved in person at the Hampton Court box office, or in advance at www.hamptoncourticerink.com. The annual **Hampton Court Flower Show** held in the height of summer is a superb event and certainly not just for gardeners, with craft stalls, music, and displays alongside the stunning horticultural displays (www.rhs.org.uk).

### Shopping

The **Garden Shop,** overlooking the gardens on the East Front of the palace, has a selection of garden-themed merchandise including books and accessories. The **Tudor Kitchens Shop,** next to the Tudor Wine Cellar, sells jam, tea, and traditional kitchen equipment. Other shops include a Tudor-themed **Henry Shop** and the **Barrack Block Shop** for general gifts and souvenirs.

### Where to Eat

Take a mid-morning break in the Tudor-themed **Privy Kitchen Coffee Shop** near the Tudor Kitchens, open daily from 10am to 5pm (Nov–Mar until 4pm). The **Tiltyard Café** (✆ **020/8943-3666**), in the palace gardens, is a buffet cafe-restaurant that serves sandwiches as well as hot meals. Open daily 10am to 5:30pm (Nov–Mar until 4:30pm).

## KNOLE

Built in the 15th century by an archbishop of Canterbury, the stone turrets and sturdy walls of the great house at Knole form a fine example of pure, Tudor architecture. Amid sprawling grounds—with miles of rolling hills and shallow valleys where herds of delicate deer wander—the house stands out not just for its extraordinary architecture but also for its sheer size. The place is enormous—the building alone covers 7 acres (2.8 hectares). Its design is tied into the calendar: 365 rooms, 52 staircases, and 7 courtyards. You only have access to a small part of the building, but its dark, labyrinthine hallways, rooms, and galleries are a treasure-trove of antique furniture, textiles, and art.

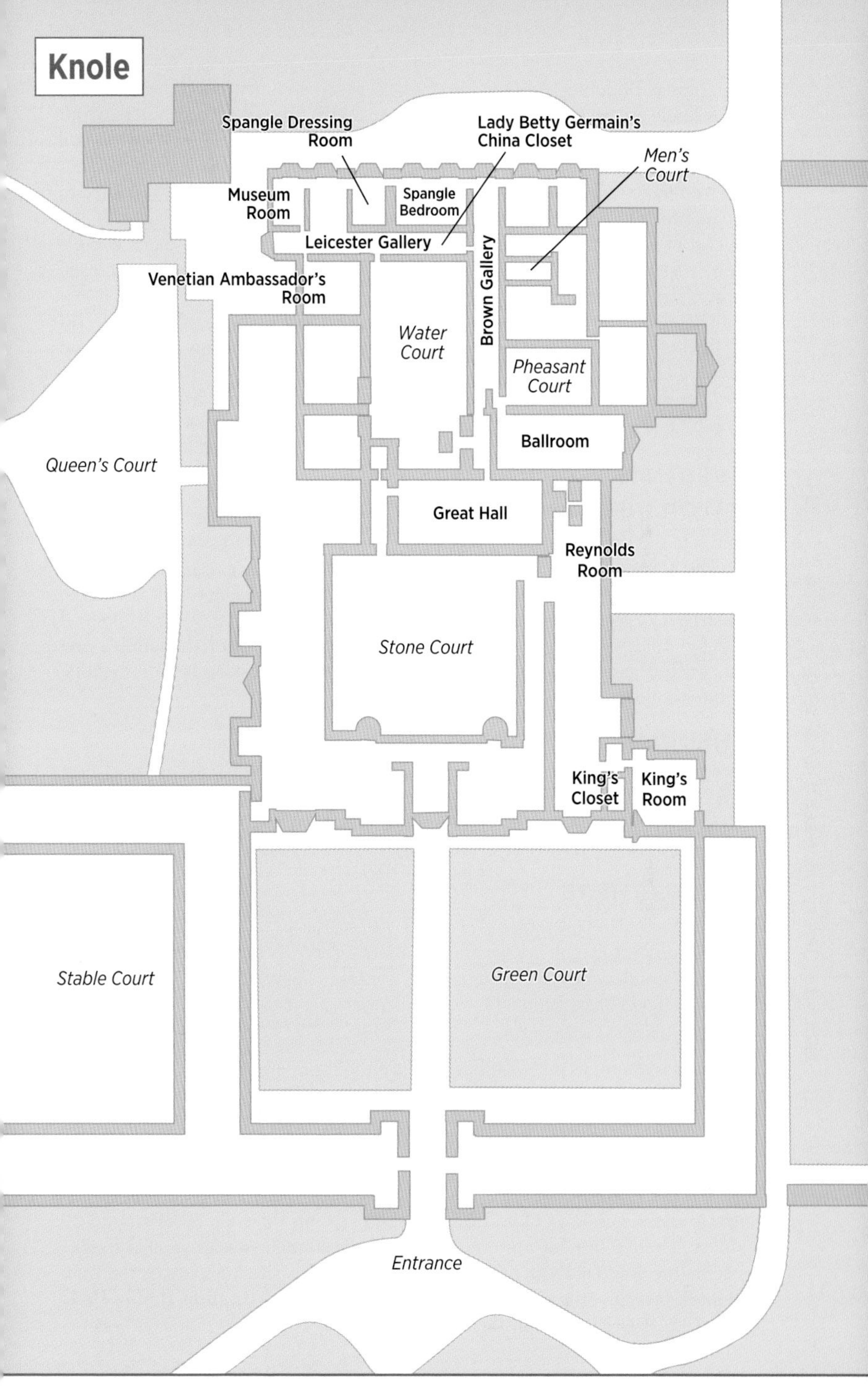

Knole
Spangle Dressing Room
Lady Betty Germain's China Closet
Men's Court
Museum Room
Spangle Bedroom
Leicester Gallery
Brown Gallery
Venetian Ambassador's Room
Water Court
Pheasant Court
Ballroom
Queen's Court
Great Hall
Reynolds Room
Stone Court
King's Closet
King's Room
Stable Court
Green Court
Entrance

Thomas Bouchier, Archbishop of Canterbury, commissioned the construction of Knole on the site of a medieval farm in 1456. The palace was home to four of Bouchier's successors, until the early 16th century, when Henry VIII took a liking to it and seized it for himself. He spent a fortune renovating the house but there's no indication that he spent much time here. When it eventually passed to his daughter, Queen Elizabeth I, she gave it to her cousin, Thomas Sackville, the first earl of Dorset, and it has been in the Sackville family ever since. Virginia Woolf, a friend of Vita Sackville-West and often a guest of the Sackvilles, used Knole as the setting for her novel Orlando.

The elaborate paneling and plasterwork provide a background for the 17th- and 18th-century tapestries and rugs, Elizabethan and Jacobean furniture, and collection of family portraits.

Less than an hour from London, you can easily do this day trip in half a day, or combine it with a visit to Ightham Mote or Chartwell. See p. 90.

## Essentials



### VISITOR INFORMATION

Knole is in the leafy town of Sevenoaks, about 30 miles (48km) southeast of London. The house (✆ **01732/450-608;** www.nationaltrust.org.uk) is open March to October Wednesday through Sunday noon to 4pm. The Deer Park is open to pedestrians for free, year-round. Admission to the house is £10.40 for adults and £5.75 for children. On Tuesdays from April through September, the family's **private, walled gardens** are open from 11am to 4pm. Admission is £5 for adults, £2.50 for children.

### SCHEDULING CONSIDERATIONS

As it's often extremely busy on weekends in the summer, Knole house is best visited on weekday mornings, when you can explore it in relative peace. Although you're welcome to wander the grounds on foot at any time, no parking is allowed on the property when the house is closed.

### GETTING THERE

#### By Train

Southeastern trains run to Sevenoaks about every 30 minutes from Charing Cross and London Victoria stations. The trip takes approximately 35 minutes. A round-trip ticket costs from £14.

#### By Car

Sevenoaks is about 30 miles (48km) from central London, and the drive from the city takes about 45 minutes. Take the M25 to the A21 and follow signs for Sevenoaks. The entrance to Knole is well-signposted at the south end of the town center off the A225 Tonbridge Road.

### GETTING AROUND

Knole is about 1 mile (1.6km) from the train station; the walk takes around 20 minutes. There's another mile of grounds to cross once you arrive at the gatehouse before you reach the house itself. A taxi stand is situated outside the train station, or you can arrange a pickup in advance by calling **Beeline Radio Taxis** (✆ **01732/456-214**) or **Knole Taxis** (✆ **01732/465-002**).

## Walking Around Knole

Knole's deer park is criss-crossed with unmarked paths that go on for miles. There are a number of good walks to be had here; ask for a brochure on walks at the visitor center, or download a walking map from the National Trust website (www.nationaltrust.org.uk). One 3-mile (5-km) walk starts at the front gate—follow the path along the inside of the wall, turning onto a paved drive known as "Broad Walk," and then onto a small road that passes it. This leads you past ponds and forests to a pathway lined with sweet chestnut trees, which eventually returns you to Broad Walk. The garden is so enormous that a map is essential to finding your way back to your starting point.

## A Day at Knole

There are only 13 rooms at Knole open to the public, but the house is so immense that you'll feel as if you've covered acres.

After passing through two courtyards, the first room you visit is the **Great Hall ★★★**. Thomas Bouchier, Archbishop of Canterbury who built the house between 1456 and 1480, used to dine on the dais at the far end of the cavernous space. When Thomas Sackville took possession of Knole in 1603, he added a minstrels' gallery where his private orchestra would play throughout the meal.

The staterooms at Knole are laid out as apartments with long galleries, bedchambers, and dressing rooms. As you pass through the first of these, the **Brown Gallery ★** and the adjoining **Lady Betty Germain's China Closet ★★**

The Spangle Bedroom at Knole.

### Nearby

From Knole you can visit two other great houses. The first, **Ightham Mote ★**, is a perfectly preserved medieval, moated manor house, dating from the 14th century. Once home to medieval knights, the house is beautifully maintained, with rooms filled with textiles, paneling, and furnishings accumulated over the centuries. Ightham Mote is in the tiny village of **Ivy Hatch,** 6 miles (9.5km) east of Sevenoaks on the A227 (✆ **01732/811-145;** www.nationaltrust.org.uk). Admission is £11 for adults and £5.50 for children 5 to 15.

**Chartwell ★**, the home of Sir Winston Churchill from 1922 until his death in 1965, isn't as grand as his birthplace at Blenheim Palace, but it's a must-see for Churchill fans. There are displays of his trademark suits and hats, as well as maps, documents, photographs, pictures, and mementos. Many of the former prime minister's watercolor paintings are displayed in a garden studio. Chartwell (✆ **01732/868-381;** www.nationaltrust.org.uk) is 7 miles (11km) from Sevenoaks on Mapleton Road near the town of Westerham—it's well-signposted. Admission is £11.80 for adults; £5.90 for children.

(which houses a notable collection of Delft), glance out of the window into the **Water Court ★★**—this half-timbered courtyard surrounded by bow windows is one of the few charming nooks and crannies at Knole.

Later you'll pass the **Leicester Gallery,** and then the **Venetian Ambassador's Room** where the bed is said to be the one in which King James II awoke in 1688 on the day William of Orange forced him into exile. A few rooms down in the **Spangle Bedroom,** the 17th-century bed is covered with thousands of silver panels that sparkle in sunlight.

The next rooms hold Knole's most famous paintings. A Van Dyck portrait of Frances Cranfield, who married a 17th-century owner of Knole, is in the grand **Ballroom ★★**, and a collection of paintings by Sir Joshua Reynolds hangs in the **Reynolds Room ★★**.

The **King's Room ★★** shows off a grandiose bed made for King Charles II, as well as a set of rare silver furniture—one of Knole's great treasures.

## Where to Eat

The estate's former brewer, now the **Brewhouse Tearoom** (✆ **01732/462-100**), is located near the stable yards behind the house. It's a pleasant setting to stop for sandwiches, soup, and salads, as well as tea and cake, and ice cream in summer (most options £3–£7).

# SANDRINGHAM

The queen's Norfolk estate is known to be one of her favorite houses, and has been a retreat for British royalty for more than a century. Set amid a vast spread of picturesque gardens and parkland, the house is a rambling country mansion built in 1870 by King Edward VII and has been famously described as "the most comfortable house in England." The ground-floor rooms are open to the public

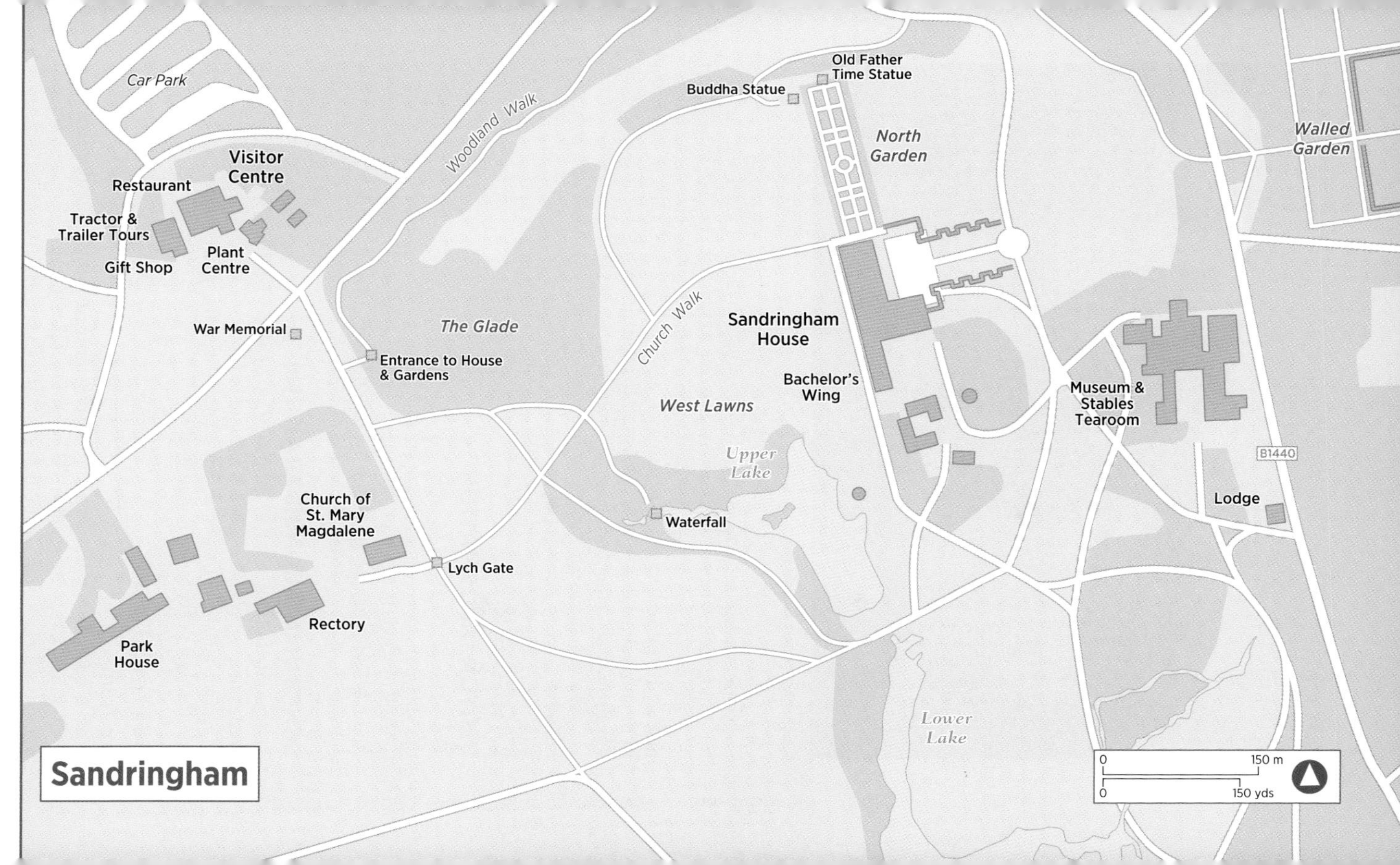
Sandringham
Car Park
Visitor Centre
Restaurant
Tractor & Trailer Tours
Gift Shop
Plant Centre
War Memorial
Woodland Walk
The Glade
Entrance to House & Gardens
Church Walk
Buddha Statue
Old Father Time Statue
North Garden
Walled Garden
Sandringham House
Bachelor's Wing
West Lawns
Upper Lake
Waterfall
Museum & Stables Tearoom
B1440
Lodge
Church of St. Mary Magdalene
Lych Gate
Rectory
Park House
Lower Lake
0
150 m
0
150 yds

Sandringham estate and gardens.





and these are largely furnished in the Edwardian style, and filled with art and furnishings collected by four generations of the royal family.

The house was always designed to be a getaway for the monarch, and not intended to be a palace for state purposes, and so it has an informal air compared to the official palaces. Queen Elizabeth II regularly spends Christmas at Sandringham, and by tradition the royal family sees in every New Year here.

You can spend an easy-going half day exploring the house, gardens, and museum.

## Essentials

### VISITOR INFORMATION

The estate (✆ **01485/545-408;** www.sandringhamestate.co.uk) is just outside the village of Dersingham. It's open daily April to late October from 11am to 4:45pm (3:45pm in October). Admission to the house is £11.50 for adults, £9.50 students and senior citizens, and £6 for children. A small discount is given on entry if you show your public transport train or bus ticket.

### SCHEDULING CONSIDERATIONS

The **Sandringham Flower Show** (✆ **01485/545-400;** www.sandringham flowershow.org.uk) takes place at the end of July every year and the house closes to regular guests at that time. You can still see the gardens and museum by purchasing a ticket to the flower show.

### GETTING THERE

#### By Train

First Capital Connect trains run to the town of **King's Lynn** every hour from King's Cross in London. The journey takes about 1½ hours; advance round-trip tickets start at around £35. Kings Lynn is 10 miles (16km) from

## Nearby

Sandringham sits at the edge of a beautiful stretch of the North Norfolk Coast, a beautiful wilderness set around beaches, dunes, and marshes. The main A149 road passes through **Salthouse** (a bird reserve of lagoons and marsh protected from the sea by a shingle bank), and on to the eco-friendly **Cley Marshes Wildlife Trust** (✆ **01263/740-008**; www.norfolkwildlifetrust.org.uk). Access to the reserve that runs down to the sea costs £4. **Wells-next-the-Sea** is a pleasant town with a bustling quayside. Parking at the main beach carpark offers a walk along the water's edge (and views of the occasional seal). The beach is backed by pine forest with mountainous dunes reaching all the way around to **Holkham beach** ★★—which itself stretches for miles with flat, golden sand backed by protected dunes. The impressive **Holkham Hall** ★ (image below), on the A149 (✆ **01328/710-227**; www.holkham.co.uk), was the magnificent stately home of several of the Earls of Leicester. Its deer park is enormous and free to visit on foot; you're very likely to catch sight of majestic stags and fey does. It's open April through October, Sunday, Monday, and Thursday, from noon to 4pm. Admission to the house is £11 for adults and £5.50 for children.

Sandringham, and so you can catch a local bus no. 11 or take a taxi. **King's Lynn Taxis** (✆ **01553/763-636**) or **A1 Cabs** (✆ **01553/772-616**) charge around £15.

### By Car

Sandringham is 110 miles (177km) northeast of London. Take the M11 north, turning onto the A10 at Cambridge. At King's Lynn take the A148 north and follow signs to Sandringham. The house is well-signposted.

### GETTING AROUND

Sandringham estate has miles of footpaths that you can traverse, through forests and across formal gardens. The grounds can be muddy, and so wear good walking shoes. There is wheelchair access throughout the house, museum, and visitor center.

## A Day at Sandringham

As you enter the house, walk through to the vast entrance hall or **Saloon** ★★ where the high-reaching walls hold portraits of Queen Victoria and Prince Albert painted by Franz Xavier Winterhalter.

Nearby, the **small drawing room** has further family portraits, exquisite porcelain from the queen's collection, and wooden chairs adorned with embroidery, stitched by Princess Alexandra's own hand.

The **main drawing room ★** is dominated by a portrait of Alexandra painted by Edward Hughes, and has a painted ceiling and wall panels. Some of the items on view include sterling silver Russian glasses, and Chinese figurines that date to the early 1800s.

Down the hall, the **dining room** is draped in Spanish tapestries—a gift to Edward VII, the Prince of Wales in 1875, from Alphonso XII of Spain—and the table is set with antique china and crystal.

Outside, the garden gates—ornamented with a wrought iron design of flowers and leaves—open onto a green and verdant expanse stretching across 59 acres (24 hectares). Each generation has added to the gardens over the last 140 years, and so they vary from the formal straight lines of the **North Garden** to an element of wildness along **Stream Walk.**

Walk around the house to the former coach house that holds a **museum ★** displaying the gifts given to the royal family on state visits alongside various collectables, including a clock used to time Her Majesty's racing pigeon and a 1939 Merryweather fire engine.

## Where to Eat

Next to the visitors' center, the **Sandringham Restaurant,** the largest dining area on the estate, overlooks the gardens and serves snacks and sandwiches all day, hot meals from 11:30am to 2:30pm. Nearby, the **Terrace Coffee Shop** and the **Stables Tea Room** offer mainly teas, cakes, and lighter dishes. There's even a picnic lunch service available, but this must be ordered in advance—see the website for details (www.sandringhamestate.co.uk).

# SISSINGHURST CASTLE GARDEN

Many English castles have impressive surroundings, but the exquisite gardens at Sissinghurst are so extraordinary that it has come to be seen as a garden foremost and a castle second. The project of the bohemian writer and Bloomsbury Group member Vita Sackville-West and her partner, the diplomat Harold Nicholson, the gardens were an elaborate labor of love. When they bought the Elizabethan castle in 1930, it lay in ruins and the grounds were a jungle. By the time they'd finished, Sissinghurst was truly spectacular.

Inspired by Britain's best-known garden designers of the early 20th century, Sir Edwin Lutyens and Gertrude Jekyll, Harold and Vita divided the precincts into 10 outdoor "rooms," each with a distinct look and feel, separated by hedges and stone walls, and each planted with a rich diversity of foliage and flowers. In spring, the gardens are awash with flowering bulbs and daffodils, while the famed white garden reaches its peak in June. The couple also restored the gatehouse, stables, and tower—enough to give you an idea of how spectacular the castle must once have been.

The trip down from London to Sissinghurst is relatively quick, making the castle and gardens an excellent choice for a half-day excursion.

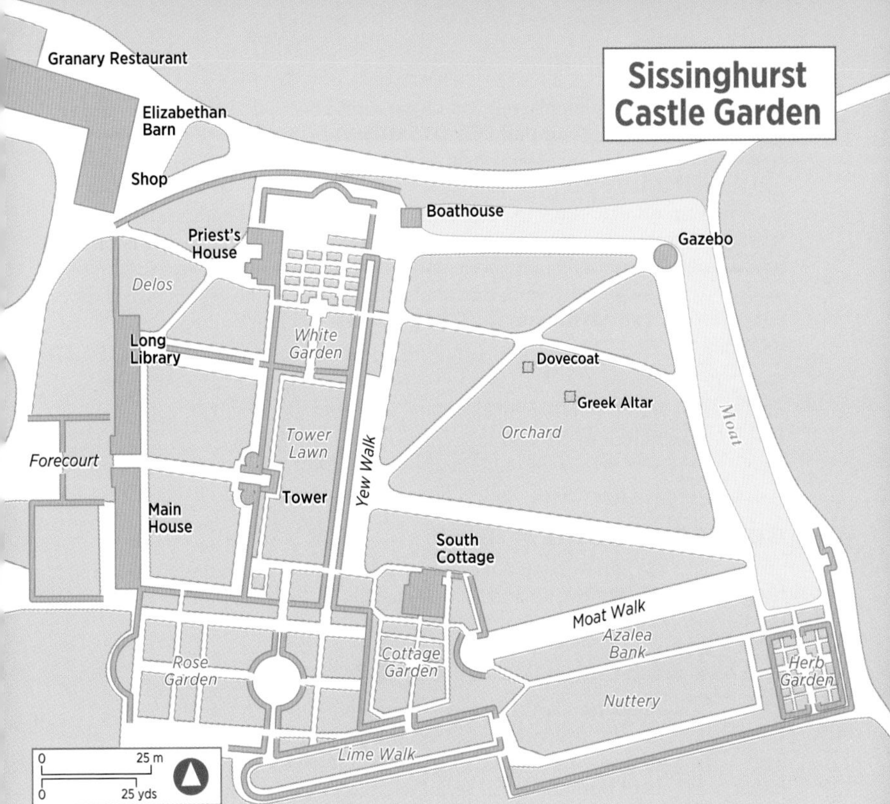


# Essentials

## VISITOR INFORMATION

The garden is open from mid-March to late October Friday through Tuesday from 10:30am to 5pm. Admission is £10 for adults and £5.50 for children 5 to 15 years old. For more information, call ✆ **01580/710-701** or visit www.nationaltrust.org.uk.

## SCHEDULING CONSIDERATIONS

The charms of Sissinghurst are well-known and the garden is one of England's most popular attractions. Try to visit when the garden isn't crowded—Sissinghurst is always spectacular and so you can enjoy a visit even outside of the summer months, although it's most beautiful during late spring and summer. Only a set number of visitors are allowed into the garden at a time, so expect a wait on sunny summer weekends. It's best to visit during the week if you can.

## GETTING THERE

### By Train

The train station closest to Sissinghurst is in the village of Staplehurst, about 7 miles (11km) away. Trains run from London Charing Cross to Staplehurst every 30 minutes. The journey takes about 1 hour and the standard day round-trip fare is £17.50. From Staplehurst you can take a taxi to Sissinghurst for about £12—try **Maidstone Taxi Company** (✆ **01580/890-003**). Arrange for your driver to pick you up at the end of your visit, or get a card to call the taxi company when you're ready to leave.

You can also continue to Sissinghurst by bus no. 4/5 (Maidstone–Hastings service). Buses run roughly every 1½ hours throughout the day, and the fare is £2.30. Get off in Sissinghurst village and follow the well-marked footpath to the garden. A special bus runs from the Staplehurst station to the garden on Sundays and Tuesdays; call **Sissinghurst** (✆ **01580/710-701**) for times and additional information.

### By Car

Sissinghurst is in the rolling hills of Kent, about 50 miles (80km) southwest of London. The trip from London takes just over an hour. Take the M25 to Maidstone, where you get on the A229 and travel south through Staplehurst to the A262; Sissinghurst is about 3 miles (5km) west of the junction. Parking is free.



### GETTING AROUND

The gardens are sprawling and paths are often muddy; wear comfortable mud-friendly shoes. A limited number of wheelchairs are available for travelers with disabilities, but the tower and libraries both have steps.

## A Day at Sissinghurst Castle Garden

You enter Sissinghurst Castle Garden—through an arch in the stable and servants' block into the courtyard and past the base of a tall tower of pale pink brick—the same way that Queen Elizabeth I did when she paid a visit to its owner Sir Richard Baker in 1573. Baker had built a grand Elizabethan manor at Sissinghurst on the foundations of a medieval house. The two rooms inside the house you can visit, the Long Library and Vita's study in the Tower, are reached off the courtyard, but save them for later; instead, focus on the gardens that lie just on the other side of the Tower.

As you move from one garden to another, take note of the way the design incorporates classical symmetry and romantic abandon—in this way, the garden is said to capture the personalities of the couple who created it. In the **Rose Garden ★★★**, to your right as you pass through the arch at the base of the Tower, Harold designed the disk of mowed lawn surrounded by yew hedges; and Vita, whose preference was for colorful beds and flowers straying over paths,

#### Nearby

**As a child, Vita Sackville-West grew up in Knole (see p. 86), a glorious, rambling mansion and estate 24 miles (39km) to the west of Sissinghurst. As the only heir of her father, Lionel, the third Lord Sackville, she would have inherited it had she been male. She was close friends with the writer Virginia Woolf and her sister the artist Vanessa Bell, and frequently visited them in Lewes (see p. 31), 26 miles (42km) south of Sissinghurst, at Charleston (p. 35).**

Sissinghurst Castle Garden.

planted the luxuriant, old-fashioned varieties that bloom in June. In the **White Garden ★★★**, Vita planted all white flowers that bloom throughout the spring and summer. The **Cottage Garden ★★★** combines formality and a sense of abundance, and in it grows a white rose the couple planted the day they bought Sissinghurst. The classically oriented Harold planted the formal, Italianate **Lime Walk ★★** and Vita lavished care on the **Herb Garden ★★**; she claimed she could identify every herb with her eyes closed.

Once you've seen everything outside, return to the **Tower ★★★**, where you can look into Vita's study. Climb the winding staircase to the top for sweeping views of the gardens and surrounding green hills. Just across the courtyard, the **Long Library ★★** is a handsome room dating from 1490 and filled with centuries-old family furniture.

## Where to Eat

An airy building on the estate near the garden entrance, **The Granary** (✆ **01580/710-704**) is an unusually pleasant setting for a cafe-style restaurant overlooking fields through a wall of glass. It serves sandwiches, salads, and a few hot dishes, along with tea, scones, and cakes. Most plates are priced from £3 to £7.

# MEDIEVAL CASTLES & TUDOR FORTRESSES

5

These stone castles offer insight into the country's long regal and military history, in times of conflict and stately concord. Sturdy Dover Castle still glares across the channel toward France, the warren of secret defensive tunnels that lie beneath were built in the medieval period and put to use during both the Napoleonic War and WWII. The moated castle at Hever was the childhood home of Anne Boleyn, the unfortunate second wife of Henry VIII. Here you can delve further into the Tudor King's tempestuous love-life in the Long Gallery's exhibition and watch some medieval jousting in the grounds. A swan- filled lake surrounds the turreted Leeds Castle. Built in the 9$^{th}$ century it briefly operated as a hospital for injured soldiers in WWII. Today the gardens encompass a yew tree maze, impressive modern aviary and the eccentric Dog Collar Museum.



---

Windsor Castle holds many fine paintings from the Royal Collection, an intricate, fully functioning dolls house designed by architect Sir Edwin Lutyens and has its own Changing of the Guard ceremony to rival that of Buckingham Palace. Nearby the Great Park provides woodlands, a lake and formal gardens for wandering and is an idyllic spot for a picnic.

## DOVER CASTLE

A castle has stood high atop a cliff, hundreds of feet above the port town of Dover, for more than 2,000 years. Today it still stands like a sentinel, low and sturdy, with walls almost 10 feet (3 meters) thick surrounded by swirling rings of ancient earth and stone walls. While exploring the castle and its grounds, you walk through millennia of British history—from a Roman lighthouse to a magnificent keep, and down to secret tunnels first burrowed into the chalky ground in medieval times.

The first castle stood on this site in Anglo-Saxon times, but it took on its present appearance in the 12th century, when Henry II strengthened its walls and built the keep, still the largest in Britain. Fearing an invasion by French forces from across the Channel, the monarchs who followed him each expanded the fortress. The Napoleonic Wars spurred the extension of a labyrinth of defensive tunnels that housed thousands of soldiers to fend off an invasion, and the underground complex was back in action again during World War II.

FACING PAGE: **Hever Castle.**

Plan on devoting a full day to this trip, giving you time to tour the castle at leisure and for a walk atop the White Cliffs.

## Essentials

### VISITOR INFORMATION

Dover is 78 miles (126km) southeast of London. **Dover Castle** (✆ **01304/211-067;** www.english-heritage.org.uk), at the eastern edge of the town, is open daily April through September 10am to 6pm (from 9:30am in Aug); October daily 10am to 5pm; November through January Thursday through Monday 10am to 4pm; and February and March daily 10am to 4pm. Admission is £16 for adults, £14.40 for students and seniors, and £9.60 for children 5 to 15.

The **Dover Visitor Information Centre** (✆ **01304/205-108;** www.whitecliffscountry.org.uk), on Biggin Street, has maps and loads of information. It's open Monday through Friday from 9am to 5:30pm, Saturday and Sunday from 10am to 4pm (closed Sun Oct–Mar).

### SCHEDULING CONSIDERATIONS

Dover Castle isn't a place to save for a rainy day. You'll get soaked as you cross the vast castle compound, and the cliffs can be a bit dangerous in stormy weather.

### GETTING THERE

#### By Train

Southeastern trains run about every 30 minutes throughout the day from London Victoria and Charing Cross stations to Dover Priory station. The trip takes about 2 hours. Round-trip tickets start at £32.

#### By Bus

Buses operated by **National Express** (✆ **08717/818-178;** www.nationalexpress.com) run hourly or half-hourly from London Victoria bus station to Dover

Dover Castle, perched high above the town.

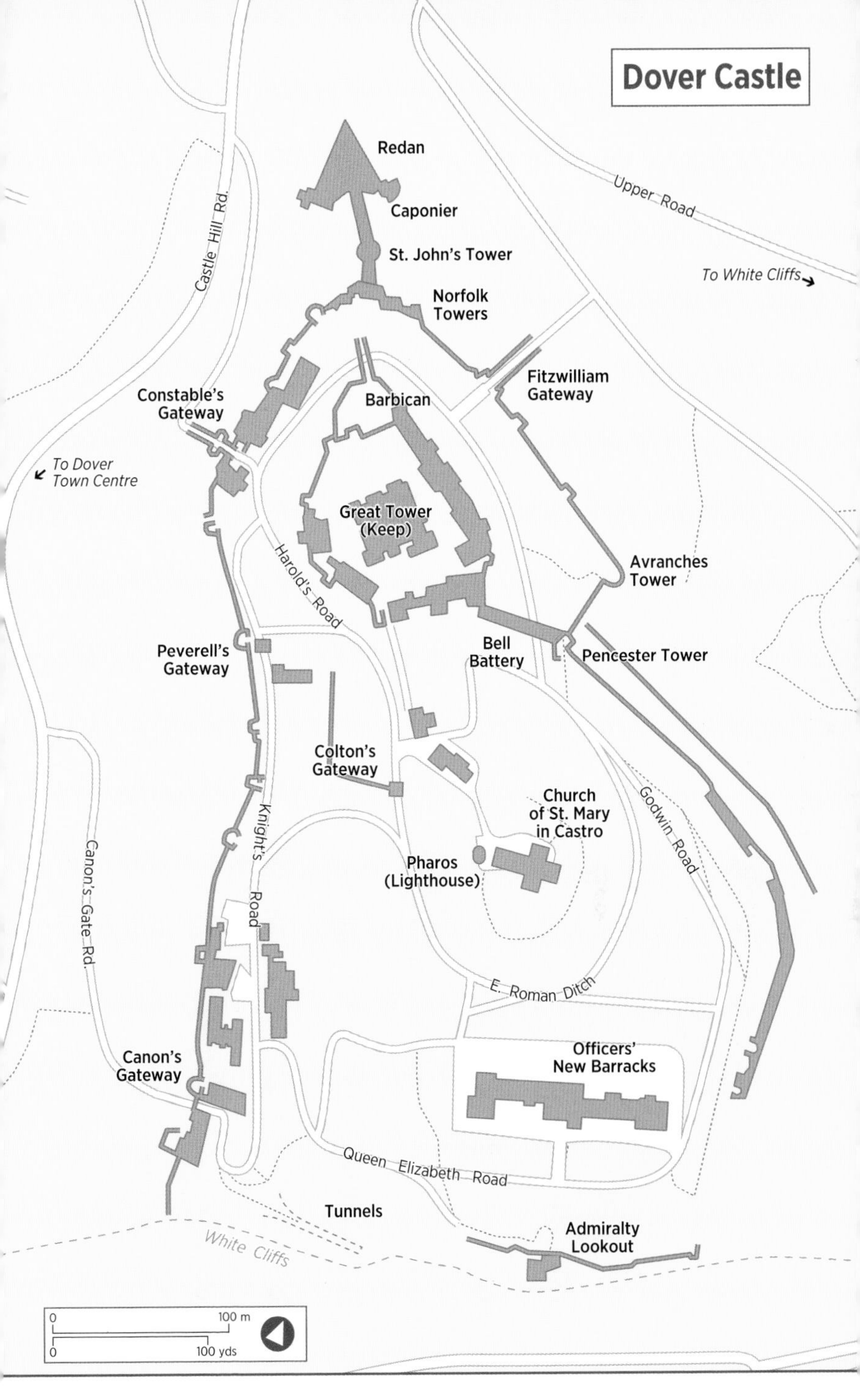
Dover Castle
Redan
Caponier
St. John's Tower
Norfolk Towers
Upper Road
To White Cliffs
Castle Hill Rd.
Fitzwilliam Gateway
Constable's Gateway
Barbican
To Dover Town Centre
Great Tower (Keep)
Harold's Road
Avranches Tower
Bell Battery
Pencester Tower
Peverell's Gateway
Colton's Gateway
Church of St. Mary in Castro
Godwin Road
Knight's Road
Pharos (Lighthouse)
Canon's Gate Rd.
E. Roman Ditch
Officers' New Barracks
Canon's Gateway
Queen Elizabeth Road
Tunnels
Admiralty Lookout
White Cliffs
0
100 m
0
100 yds

town center. The trip takes about 2½ hours and the same-day round-trip fare is £13.

### By Car

The trip from London takes about 1½ hours, depending on traffic. Take the M25 to the M20 for the speedy drive down to Folkestone, and then the A20 to Dover. As you approach Dover on the A20, there's a well-marked exit to the castle, where you'll find several parking areas.

### GETTING AROUND

The castle is up a very steep hill from the train station in town; the route is well-marked and takes about 15 minutes. Alternatively, Stagecoach buses nos. 15/X and 593 make the trip from the bus station to the entrance of the castle; tickets costs £2 (www.stagecoachbus.com). You can also take a taxi—there's a taxi stand outside the station or call **Heritage Taxis** (✆ **01304/225-522**). The taxi fare costs around £5.

## A Day at Dover Castle

Dover Castle spreads across 70 acres (28 hectares) and is packed with things to see. At the top of the castle hill, the sturdy Saxon church **St. Mary-in-Castro** dates back more than 1,000 years. The battered-looking round tower behind it is even older—the pharos **lighthouse ★** was constructed by the Romans to guide their ships across the Channel and is claimed to be the oldest structure in Britain.

Between 1160 and 1180, Henry II transformed Dover into one of the mightiest fortifications in Europe, expanding and enhancing its defenses. At the heart of the king's project was the construction of the **keep ★★★**, or great tower, where you can step into the hulking remains of the Great Hall and two graceful

A bedroom fit for a king within the castle keep.

A brisk stroll along the White Cliffs.

stone chapels, one dedicated to Thomas à Becket, murdered in Canterbury Cathedral by Henry's knights in 1170 (see p. 56). Also in the keep are rooms filled with furniture, documents, and other effects of Henry VIII, who came to Dover in 1539 soon after his divorce from Catherine of Aragon (a divorce she neither wanted nor accepted) and his excommunication from the Catholic Church. European sentiment had turned against him and the king was seeking assurance that the castle could withstand an invasion that then seemed inevitable.

Just south of the keep is the entrance to the **medieval underground tunnels ★** that allowed soldiers to travel from one part of the castle to another safely during a siege. Dover's greatest strength was always its sturdy **walls ★★★** that still completely encircle the compound. You can climb to the top and walk the complete circuit, stopping to take in the view of the port from **Admiralty Look-Out ★**. Back on the ground—or rather below ground—are the **secret wartime tunnels ★★★**. This 18th-century tunnel system, first used by British soldiers housed here to ward off a French invasion during the late-18th-century Napoleonic Wars, was pressed into use in 1940, when it became the command center

## Walking the White Cliffs

One of the most breathtaking sights in England is the view from atop the famous **White Cliffs of Dover (✆ 01304/ 202-756;** www.nationaltrust.org.uk). On a clear day, you can see all the way to France. The footpath at the top leads you to the Victorian **South Foreland Lighthouse,** with its square, sturdy tower. You can climb up to take in the view and learn the history of shipwrecks on the Kentish coast. Generally, the lighthouse is open all year Monday and Friday to Sunday 11am to 5:30pm, but mid-week opening varies depending on the month, so check the **National Trust** website first (www.nationaltrust.org.uk). Admission is £4 for adults, £2 for under-16s. The cliffs are signposted from the Dover Castle entrance, and start about a quarter of a mile (half a kilometer) beyond the castle. A 2.5 mile (4km) path follows the top of the chalk cliffs.

for Operation Dynamo. This involved the evacuation of 340,000 British troops from Dunkirk, across the Channel in France, after it became clear they couldn't fend off the German army. By the time the war ended the tunnels housed an underground city of barracks, military headquarters, a communications center, and hospital. The hour-long guided tours of the tunnels include dramatic sound-and-light effects.

South Foreland Lighthouse.

## ORGANIZED TOURS

See the cliffs from below and above on a **Dover White Cliffs Tour** (✆ **01303/271-388;** www.doverwhiteclifftours.com). These combine a 40 minute boat trip to see Dover's cliffs from the English Channel, with a bus trip to the top of the cliffs and a short guided walk. The bus then drops you off at the castle or station. Fares for a 2-hour tour begin at £15.

## MORE THINGS TO SEE & DO

Down in Dover town, the 1,800-year-old **Roman Painted House,** New St. (✆ **01304/203-279**), has astonishingly complete frescoes, as well as walls and heating systems that once kept Romans warm. It's open April through September Tuesday to Saturday 10am to 4:30pm and Sunday 1 to 4:30pm. Admission is £3 adults and £2 seniors and children. The **Maison Dieu,** in the town hall on Biggin St. (✆ **01304/201-200;** www.dover.gov.uk), dates to the early 12th century and was built as a hostel for pilgrims traveling from the European continent to Canterbury (open Tues–Sat 10am–4:30pm and Sun 2–4:30pm, with free admission). The wooden Bronze Age boat is the chief draw of the **Dover Museum,**

### Nearby

Dover is 18 miles (29km) south of the lovely cathedral city of **Canterbury** (see p. 51).

The seaside town of **Folkestone** 9 miles (14.5km) from Dover, is a charming place with winding streets, arty shops, a grassy, cliff-top promenade, and a small quayside (with views of the White Cliffs). The beach, a short walk down the hill, stretches as far as you can see. Just south of Folkestone in **Hythe,** the Romney, Hythe, and Dymchurch narrow-gauge steam railway (✆ **01797/362-353;** www.rhdr.org.uk) runs along the coast to the wild and windy shingle beach at **Dungeness,** where fishing cottages made from old railway carriages provide stark contrast to the huge modern power station behind them. See **www.discoverfolkestone.co.uk** for more information on the area.

Market Square (✆ **01304/201-066**), alongside exhibitions on local history. It's open April through September Monday to Saturday 10am to 5:30pm, Sunday noon to 5pm. Admission is £3 adults, £2 seniors, students, and children.

## Where to Eat

There are several places to eat at Dover Castle, including the **NAAFI Restaurant,** which serves hot food and snacks, with views overlooking the Channel. The **Great Tower Café** offers sandwiches, tea, and cakes near the tower, while the **Secret Wartime Tunnels Café** serves similar fare in the tunnels. All eateries are open the same hours as the castle; expect to pay £3.50 to £6.95 for most lunch dishes.

# HEVER CASTLE

Hever has everything you expect of a castle—ancient stone walls, tall towers, moat and drawbridge, and grounds that spread for miles. William de Hever built the first structure in 1270, which was added to by the next owner Sir Geoffrey Bullen (or "Boleyn" in modern spelling) in 1462, with a large Tudor house. This is where Anne, the doomed second wife to King Henry VIII and mother to Queen Elizabeth I, grew up.

After Anne's execution, Henry callously gave Hever Castle to a later wife, Anne of Cleves, as part of their divorce settlement. After that, the house passed from one family to another and ultimately fell into decay. By the early 20th century it was nearly ruined—the roof had collapsed in places and the owners couldn't afford to fix it. William Waldorf Astor (1848–1919), heir to an American fur-trading fortune, bought the castle in 1903, and he and his wife, Mary, devoted

Hever Castle.

## Walking to Hever

The tiny village of Hever is about 1 mile (1.6km) from the castle gates. The best walk to the castle crosses farms and fields on public footpaths. You can download a rudimentary map from the castle website (www.hevercastle.co.uk). To begin, follow the lane leading from the station to the road—almost directly across that road, a public footpath sign directs you onto the trail. Follow it as it winds to the right and when it joins another footpath, turn left. When the path reaches a road, follow it past the **Henry VIII Inn** (p. 110) to the castle entrance 5 minutes' walk away.

years and huge amounts of money to the process of restoring it. The Astors insisted that their workers used traditional tools for the work, and today you can still see the marks their antique tools made as they replaced bricks and created elaborate plaster designs. They even created a Tudor village inside the castle walls, as it might have existed centuries before.

Their work gave Hever a magical atmosphere; its rooms are well-restored, and the gardens are lush and delightful, filled with topiary. It's a perfect setting for the events, such as medieval jousting tournaments, that are held here throughout the year. Aim to spend half a day here—possibly longer on a sunny day.

# Essentials

## VISITOR INFORMATION

**Hever Castle** (✆ **01732/865-224;** www.hevercastle.co.uk) is 30 miles (48km) southeast of London, in Kent. It's open April through October daily 10:30am to 5pm, and November through March daily 10:30am to 4pm. Admission to the castle and gardens is £14 for adults, £12 for seniors, and £8 for children 5 to 15.

## SCHEDULING CONSIDERATIONS

The gardens at Hever are especially lush during **Spring Garden Week** in mid-March and **Rose Week** in late June. In December, the house is decorated for Christmas, and crafts fairs are frequently held on weekends. Otherwise there are seasonal events throughout the year; further details can be found on the website.

## GETTING THERE

### By Train

From London Bridge station, trains depart hourly throughout the day for Edenbridge and Hever stations. The trip takes 45 minutes, and round-trip tickets cost around £10. The castle is 1 mile (1.6km) from Hever station, which is the ideal stop for those planning to walk. Edenbridge station is 3 miles (5km) away, and is best for those who would prefer to take a taxi. Try **Edenbridge Cars** (✆ **01732/864-009**). Book your taxi in advance.

### By Car

Hever is about 30 miles (48km) from London, near the town of Edenbridge. From the M25, take exit 5 and follow the A22 about 5 miles (8km) south to Bindley Heath; from there follow small country lanes (to the B2026). The route is well-signposted.

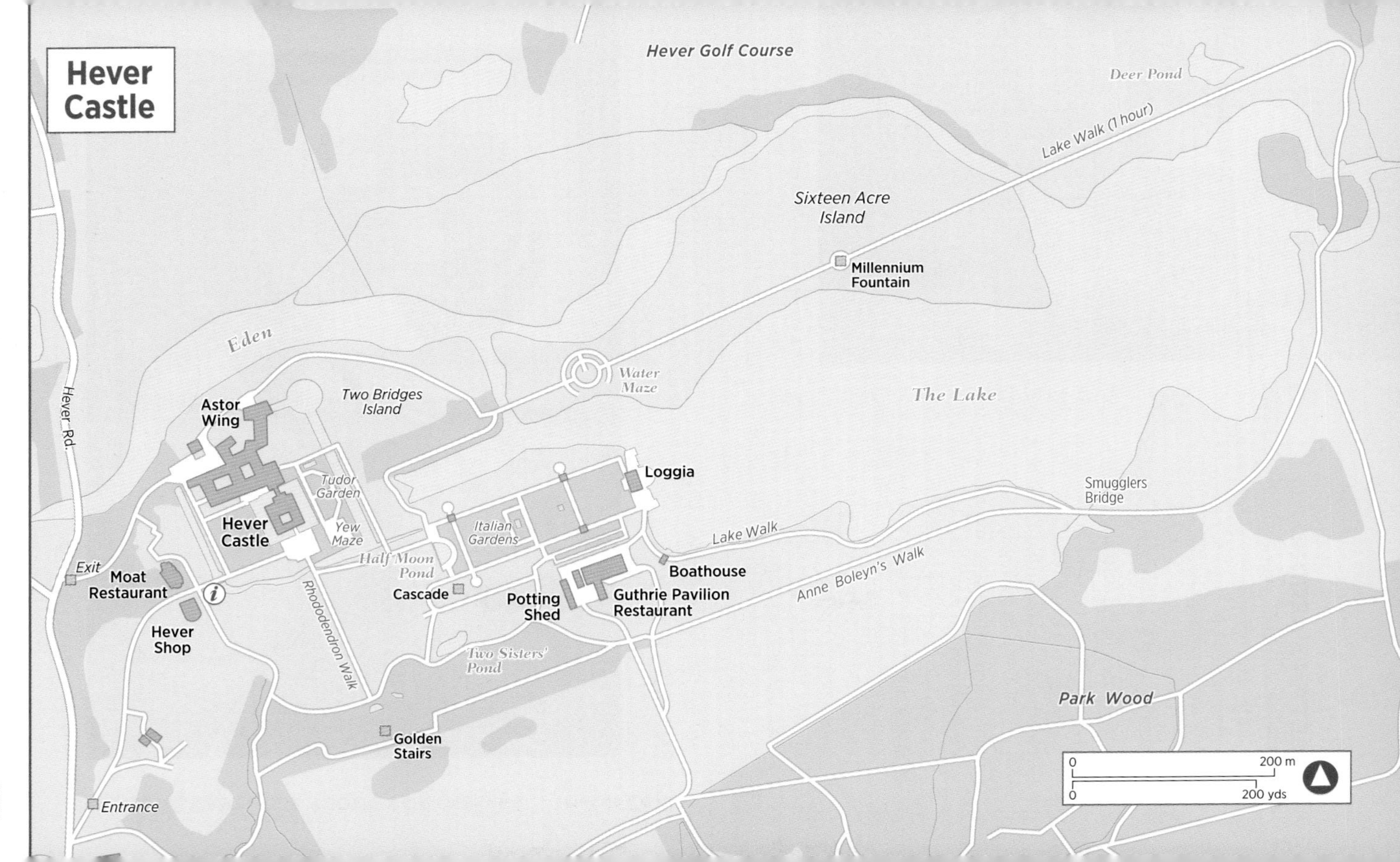
Hever Castle
Hever Golf Course
Deer Pond
Lake Walk (1 hour)
Sixteen Acre Island
Millennium Fountain
Eden
Water Maze
The Lake
Two Bridges Island
Astor Wing
Hever Rd.
Tudor Garden
Loggia
Smugglers Bridge
Hever Castle
Yew Maze
Italian Gardens
Lake Walk
Half Moon Pond
Boathouse
Anne Boleyn's Walk
Exit
Moat Restaurant
Cascade
Potting Shed
Guthrie Pavilion Restaurant
Hever Shop
Rhododendron Walk
Two Sisters' Pond
Park Wood
Golden Stairs
0
200 m
0
200 yds
Entrance

## GETTING AROUND

There's no public transportation to Hever Castle, and so plan to either walk from Hever station or book a taxi to take you from nearby Edenbridge.

## A Day at Hever Castle

The castle's grand **entrance hall** is dimly lit, with wood-paneled walls hung with portraits of Henry VIII and his wives. Nearby, the grand **dining room ★★** is set up as if for a Tudor feast, with a long oak table, gigantic fireplace, and minstrels' balcony above (you can climb up a tiny staircase to see the dining hall as the musicians would have viewed it). Up the main staircase, you pass through a series of bedrooms and drawing rooms furnished with antiques and historic artifacts. At the end of one hallway, a small exhibition room holds a display on Anne Boleyn and Henry, featuring a **Book of Hours ★** signed by a young Anne "Le temps viendra" ("The time will come"). Nearby, the bedroom where Henry stayed when visiting the Boleyns is richly furnished as it was during his rare visits to the castle. In it hangs a much-reproduced portrait of the king attributed to Hans Holbein.

One of many antique filled rooms inside the castle.

Anne Boleyn in the Long Gallery.

## THE SIX *wives* OF HENRY VIII

Among the lures of Hever Castle is its connection to King Henry VIII and his many marriages. Wax figures of Henry's queens are lined up in the Long Gallery, and they provide an illuminating lesson in a juicy episode in English Tudor history. **Catherine of Aragon** (1485–1536), the daughter of King Ferdinand and Queen Isabella of Spain, had been married to Henry's brother Arthur, and upon his death a year after the marriage, Catherine became betrothed to Henry, who was then too young to marry. After 20 years of marriage, Catherine failed to produce a male heir (she had one daughter, who would later reign as Mary I, or "Bloody Mary"), and Henry sought to annul the union. The pope refused, and so Henry installed a new Archbishop of Canterbury, Thomas Cranmer, to carry out his wishes, thereby creating the Church of England. Catherine never accepted the divorce and until her dying day always thought of herself as Henry's wife.

One of the chief reasons for divorcing Catherine was so that Henry could officially marry the spirited **Anne Boleyn** (1500–36), whose family lived at Hever at this time. While queen, she produced a daughter (who would become Elizabeth I) but no male heir, and despite Henry's initial infatuation with her, he became convinced the union was doomed. He had Anne executed on (trumped-up) grounds of adultery and 11 days later married **Jane Seymour** (1509–37), who within the year finally gave Henry a son (the future Edward VI) but herself died in childbirth. Henry next married **Anne of Cleves** (1515–57) to further his alliances with Germany, but it was an unsuccessful match from the start, and the two were soon divorced. Fortunately for Anne it was an amicable arrangement and Hever was given to her as part of her settlement.

Sixteen days after freeing himself of Anne, Henry married **Catherine Howard** (1521–42), more than 30 years his junior. The king had his young queen, who was a first cousin of Anne Boleyn, executed on suspicion she was taking lovers. In 1543, Henry married the level-headed **Catherine Parr** (1512–48), who outlived the king and went on to marry Thomas Seymour, brother of Henry's third queen.

You can trace the tawdry history of Henry's love-life in lavish detail in the **Long Gallery** ★, which stretches nearly the length of the house and is filled with mannequins depicting the monarch and his six wives.

Head through a confusing warren of hallways to the **Gatehouse** ★—the oldest part of the building, it dates to 1270 and houses a grisly display of torture devices.

### OUTDOOR ACTIVITIES

Half the joy of visiting Hever is wandering the grounds and extraordinary gardens. The Astors' 1,800 gardeners toiled for 4 years to create the landscape. Formal **Italian Gardens** ★★ surround an artificial lake with classical sculptures. Nearby, the **yew maze** ★ will take you no time at all to conquer, while the kids can amuse themselves splashing in the **water maze** or climbing in the **adventure playground** ☺.

## Where to Eat

There are two restaurants within the grounds: the **Moat Restaurant** next to the gift shop and the **Guthrie Pavilion** near the boating lake. Both serve seasonal homemade food and fairtrade hot drinks. There are also four food kiosks around the grounds where you can buy ice creams and snacks. In the nearby village of Hever, the handsome **Henry VIII Inn** (✆ **01732/862-457;** www.kinghenryviiiinn.co.uk) dishes-up substantial hot meals, along with smaller snacks, and on Sundays, a satisfying roast lunch (most meals priced from £6 to £9).

Stained glass window in the Long Gallery.

## Where to Shop

Apart from the usual gift shop well-stocked with Hever-influenced products, the **Courtyard Shop,** close to the Guthrie Pavilion, will appeal to gardeners inspired by Hever's lush gardens, with plants and various horticultural paraphernalia for sale.

### Nearby

Well-maintained public footpaths criss-cross the countryside all around Hever. One of the most pleasant walks takes you through woods and fields from the church near the castle gate for about 1.5 miles (2.5km) to **Chiddingstone ★,** where the half-timbered houses look like they've stepped out of the pages of a history book. **Chiddingstone Castle ★** on Hill Hoath Rd. (✆ **01892/870-347;** www.chiddingstonecastle.org.uk) is a 19th-century house designed to look like a medieval castle, and it holds an eclectic collection of eastern art and artifacts. (Gardens open year round; house opens Apr–Oct Sun–Wed 11am–5pm. Tickets £7 adults, £4 children 5–13. Parking is £2.50.)

If you're feeling energetic, you can continue to **Penshurst Place ★** (✆ **01892/870-307;** www.penshurstplace.com), but stop at the post office or a shop on the main street and ask for detailed directions; it can be really hard to find your way on the intersecting footpaths. A spectacular example of a complete 14th-century manor house, Penshurst contains an extensive collection of tapestry, art, and armor. It's open April through October daily 10:30am to 6pm (house closes at 4pm). Admission is £9.80 adults and £6.20 children 5 to 16.

The lake within Hever Castle's grounds.



## LEEDS CASTLE

Leeds Castle is a vision of turrets, towers, and light gray stone that seems to float in the middle of a swan-filled lake. It has a long history: its roots trace back to the 9th century, when Leed, a minister of the king of Kent, built a wooden fortress here on two islands in the River Len, and the fort was transformed into a royal palace for Edward I in 1278; the castle's vineyard, still producing grapes, is listed in the 11th-century Domesday Book. King Henry V imprisoned his stepmother, Queen Joan, at Leeds on charges of witchcraft, and then turned the castle over to his wife, Catherine de Valois. Henry VIII made substantial improvements to Leeds for his first queen, Catherine of Aragon. The castle was later the country seat of Lord Culpeper, colonial governor of the state of Virginia.

The last private owner of the castle was Lady Olive Baillie, an Anglo-American heiress who bought it in 1926. She restored some of Leeds to its medieval splendor and created in other parts of the castle one of the most sophisticated and tasteful homes of 20th-century Britain. During World War II, she donated it for use as a hospital for injured servicemen, and when she died in 1974, she left it to a private foundation to be preserved for the nation.

Although Leeds is beautiful and the setting for a great many moments in Britain's past, it's also a lot of fun. Mazes enliven the gardens, balloons take off from the grounds, fireworks frequently burst overhead, and strains of orchestras float through the woods during summer concerts. All in all, Leeds is probably the showiest castle in the land. To take advantage of the place in all its glory, try to arrange a visit on a day when the weather permits you to enjoy the grounds as well as the castle.

Leeds Castle and grounds.

## Essentials

### VISITOR INFORMATION

**Leeds Castle** (✆ **01622/765-400;** www.leeds-castle.com) is in the county of Kent, about 35 miles (56km) southeast of London. It's open April through September daily 10am to 5pm, closing at 4pm at all other times. Admission costs £18.50 for adults, £15 for seniors and students, and £11 for children 4 to 15. Your ticket is good for repeat visits throughout the year.

### SCHEDULING CONSIDERATIONS

In the summer and autumn, events at Leeds Castle are constant—knights joust one weekend, balloons take off around the lake the next. There are also plays, flower shows, firework displays, and concerts. Check the website for events when you'll be visiting—some involve an extra charge or advance booking.

### GETTING THERE

#### By Train

The closest train station is in the village of Bearsted, about 7 miles (11km) away. Southeastern trains run to Bearsted from London Victoria every 30 minutes or so, the trip takes just over 1 hour. Round-trip tickets start at £16. From March to October a private shuttle bus service meets trains for the trip from the station to the castle (£5 round-trip).

#### By Bus

There are no regular direct bus routes from London to Leeds Castle, but you can book a bus trip from various companies, which can include entrance fees as part of the package. **Premium Tours** (✆ **0207/713-1311;** www.premiumtours.co.uk) often include a private tour of the castle outside of normal open hours.

#### By Car

The trip from central London takes just under 1 hour, depending on traffic. Follow the M25 to the M20, and then take exit 8 and look out for signs to the castle entrance. Parking is free.

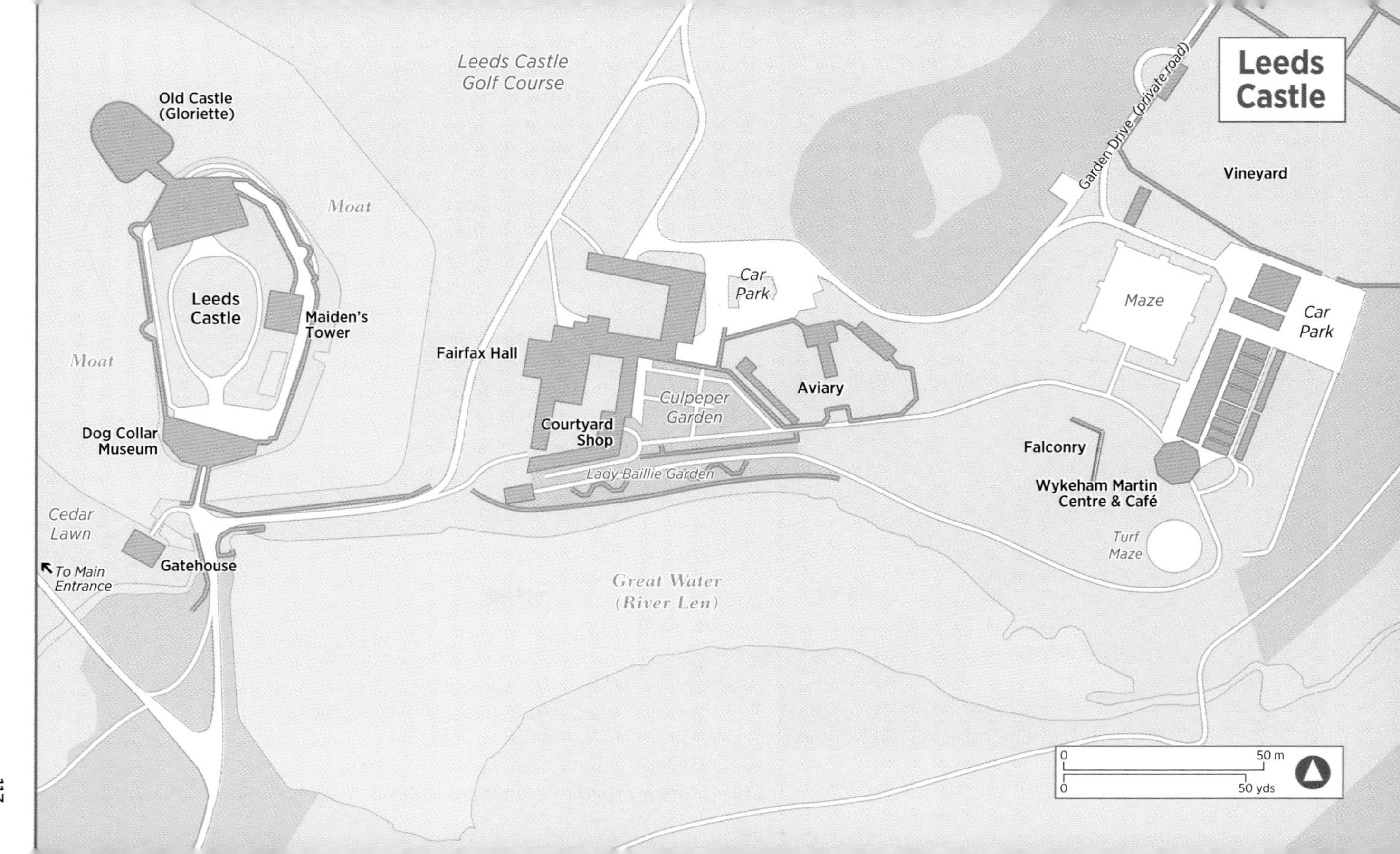
Leeds Castle
Leeds Castle Golf Course
Old Castle (Gloriette)
Moat
Leeds Castle
Maiden's Tower
Moat
Fairfax Hall
Dog Collar Museum
Cedar Lawn
Gatehouse
To Main Entrance
Car Park
Culpeper Garden
Courtyard Shop
Lady Baillie Garden
Aviary
Great Water (River Len)
Garden Drive (private road)
Vineyard
Maze
Car Park
Falconry
Wykeham Martin Centre & Café
Turf Maze
0
50 m
0
50 yds

Henry VIII's Banqueting Room.



### GETTING AROUND

A free, open-air bus travels from the main entrance to the castle (a distance of about a quarter-mile/400m) and other attractions on the grounds. Much more enjoyable, however, is to walk along the paved paths that curve around ponds and cross lawns and woods.

## A Day at Leeds Castle

To get a good overview of the extent and grandeur of Leeds, and to enjoy views of its moat, turrets, and towers, walk around the grounds before entering the castle. The rooms are intimate and appealing—**Henry VIII's Banqueting Room ★★**, one of many additions the king made to the castle, is handsome, but not overwhelming, and overlooks the grounds through a large bay window. One of the pleasures of exploring the castle is coming upon treasure after treasure: In the Banqueting Room, the prize is a spring scene by Pieter Bruegel the Younger; in the **Chapel ★★** are exquisite limewood carved panels and four paintings by the late-14th-century Florentine Niccolò di Pietro Gerini that depict the Passion of Christ—they are some of the earliest known works on canvas. Probably the most charming of the castle's many works of art is Giambattista Tiepolo's The Punchinello's Kitchen, which hangs above the mantle in the **Yellow Drawing Room ★** and provides an 18th-century view of the Venice Carnival.

After the castle tour, return to the grounds and take some time to relax in a nice spot—the benches overlooking the lake known as the **Great Water ★** are a good choice. The grounds are filled with touches that reflect the quirks of past owners including the odd **Dog Collar Museum,** with 400 hundred years of canine accessories, and the state-of-the-art **aviary**, built in the memory of bird

### Nearby

Seven miles (11km) away from the castle, the village of **Bearsted ★★** surrounds a large, beautifully maintained green, with the steep, conical roofs of oast houses (used for drying hops) notable on the east side. The 13th-century **Holy Cross church** south of the square is worth a visit—with the three stone beasts on its parapet, it's an intimidating structure.

collector Lady Baillie, which houses parakeets, macaws, and other feathered species.

The lush **maze ★★** ☺, made of 2,400 yew trees, follows a simple puzzle path leading you to a grotto filled with mythical beasts crafted from shells and minerals.

While you're wandering the grounds, look out for the **Culpeper Garden ★**, a colorful and delightfully informal bower, and the **Lady Baillie Garden ★★**, where Mediterranean plantings cascade down lakeside terraces.

## OUTDOOR ACTIVITIES

If you like golf, you might want to try out the **9-hole course** (open daily, greens fees £10 per person). Kids can amuse themselves in the **Knights Realm** ☺—a free playground set up to look like a child-sized castle. Teens might prefer to climb the trees at **Go Ape** ☺ (www.goape.co.uk), a tree-top climbing course with zip lines that takes you 65 feet (21m) above the ground. There are **falconry courses** (£70 per person) and **hot air balloon flights** (£90 per person) and more. Call or check the website to book your place.

The brightly colored grotto.

The yew tree maze.

## Where to Eat

The **Fairfax Hall Restaurant** ★ in an oak-beamed 17th-century house on the castle grounds sells homemade meals and cakes, with amazing views of the castle. Over the summer months, the **Maze Market Grill** sells sandwiches and ice cream. Both eateries are open the same hours as the castle. In the nearby village of Bearsted (see below), the historic **White Horse** pub (✆ **01622/738-365;** www.thewhitehorsebearsted.co.uk) is a cozy alternative to eating at the castle, especially in winter when you can warm up next to the fire and tuck into pasta and pizza (£6.25–£10.75) and British classics such as ribeye steak with chips (£16.95).

## Where to Shop

The main gift shop at the castle stocks a wide range of gifts and souvenirs, from jewelry and foodstuffs to children's books and games.

# WINDSOR & ETON

Located in Windsor, Berkshire, 20 miles (32km) from the center of London, Windsor Castle is the second-most-visited historic building in England (just behind the Tower of London) and one of the queen's official residences. The home of royalty since Henry I moved in 900 years ago, the imposing building is the largest inhabited castle in the world and the oldest in continuous use. Unsurprisingly, it dominates the town's narrow streets, lined with chocolate-box storefronts and twee teashops. Given that Eton College, an exclusive boys' boarding school, sits just across the river, the whole place has an entirely appropriate air of aristocracy.

The castle is lavishly decorated and filled with exceptional paintings from the Royal Collection. The changing of the guard is much easier to see here than at Buckingham Palace—there's no peering through a fence, in Windsor the soldiers in their towering hats march right down the main street. Having tea in town after a bit of window-shopping is a great way to cap off your day.

Allow at least half a day to explore Windsor, but a full day would give you time to enjoy all that this town has to offer.

## Essentials

### VISITOR INFORMATION

The **Royal Windsor Information Centre** is at the Old Booking Hall, Windsor Royal Shopping Center on Thames Street in the center of town (✆ **01753/743-900;** www.windsor.gov.uk). It's open May through August, Monday to Friday 9:30am to 5:30pm, Saturday 9:30am to 5pm and Sunday 10am to 4pm; and September through April, Monday to Saturday 10am to 5pm and Sunday 10am to 4pm.

### SCHEDULING CONSIDERATIONS

**Windsor Castle** is open year-round, but often closes for official engagements—and so check before you travel. To watch the 11am **Changing of the Guard** (daily in summer, alternate days Aug–Mar), be on High Street or in the castle by 10:50am. **Eton College** is open to visitors from late March to early October, with daily guided tours at 2pm and 3:15pm in school holidays, restricted to

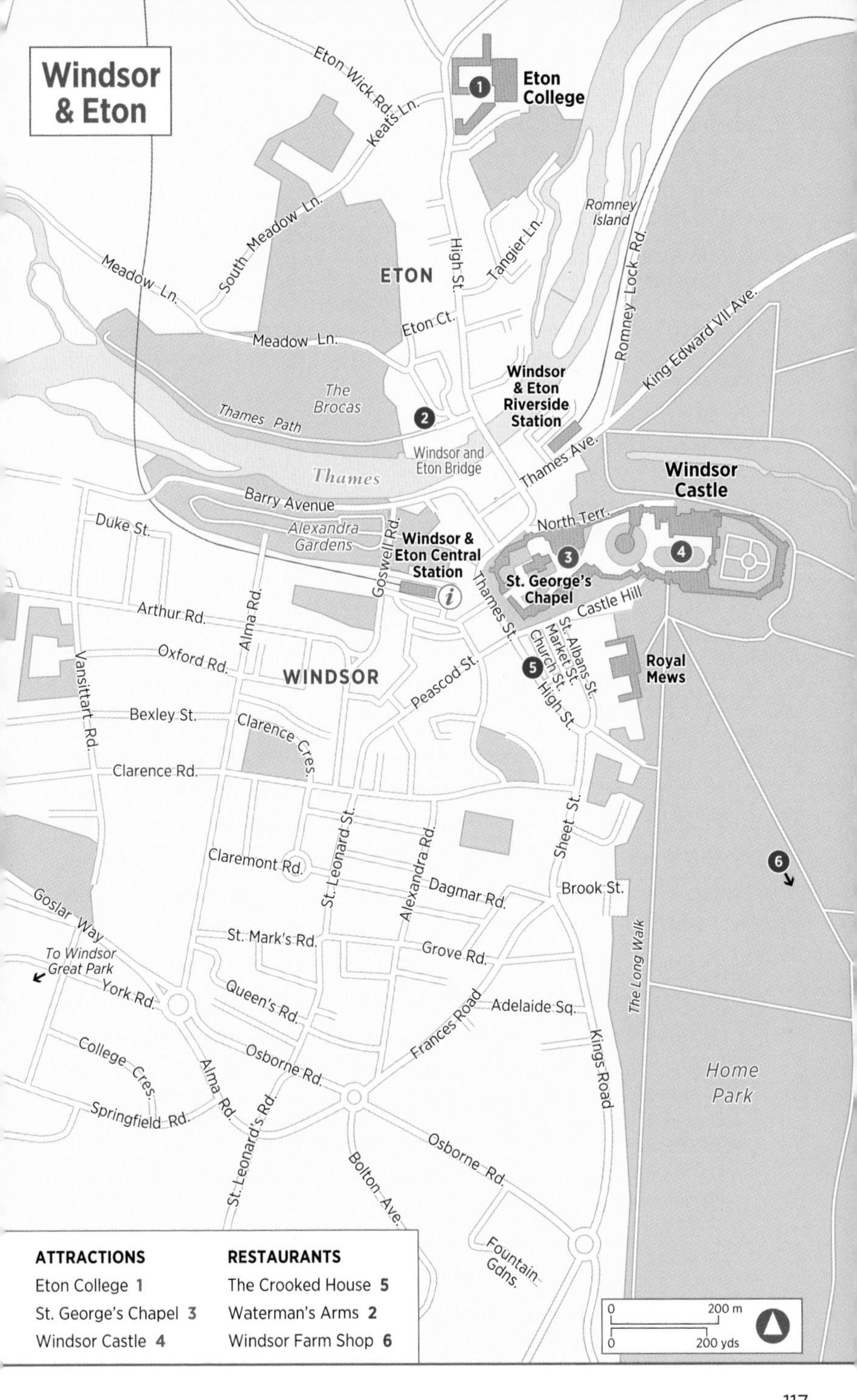

Windsor & Eton
Eton College
ETON
WINDSOR
Windsor & Eton Riverside Station
Windsor Castle
Windsor & Eton Central Station
St. George's Chapel
Royal Mews
Romney Island
The Brocas
Thames
Alexandra Gardens
Windsor and Eton Bridge
Home Park
The Long Walk
To Windsor Great Park
Eton Wick Rd.
Keats Ln.
South Meadow Ln.
Meadow Ln.
High St.
Tangier Ln.
Eton Ct.
Romney Lock Rd.
King Edward VII Ave.
Thames Path
Thames Ave.
Barry Avenue
North Terr.
Duke St.
Goswell Rd.
Thames St.
Castle Hill
Arthur Rd.
Alma Rd.
Oxford Rd.
Peascod St.
St. Albans St.
Market St.
Church St.
Vansittart Rd.
Bexley St.
Clarence Cres.
Clarence Rd.
Sheet St.
St. Leonard St.
Alexandra Rd.
Claremont Rd.
Dagmar Rd.
Brook St.
Goslar Way
St. Mark's Rd.
Grove Rd.
York Rd.
Queen's Rd.
Adelaide Sq.
Frances Road
Kings Road
College Cres.
Osborne Rd.
Springfield Rd.
St. Leonard's Rd.
Bolton Ave.
Fountain Gdns.
0 200 m
0 200 yds
ATTRACTIONS
Eton College 1
St. George's Chapel 3
Windsor Castle 4
RESTAURANTS
The Crooked House 5
Waterman's Arms 2
Windsor Farm Shop 6

Wednesday, Friday, and weekends during term time. The charge is £6.50 for adults and £5.50 for seniors and children under 14. The college is closed on various days and so it's always wise to phone ahead or check the website before you travel (✆ **01753/671-000;** www.etoncollege.com).

## GETTING THERE

### By Train

**First Great Western** trains run about every 20 minutes or so from London Paddington to Windsor and Eton Central (you have to change trains at Slough). The trip takes 30 minutes. Trains also run direct from London Waterloo to Windsor Riverside, but the journey takes 1 hour. Expect to pay about £9 for a round-trip fare.

### By Bus

**Green Line** (✆ **0871/200-2233;** www.greenline.co.uk) buses (nos. 701 and 702) depart from the colonnades outside London Victoria station to Windsor every 30 minutes. The journey takes about an hour. For a round-trip ticket, expect to pay around £8.

### By Car

If you're driving from London, take the M4 west and follow signs for Windsor—the drive should take about 45 minutes. Signs direct you to parking areas as you approach the town center. Follow the "Long Stay" signs for cheaper all-day parking.



## GETTING AROUND

Walking is the best way to see Windsor and the town of Eton. A hop-on/hop-off bus service makes a circuit of all the main sights in town (see "Organized Tours" below). Taxis are usually available outside both train stations. If you want to call one, try **Windsor Radio** (✆ **01753/677-677**) or **5 Star** (✆ **01753/858-888**).

# A Day in Windsor & Eton

Almost everybody visiting Windsor starts their tour at **Windsor Castle ★★★** (✆ **0207/766-7304;** www.royalcollection.org.uk), one of three official residences of Queen Elizabeth II. When the queen's in residence, the Royal Standard flies from the **Round Tower;** at all other times you'll see the Union Flag. The castle is visible and signposted from both train stations.

### Walking in Windsor

The splendid 180-mile (288-km) **Thames Path National Trail** begins at Thames Head near Kemble in the Cotswolds and runs all the way to the Thames Barrier, east of London. Around Windsor it has flat, paved paths along the river. The path follows the river for miles, and along the way there are great views of the castle. To find the path, cross the river at Windsor Bridge. Once on the Eton side, turn left on Brocas Street. The footpath starts at the end of the road.

Less ambitious walks can be had in **Windsor Park ★**, which has miles of paths through forests, around lakes, and past formal gardens. The tourist office has park maps.

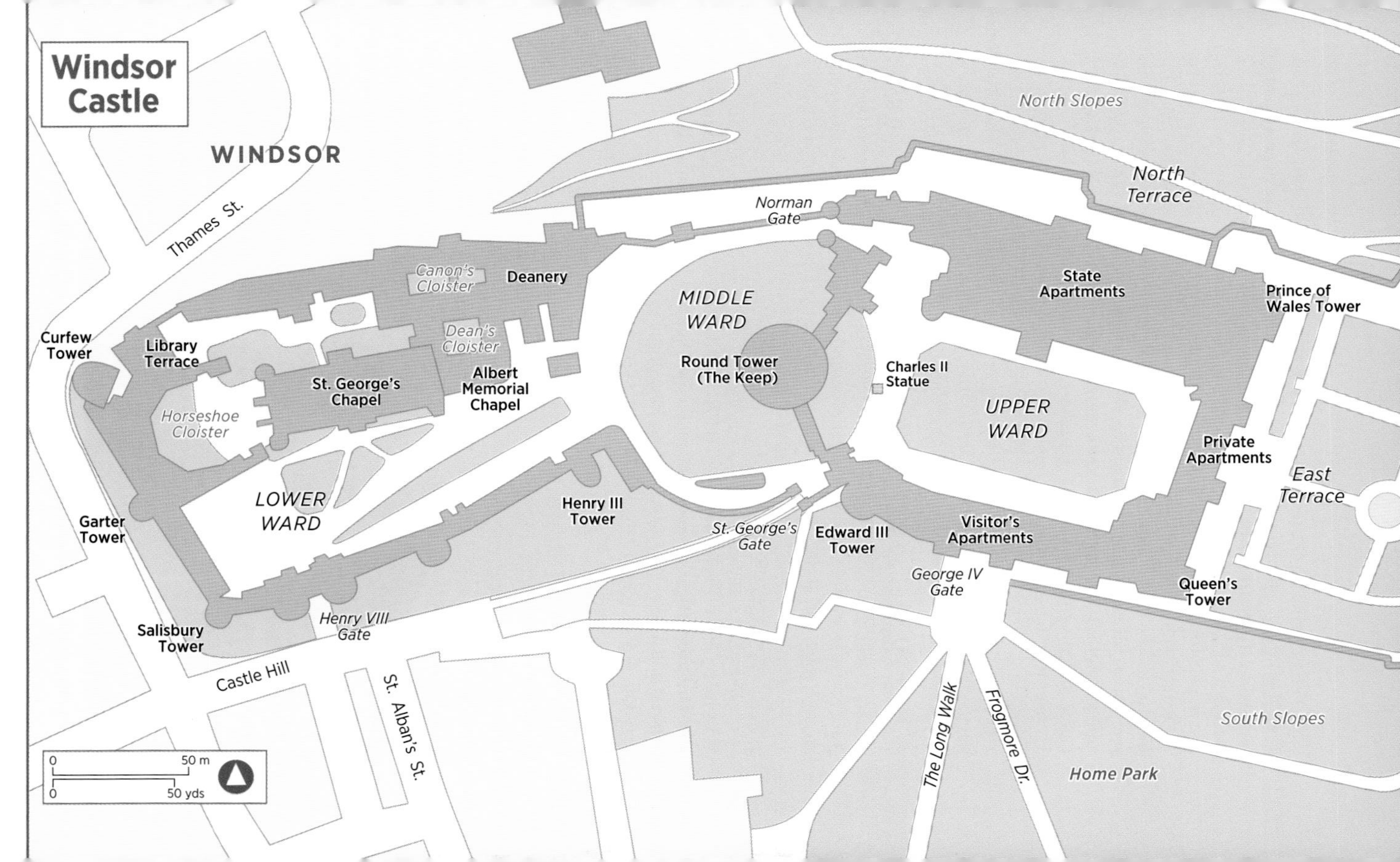

Windsor Castle
WINDSOR
Thames St.
North Slopes
North Terrace
Norman Gate
Canon's Cloister
Deanery
MIDDLE WARD
Round Tower (The Keep)
State Apartments
Prince of Wales Tower
Curfew Tower
Library Terrace
St. George's Chapel
Dean's Cloister
Albert Memorial Chapel
Charles II Statue
UPPER WARD
Horseshoe Cloister
Private Apartments
East Terrace
LOWER WARD
Henry III Tower
Garter Tower
St. George's Gate
Edward III Tower
Visitor's Apartments
George IV Gate
Queen's Tower
Salisbury Tower
Henry VIII Gate
Castle Hill
St. Alban's St.
The Long Walk
Frogmore Dr.
South Slopes
Home Park
0
50 m
0
50 yds

The magnificent **State Apartments ★★★** are furnished with classical art from the Royal Collection, including works by Rembrandt, Rubens, and Gainsborough. The **Semi-State Rooms ★★** (only open Oct–Mar) were created by George IV in the 1820s as a personal apartment, and they continue to be used by the queen for official entertaining. The **semi-staterooms** include the Green Drawing Room, Crimson Drawing Room, State Dining Room, and Octagon Dining Room. The queen uses its flamboyantly decorated dining and drawing rooms for parties. Elsewhere in the building, **St. George's Chapel** (www.stgeorges-windsor.org) is a fine gothic structure containing the tombs of 10 English sovereigns, including Henry VIII and Charles I. Look out for **Queen Mary's Dolls House ★★** ☺—an intricate miniature palace designed by the architect Sir Edwin Lutyens in 1924. It took nearly 1,500 artists and craftsmen 3 years to create its working lights, hot and cold running water, and flushing toilets. The castle opens daily at 9:45am and closes at 4:15pm, last entry is at 3pm. Admission is £16.50 for adults, £15 for seniors and students, and £10 for children aged 5 to 16.

The **Changing of the Guard ★★★** is an even bigger event at Windsor than at Buckingham Palace. The guards march up High Street to the castle, and the changeover happens on the castle grounds; if you want to see that part, arrange your visit to the castle so that you're there late morning. The ceremony takes place April through July Monday through Saturday at 11am. The rest of the year, it happens on alternate days.

On Park Street you'll see signs leading you to the 4,800 acre (1,920 hectare) **Windsor Great Park ★★★** (✆ **01753/743-900**). Once a favored hunting spot for Saxon kings, it's now a fine picnic spot surrounded by woodlands, formal gardens and a lake. Pick up a footpath map of the park from the tourist office.

Cross the river from Thames Street and you'll find yourself on Eton High Street, which inevitably leads to **Eton College ★** (✆ **01753/671-000;**

The round tower of Windsor Castle.

St George's Chapel Windsor.

www.etoncollege.com). Founded in 1440 by the 18-year-old King Henry VI, the famously exclusive boys school's alumni include 18 former British prime ministers, uncounted heirs to the throne (Prince William studied here), and leading literary figures such as George Orwell and Ian Fleming. It's open to visitors only when school's not in session, usually late March to early October. Visits are by guided tour only at 2pm and 3:15pm. It's sometimes closed for activities and so check the website before traveling. Admission is £6.50 for adults, £5.50 for seniors and children 8 to 13. Military personnel and their families can tour for free with a military ID.

## ORGANIZED TOURS

**City Sightseeing** (✆ **01708/865-656;** www.city-sightseeing.com) offers hop-on/hop-off guided bus tours through Windsor and Eton. Buses depart from outside the castle, across from Ye Harte and Garter Hotel, to the left of the statue of Queen Victoria. Tickets cost £8.50 for adults, £7.50 for seniors and students, and £4 for children.

**Orchard Poyle Carriage Hire** (✆ **01784/435-983;** www.orchardpoyle.co.uk) provides a fun and elegant way to tour Windsor in a horse-drawn carriage. You're taken along High Street, into Park Street, and then down the Long Walk into Windsor Great Park. Rides lasting 30 minutes cost £40 per carriage carrying 4 to 6 people. The carriage collects visitors from High Street, opposite the statue of Queen Victoria. In high season, it's wise to book in advance. Carriage rides aren't available in January or February, and possibly other months if the weather is unsuitable.

**French Brothers Ltd.** (✆ **01735/851-900;** www.boat-trips.co.uk) organizes boat rides down the Thames, daily from April to October. Find the boats off the promenade, next to the bridge to Eton. Rides are available all year, from mid-February through October daily 10am to 5pm and weekends during winter (until 4pm). Boat trips last 40 minutes or 2 hours with costs for the shorter tour at £5.40 for adults, £5.15 seniors, and £2.70 for children.

### Nearby

If you're traveling with children, you may want to combine your trip to Windsor Castle with a visit to nearby **Legoland** (✆ **08705/040-404;** www.legoland.co.uk), a popular amusement park themed around one of the nation's favorite toys. There are rides, shops, and games, and kids love it, but all that fun doesn't come cheap with tickets priced £38 for adults and £29 children aged 4 to 16. Legoland is on Winkfield Road at the edge of Windsor, and is well-signposted. Located 3 miles (4km) southeast of Windsor on the banks of the Thames, **Runnymede** is the famous meadow where King John sealed the Magna Carta in 1215 (after enormous pressure was put on him by his feudal barons and lords), establishing the principle of the constitutional monarchy and affirming the individual's right to justice and liberty. High on the hill is a memorial to the men and women of the Air Forces of the British Commonwealth who lost their lives in WWII. Runnymede is a peaceful place with magnificent views across the Thames Valley. By car it can be reached on the A308 from Windsor toward Staines.

## Where to Shop

Windsor's historic High Street has a diverse range of small family businesses, including clothing boutiques, jewelers, bookshops, art galleries, and gift shops. Eton's High Street is similar. Pop in to **Windsor Farm Shop,** Datchet St. (✆ **01753/623-800;** www.windsorfarmshop.co.uk), for fresh meat, cream, and ice cream, all from royal estates. There's even royal whisky from Balmoral Castle in Scotland.

## Where to Eat

The tea and coffee shop at **Windsor Farm Shop ★★** (see above) makes a fabulous cup of tea, as well as sandwiches and cakes, using ingredients sourced from the queen's farms. In Windsor, **The Crooked House ★** tearoom, 51 High St. (✆ **01753/857-534;** www.crooked-house.com), serves lovely scones, as well as light meals throughout the day. In Eton, the **Waterman's Arms ★**, Brocas St. (✆ **01753/861-001;** www.watermans-eton.com), dates to 1542, and serves local ales as well as the usual British pub standards of fish and chips, and steak and Guinness pie. A lunchtime sandwich will cost you around £3.50, hot dishes from £6.50 to £12.

6

# ROMAN BATHS & RIVER PUNTING

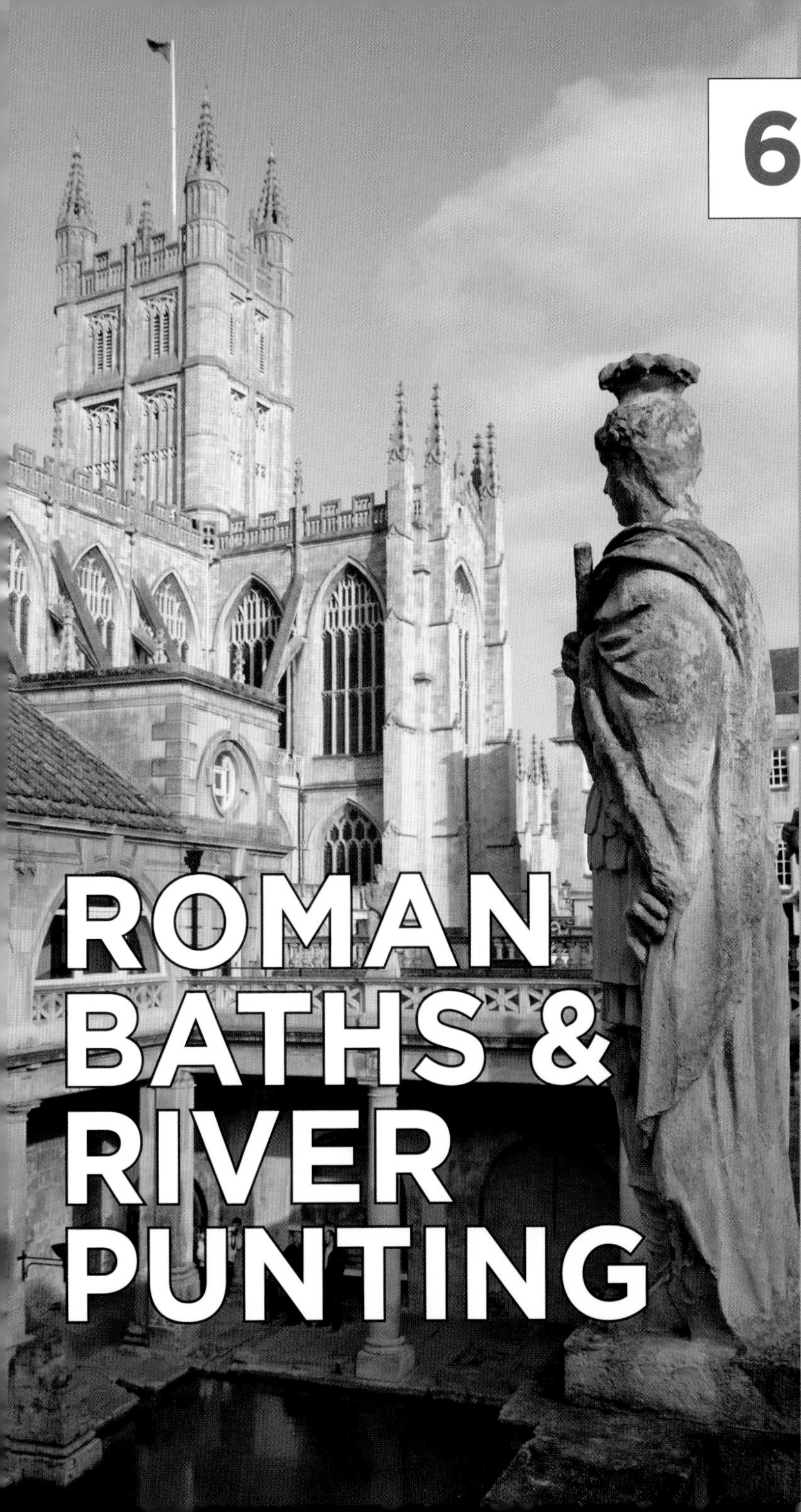

Cambridge and Oxford are not only filled with historic buildings and cobbled lanes, but also traversed by slow-moving rivers, perfect for boating alongside river meadows and absorbing the medieval architecture. Much can be credited to the universities in these cities and the great minds that have studied there, including scientists Darwin and Newton at Cambridge, and literary favorites C.S. Lewis and J.R.R. Tolkien at Oxford.

---

The spa towns of Bath and Tunbridge Wells were once the social epicenters of polite society, who came to drink and bathe in the therapeutic waters, particularly during the 18th and 19th centuries. Jane Austen lived in Bath for a period, taking much inspiration for her characters and stories from the many social gatherings. These days you can taste a cup of the mineral waters at the Pump Room, and take a tour of the adjoining Roman Baths museum which reveals how it all began. The wide lanes of the Pantiles in Tunbridge Wells are lined with book stores, art galleries and cafes to peruse, or you can take to the Kennet and Avon Canal towpath in Bath on foot or bicycle and go as far as you please.

# BATH

Graceful Georgian houses line pristine squares and arch alluringly in creamy crescents, while the extraordinary Roman baths, still burbling with sulfurous mineral water as it has for millennia, has been the main allure of the city of Bath for centuries. These days, millions of visitors come to this city of soft, mellow stone—designated by UNESCO as a World Heritage Site—not to take the waters (although that can be done) but simply to enjoy Bath's unique beauty. The ravishing architecture, including the Palladian mansions and historic pubs, has been virtually untouched by modern development, making this city a destination to visit any time of year.

In the leafy Avon Valley, Bath was first established by the Romans as a hot-spring spa in A.D. 43, although the springs in Bath were known and used by the Celts as long ago as 875 B.C. The curative waters were thought to alleviate health problems, and the city boomed in the 18th century, when England's high society flocked here to "take the waters." Among those who found themselves amid the city's swirling social milieu was Jane Austen, who lived here in the early 19th century. In the end, she didn't care for the place, but in the salons and ballrooms she found plenty of fodder for her novels of manners.

Bath is an ideal choice for a full-day trip from London—the train journey takes only 1½ hours, and there are plenty of sights to fill a day, as well as many places to enjoy a superb lunch or afternoon tea.

PREVIOUS PAGE: **The Roman Baths Museum.**

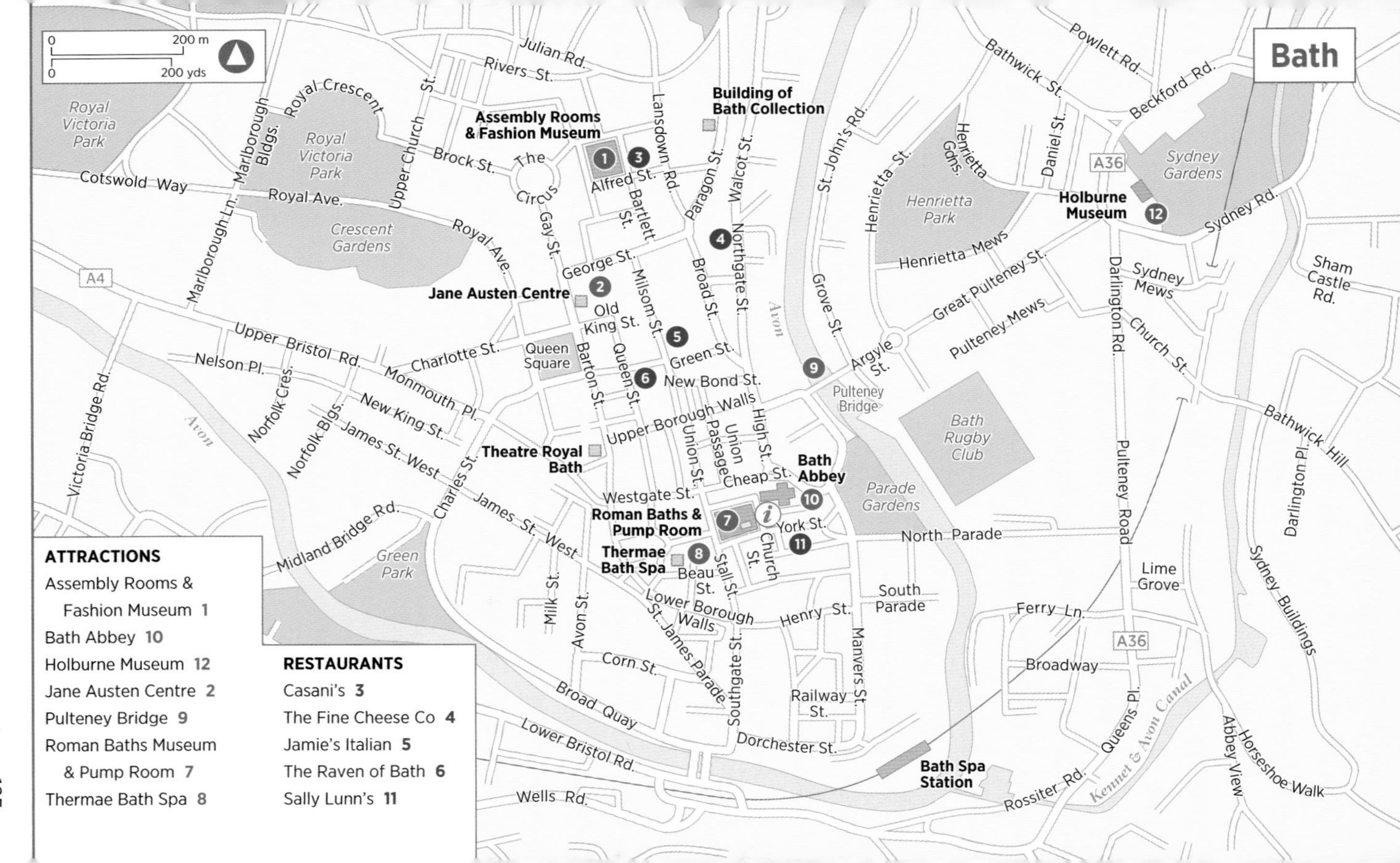

Bath
ATTRACTIONS
Assembly Rooms & Fashion Museum 1
Bath Abbey 10
Holburne Museum 12
Jane Austen Centre 2
Pulteney Bridge 9
Roman Baths Museum & Pump Room 7
Thermae Bath Spa 8
RESTAURANTS
Casani's 3
The Fine Cheese Co 4
Jamie's Italian 5
The Raven of Bath 6
Sally Lunn's 11
0 200 m
0 200 yds
Assembly Rooms & Fashion Museum
Building of Bath Collection
Jane Austen Centre
Theatre Royal Bath
Roman Baths & Pump Room
Thermae Bath Spa
Bath Abbey
Holburne Museum
Bath Spa Station
Royal Victoria Park
Crescent Gardens
Queen Square
Green Park
Henrietta Park
Sydney Gardens
Bath Rugby Club
Parade Gardens
Pulteney Bridge
Avon
Kennet & Avon Canal
Julian Rd.
Rivers St.
Royal Crescent
Marlborough Bldgs.
Upper Church St.
Brock St.
The Circus
Cotswold Way
Royal Ave.
Marlborough Ln.
Alfred St.
Bartlett St.
Lansdown Rd.
Paragon St.
Walcot St.
Gay St.
George St.
Old King St.
Milsom St.
Broad St.
Northgate St.
A4
Upper Bristol Rd.
Nelson Pl.
Charlotte St.
Monmouth Pl.
Barton St.
Queen St.
Green St.
New Bond St.
Norfolk Cres.
Norfolk Bldgs.
New King St.
James St. West
Upper Borough Walls
Union St.
Union Passage
High St.
Cheap St.
Victoria Bridge Rd.
Charles St.
Westgate St.
York St.
Church St.
Midland Bridge Rd.
Milk St.
Avon St.
Beau St.
Stall St.
Lower Borough Walls
St. James Parade
Henry St.
Corn St.
Southgate St.
Manvers St.
Railway St.
Broad Quay
Lower Bristol Rd.
Dorchester St.
Wells Rd.
St. John's Rd.
Grove St.
Argyle St.
Henrietta St.
Henrietta Gdns.
Henrietta Mews
Great Pulteney St.
Pulteney Mews
Daniel St.
Bathwick St.
Powlett Rd.
Beckford Rd.
A36
Sydney Rd.
Sydney Mews
Darlington Rd.
Church St.
Sham Castle Rd.
Bathwick Hill
Darlington Pl.
Pulteney Road
North Parade
South Parade
Lime Grove
Ferry Ln.
Broadway
Sydney Buildings
Queens Pl.
Rossiter Rd.
Abbey View
Horseshoe Walk

## Essentials

### VISITOR INFORMATION

The **Bath Tourist Information Centre** (✆ **0844/847-5257;** www.visitbath.co.uk) is in the city center, in Abbey Church Yard. It's open Monday to Saturday from 9:30am to 5pm (until 6pm in the summer) and Sunday from 10am to 4pm.

### SCHEDULING CONSIDERATIONS

You might want to plan your visit to Bath to coincide with one of the many events the city hosts throughout the year. These include the **Bath Music Festival** in late May and early June, the **Literary Festival** in March, and the **Mozartfest** in November. Find out about these and other events through the **Bath Festivals Office** (✆ **01225/463-362;** www.bathfestivals.org.uk).

### GETTING THERE

#### By Train

First Great Western trains run about every 30 minutes from London Paddington to Bath Spa station. The trip takes 1½ hours. Expect to pay about £50 round-trip. Bath's station is at the south edge of the city center, off Dorchester Street, a 5-minute walk from the center.

#### By Car

Bath is 115 miles (185km) west of London. If you're driving from London, head west on the M4 to junctions 17 (A350) or 18 (A46), and follow signs for Bath. Most of the city center is closed to traffic. Follow blue parking signs, or use one of the city's Park and Ride facilities (they're well-signposted).

#### By Bus

**National Express** buses leave London Victoria's bus station for Bath throughout the day. The journey takes just over 3 hours. Expect to pay from £12 round-trip. Bath bus station is across from the train station.

### GETTING AROUND

Bath center is relatively small and easy to get around, but it's also hilly. The easiest way to get from the south side of the city center (where Bath Abbey and the Roman Baths are located) to the north side (for the Assembly Rooms, Circus, and Royal Crescent) is to follow High Street north as it becomes Broad Street and Lansdown Road, and then turn left onto Bennett Street. City buses run from the train station, but most sights are within walking distance. If you need a taxi, they can usually be found at the train station, or you can call **AA Taxis** (✆ **01225/460-888**).

## A Day in Bath

A good place to start any exploration of Bath is in **Abbey Church Yard,** where the Bath Tourist Information Centre is located. You can pop in for maps and brochures and then walk a few steps to **Bath Abbey ★** (✆ **01225/422-462;** www.bathabbey.org). An ancient religious site, there has been an abbey here since the 8th century; this was where England's first king, Edgar, was crowned in A.D. 973. The Normans tore down the original and built their own massive cathedral here, but it was in ruins by 1499, when a new church was begun. That edifice succumbed to Henry VIII's dissolution of the monasteries in the mid-16th century,

The fan-vaulted ceiling of Bath Abbey.

but Elizabeth I ordered it restored and the abbey was promptly rebuilt in the Gothic Perpendicular style, with a graceful fan-vaulted ceiling and large expanses of stained glass that fill the church with light; it's little wonder the cathedral is nicknamed the "Lantern of the West." Climb the tower for spectacular views of the city. The abbey is open Monday to Saturday from 9am to 6pm (to 4:30pm in winter); Sundays 1 to 2:30pm and 4:30 to 5:30pm. A donation of £2.50 is requested. Tower tickets are £6.

Just across from the abbey stands the most famous structure in Bath, the **Roman Baths Museum & Pump Room** ★★★ (✆ **01225/477-785;** www.romanbaths.co.uk). The hot mineral springs here were known and used by the Celts as long ago as 875 B.C. In A.D. 75, the Romans channeled the waters into a luxurious bathing complex that rivals any of the baths in Rome or elsewhere in Italy. A terrace now overlooks the large pool where legionnaires once soaked in waters that bubble to the surface at 116°F (47°C). In a maze of subterranean chambers, which you navigate with the aid of an excellent self-guided audio commentary, are the remains of steaming pools and saunas, surrounded by elaborate paving. Allow yourself at least 1 hour to see everything. The baths are open daily, but hours vary seasonally: January to February and November to December 9:30am to 5:30pm; March to June and September to October 9am to 6pm; July and August 9am to 10pm; last entry is always 1 hour before closing. Admission is £12 for adults, £10.50 for seniors and students, and £7.80 for children 6 to 16. You can sample the famous waters in the adjacent 18th-century Pump Room (free with your admission ticket).

You can't swim in the Roman baths, but you can soak in the same mineral-laden thermal waters at **Thermae Bath Spa,** Hot Bath St. (✆ **0844/808-0844;** www.thermaebathspa.com) just a step away. Its open-air rooftop pool

has views over the city. A 2-hour soak costs from £25 and it's advisable to book in advance.

Nearby, just past Queen Square is the **Jane Austen Centre ★** (✆ **01225/443-000;** www.janeausten.co.uk), an earnest but informative collection of text-heavy displays that honor the ever-popular novelist of late 18th- and early 19th-century manners. Jane lived here from 1801 to 1806, and the city figures prominently in Persuasion and Northanger Abbey. The center is open daily 9:45am to 5:30pm in the summer (until 7pm Thurs–Sat July and Aug only); Sunday to Friday 11am to 4:30pm and Sat 9:45am to 5:30pm in the winter. Admission is £6.95 for adults, £5.50 for seniors and students, and £3.95 for children 6 to 15.

TOP: **The Roman Baths Museum;** RIGHT: **Elegant Georgian townhouses form the Royal Crescent.**

Heading north on Gay Street takes you to the elegant **Circus ★**, where three semicircular terraces of Regency town houses surround a circular park. The Circus was designed by John Wood the Elder (1704–54) in neoclassical style; note the symmetry and classical columns reminiscent of Imperial Rome. Follow Brock Street west from the Circus to Royal Victoria Park and the **Royal Crescent ★★★**, designed by Wood's son, John Wood the Younger in 1774. The exclusive residential semicircle of elegant town houses is a distinctive example of Georgian symmetry and proportion.

**Number 1, Royal Crescent ★★★** (✆ **01225/428-126;** www.bath-preservation-trust.org.uk/museums/no1) is a period museum situated within a house whose tenants included, in 1776, the Duke of York, second son of George III. The Bath Preservation Trust has restored the house using only paint, wallpapers, fabrics, and other materials available in the 18th century, and furnished each of the three floors with a superlative collection of period antiques. It's open Tuesday to Sunday 10:30am to 5pm (until 4pm Nov–Dec); last entry 30 minutes before close. Admission is £6.50 for adults, £5 for seniors and students, and £2.50 for children 6 to 18.

Just east of the Circus on Bennett Street are the **Assembly Rooms & Fashion Museum** (✆ **01225/477-789;** www.fashionmuseum.co.uk). The grand Assembly Rooms, built in 1771, evoke a lifestyle in which balls, card-playing, and gossip ranked high among life's priorities. If the Assembly Rooms aren't being used for a private function, you can stroll through the four elegant rooms that were the center of 18th-century Bath's social life. The rooms have been gloriously restored and look much as they did when Jane Austen and Thomas Gainsborough attended events here. In the same building, the Fashion Museum is one of the world's leading collections of clothing throughout the ages (about 2,000 pieces are on display at any one time), with outfits dating from the 16th century to the present day. Highlights include a gorgeous 17th-century "silver tissue" dress, and a whalebone corset. It's open March to October 10:30am to 5pm, and closes at 4pm January to February and November to December. Admission to the Assembly Rooms is £2, free to children under 17; the fashion museum costs £7.25 for adults, £6.50 for seniors and students, and £5.25 for children 6 to 18.

Historic gowns and bags on display at the Fashion Museum.

Back down at the river, the bridge at the end of the Grand Parade is the **Pulteney Bridge ★★**, an 18th-century span modeled on the Ponte Vecchio in Florence—like its Italian counterpart, the bridge is lined with touristy shops. On the far bank, Pulteney Road and Great Pulteney Street both lead to the **Holburne Museum,** Great Pulteney St. (✆ **01225/466-669;** www.holburne.org), which has a magnificent collection of antique silver and glass, as well as paintings by Turner, Gainsborough, and other masters. Once a private collection, it's now open to the public Monday to Saturday 10am to 6pm and Sunday 11am to 5pm. Admission is free.

## ORGANIZED TOURS

Among the many walking tours of Bath (the Tourist Information Centre has a complete list), you get the best overview on the free, 2-hour **Mayor of Bath's Honorary Civic Walking Tour ★★**, which stops at the Pump Room, Pulteney Bridge, Royal Crescent, and other architectural gems. The tour departs from the Pump Room at 10:30am and 2pm (10:30 only on Saturdays) daily from May through September.

**City Sightseeing** (www.city-sightseeing.com) offers a 1-hour double-decker bus tour with audio commentary (£12 for adults, £10 for seniors and students, £6.50 for children). Tickets are valid all day, and you can get off and on to explore places along the route.

## OUTDOOR ACTIVITIES

Skiffs, punts, and canoes are available for rental from the **Victorian Bath Boating Station** beneath the Pulteney Bridge (May–Sept daily 10am–6pm; ✆ **01225/466-407**). The nearby **Kennet and Avon Canal towpath** is one of many local places ideal for hiking, cycling, and boating. The **Bath and Dundas Canal Company** (✆ **01225/722-292;** www.bathcanal.com), at the canal information office, rents bikes as well as canoes and other boats for a leisurely outing in the green pastoral countryside; if you've been feeling city-bound in London, this is a good way to get out into the fresh air. It is located 5 miles (8km) south of Bath on the A36 near Monkton Combe. Take bus no. 264 or 265 from the train station for a 30 minute ride to the Old Viaduct Inn (the canal information center can be seen from the stop).

### Nearby

Just 8 miles (13km) from Bath, the charming historic town of **Bradford on Avon** (p. 17) makes for a peaceful countryside trip, and 12 miles (19km) east of Bath off the A350, the tiny village of **Lacock** is wonderfully preserved.

Nineteen miles (30km) south of Bath, the magnificent Elizabethan stately home **Longleat House ★★** (✆ **01747/841-152;** www.longleat.co.uk) is an enormous place, with an impressive art collection, including a Titian, and a vast collection of antique furnishings. It's at the edge of a massive **Safari Park ★** stocked with rare creatures including white rhinos, Siberian tigers, and Canadian timber wolves. You can tour it by car or train or even by boat to see hippos and sea lions. A day ticket costs £26 for adults and £18.50 children; tickets are cheaper if you just want to visit the house and gardens and not the safari park. You can get a map to Longleat from the Bath Tourist Information Centre (p. 126).

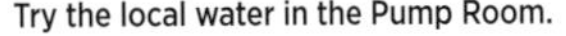

Try the local water in the Pump Room.

Jamie's Italian.

## Shopping

Bath has markets, antiques centers, specialist food stores, and boutiques in abundance. **Milsom Street** is the area to head for fashion, or you can wander the boutiques along the **Corridor** and **North and South Passages** and the independent-minded shops in **Walcot Street.**

Those in search of collectables should head to the **Green Park Arts & Craft Market** ★ in the historic Green Park train station, north of the center off Charles Street. The market's open from 9am to 5pm Tuesday through Sunday with everything from antiques to homemade crafts and farm produce for sale. Venders at the **Bartlett Street Antique Centre,** near the Assembly Rooms (Mon–Sat 9am–5pm), sell jewelry, silver, prints, and other easily portable items. At the **Bath Saturday Antiques Market,** in the Old Cattle Market on Walcot St., you can buy goods of an unusually high quality (Sat 6:30am–2:30pm).

## Where to Eat

Bath is the ideal place to indulge in that quintessentially English tradition of afternoon tea, served with jam, clotted cream, and scones. The **Pump Room** ★ at the Roman Baths (p. 127) serves tea with scones and "Bath buns" (sweet buns sprinkled with sugar). Another option is **Sally Lunn's** ★. The oldest house in Bath (built around 1483), it specializes in another Bath specialty—Sally Lunn sweet buns, similar to brioche and served with jam and cream.

A pub serving real ale and a decent selection of wines, **The Raven of Bath,** 6–7 Queen St. (✆ **01225/425-045;** www.theravenofbath.co.uk), is equally well-known for its tasty meat pies (£8.80 with mashed potato or chips). **Jamie's Italian,** 10 Milsom Place (✆ **01225/432-340;** www.jamiesitalian.com), is a popular dining spot, making excellent use of regional, fresh ingredients in the Italy-inspired fare (mains £10.95–£16.95). The authentic French menu at

**Casani's,** 4 Saville Row (✆ **01225/780-055;** www.casanis.co.uk; reservations required), features simple Provence-inspired dishes and a set lunch at £14.75 for two courses. The artisan cheesemonger **The Fine Cheese Co ★**, 29 and 31 Walcot St. (✆ **01225/483-407;** www.finecheese.co.uk), sells a selection of sandwiches that are perfect for an eat-on-the-go lunch.

# CAMBRIDGE

Cambridge, like Oxford (p. 139), is forever linked with the venerable university that has flourished here on the banks of the River Cam for eight centuries. Before the great university took root, Cambridge was known to the Romans as a place to cross the Cam, and housed several monastic settlements in the Middle Ages. Obviously, the chance to step into a few of the 31 colleges and view their architectural wonders is what brings many visitors to Cambridge, but you're in for a pleasant surprise—the town that rises from marshy lands (known as "fens") is itself a gem, an appealing blend of busy markets and shops, medieval architecture, and grassy riverside meadows and parklands. No wonder so many great minds—Sir Isaac Newton, John Milton, Charles Darwin, Virginia Woolf—were drawn to study here.

You'll want to spend a whole day in Cambridge, so get an early start. To appreciate the city fully, plan on seeing the colleges as well as the town itself, with a walk through the market and along King's Parade and other cobbled streets, with a stop in a pub; take time, too, to float down the Cam in a punt or walk along the grassy riverside parklands known as the "Backs."

## Essentials

### VISITOR INFORMATION

The **Cambridge Tourist Information Centre,** on Peas Hill by St. Edward King Church (✆ **0871/226-8006;** www.visitcambridge.org), is open year-round, Monday to Saturday 10am to 5pm (Apr–Nov also Sun 11am–3pm). If you're visiting colleges, look for signs directing visitors to either ticket offices or porters' offices. This is where you'll find that day's opening hours and admission prices.

### SCHEDULING CONSIDERATIONS

Many colleges close during exams (May–June) and are open for limited hours when school's in session from mid-January to mid-March, mid-April to mid-June, and mid-October to mid-December. The long-running **Cambridge Folk Festival** (www.cambridgefolkfestival.co.uk) on the last weekend of July is popular and sells out quickly. The **Cambridge Shakespeare Festival** (✆ **07955/218-824;** www.cambridgeshakespeare.com) in July and August has open-air Shakespeare performances in the grounds of several colleges.

### GETTING THERE

#### By Train

Trains from King's Cross take 45 minutes to 1 hour. Trains from London Liverpool St. take 1 hour 20 minutes. Expect to pay £30 for a round-trip ticket. The Cambridge train station is located south of town on Station Road. You can walk or take a bus (Citi 1, Citi 3, or Citi 7) or taxi from the train station to Market Square and the center of town, about 1 mile (1.6km) away.

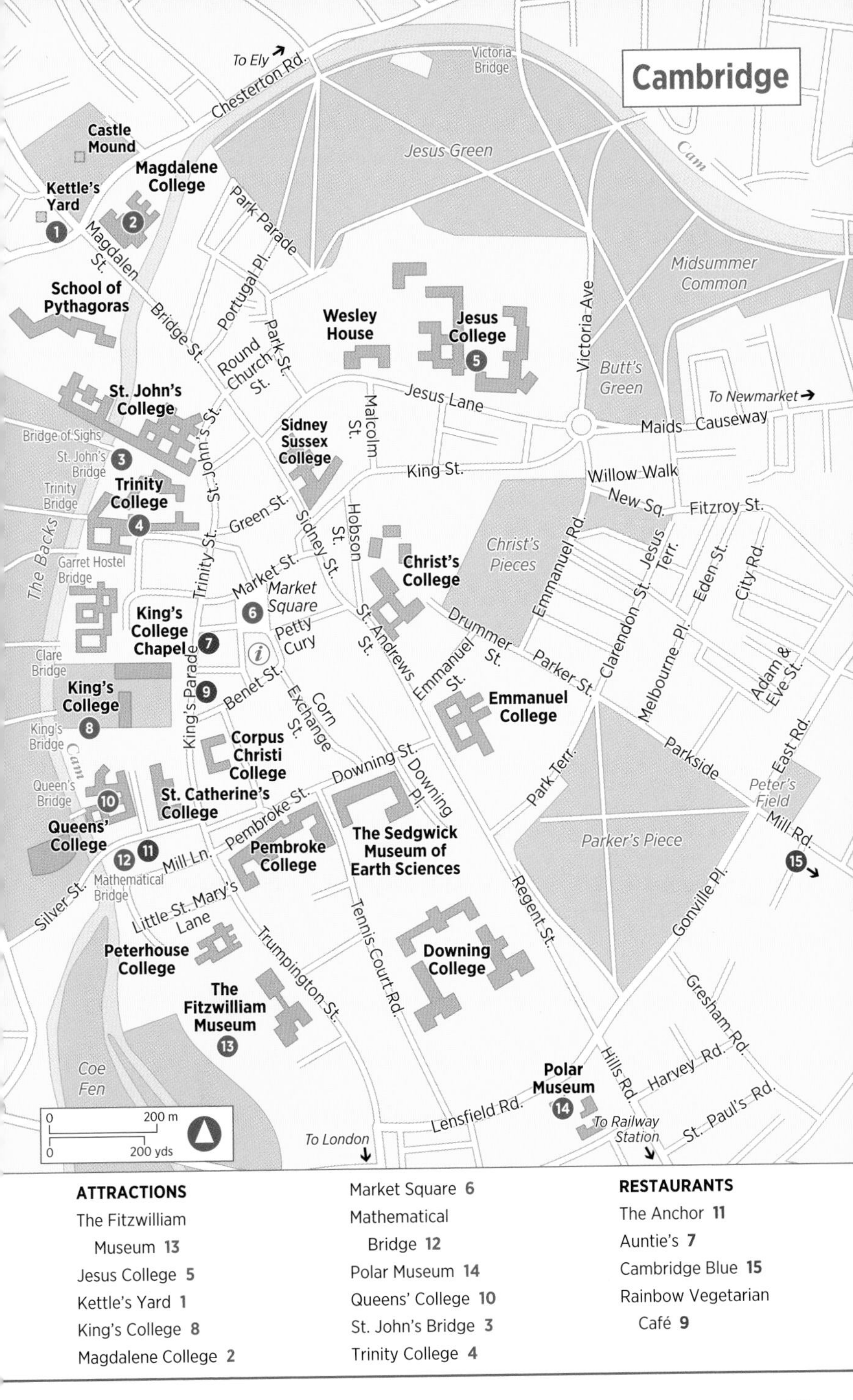
Cambridge
To Ely
Chesterton Rd.
Victoria Bridge
Jesus Green
Cam
Castle Mound
Magdalene College
Kettle's Yard
Park Parade
Magdalen St.
School of Pythagoras
Bridge St.
Portugal Pl.
Park St.
Round Church St.
Wesley House
Jesus College
Victoria Ave
Midsummer Common
Butt's Green
To Newmarket
Maids Causeway
Jesus Lane
Malcolm St.
St. John's College
Bridge of Sighs
St. John's Bridge
St. John's St.
Sidney Sussex College
King St.
Willow Walk
New Sq.
Fitzroy St.
Trinity Bridge
Trinity College
Green St.
Sidney St.
Hobson St.
Christ's Pieces
Emmanuel Rd.
Jesus Terr.
Eden St.
City Rd.
The Backs
Garret Hostel Bridge
Trinity St.
Market St.
Market Square
Christ's College
Clarendon St.
King's College Chapel
Petty Cury
Drummer St.
Melbourne Pl.
Adam & Eve St.
Clare Bridge
St. Andrews St.
Emmanuel St.
Parker St.
King's College
Benet St.
Emmanuel College
King's Bridge
King's Parade
Corn Exchange St.
Corpus Christi College
Parkside
East Rd.
Downing St.
Downing Pl.
Park Terr.
Peter's Field
Queen's Bridge
St. Catherine's College
Queens' College
Pembroke St.
The Sedgwick Museum of Earth Sciences
Mill Rd.
Parker's Piece
Mill Ln.
Pembroke College
Silver St.
Mathematical Bridge
Little St. Mary's Lane
Regent St.
Gonville Pl.
Peterhouse College
Trumpington St.
Tennis Court Rd.
Downing College
The Fitzwilliam Museum
Gresham Rd.
Coe Fen
Polar Museum
Hills Rd.
Harvey Rd.
Lensfield Rd.
To Railway Station
St. Paul's Rd.
To London
0 200 m
0 200 yds
ATTRACTIONS
The Fitzwilliam Museum 13
Jesus College 5
Kettle's Yard 1
King's College 8
Magdalene College 2
Market Square 6
Mathematical Bridge 12
Polar Museum 14
Queens' College 10
St. John's Bridge 3
Trinity College 4
RESTAURANTS
The Anchor 11
Auntie's 7
Cambridge Blue 15
Rainbow Vegetarian Café 9

### By Bus

**National Express** buses (✆ **08717/818-178;** www.nationalexpress.com) leave London's Victoria bus station for Cambridge every 30 minutes throughout the day. The journey takes around 3 hours and a round-trip fare costs £12. Cambridge bus station is on Drummer Street near the city center.

### By Car

Cambridge is about 60 miles (97km) north of London on the M11. The trip usually takes a little over 1 hour. Park in one of the public carparks around the town center; these include Lion Yard Car Park, Grafton Centre Car Park, Park Street Car Park, and Queen Anne Terrace Car Park. You'll pay about £12 for the day.

## GETTING AROUND

Cambridge is perfect for walking around, with two main streets. Trumpington Road—which becomes Trumpington Street, King's Parade, Trinity Street, and finally St. John's Street—runs parallel to the River Cam and provides easy access to several of the colleges. Bridge Street, the city's main shopping street, starts at Magdalene Bridge; it becomes Sidney Street, St. Andrew's Street, and finally Regent Street. A **Dayrider** bus pass, good all day and available from any bus driver, costs £3.50. Taxis are available at the train station; if you need one elsewhere in town, call **A1 Taxis** (✆ **01223/525-555**) or **Cabco** (✆ **01223/312-444**).

## A Day in Cambridge

A good place to start your exploration of the city is **Market Square ★**, a lively open-air market selling fresh produce, plants, and books, and surrounded by shops and restaurants. From there, follow King's Parade and take a right on Silver Street to **Queens' College ★★★** (✆ **01223/335-511;** entry £2.50). Founded by English queens Margaret of Anjou, the wife of Henry VI, and Elizabeth Woodville, the wife of Edward IV, the college dates from 1448 and is regarded by many as the most attractive of Cambridge's colleges. It includes the 16th-century handsome brick **President's Lodge** and the **Tower,** where the great scholar Erasmus lived from 1510 to 1514. The arched, wooden, self-supporting bridge connecting the college's two parts is called the **Mathematical Bridge** due to its design involving tangents, arcs, and triangles. You can get a good view of it from the less lovely Silver Street Bridge nearby.

Queens' College.

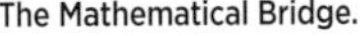

The Mathematical Bridge.

King's College Chapel.

A short walk down King's Parade is **King's College ★★** (**✆ 01223/331-100**), founded by Henry VI in 1441. The main attraction is its **chapel** which dates back to the Middle Ages and is one of Europe's finest Gothic buildings. It's a fairly transcendental place, with its magnificent fan vaulting, stained-glass windows, and behind the altar, Rubens's glorious Adoration of the Magi, painted in 1634. Carols are broadcast worldwide from the chapel every Christmas Eve and there are concerts and organ recitals throughout the year. Tickets for chapel events are sold at the Shop at King's, on King's Parade. Evensong is heavenly here (weekdays and Sat at 5:30pm, Sun at 10:30am and 3:30pm) but is held during

King's College.

school terms only. Admission to the college is £6.50 for adults, and £4.50 for seniors, students, and children aged 12 to 15.

King's Parade leads to Trinity Street, which is dominated by **Trinity College ★★★** (✆ **01223/338-400**), the largest of Cambridge's colleges. Founded by Henry VIII, this college has attracted the most famous students: Sir Isaac Newton first calculated the speed of sound here and Lord Byron used to bathe naked in the courtyard fountain with his pet bear. Pass through the enormous courtyard (called Grand Court) to the hall at the west end to see **Neville's Cloister** and the impressive **Wren Library ★★**, designed by the architect Sir Christopher Wren in 1695. Its manuscripts and books include medieval examples and early editions of Shakespeare's works.

From the library, head toward the Backs and follow the Cam up to **St. John's Bridge ★**, a replica of the Bridge of Sighs in Venice; the span joins the New Court of St. John's College, a 19th-century neo-Gothic fantasy of pinnacle and towers that students call the "Wedding Cake," with the older, authentically Tudor section of the college, founded by Lady Margaret Beaufort, the mother of Henry VII, in 1511; the poet William Wordsworth was an alumnus of St. John's.

St. John's Street leads to Magdalene (pronounced "maud-len") Street where you'll find **Magdalene College ★** (✆ **01223/332-100).** Here, you can visit the Pepys Library, which houses the diarist's collection of 3,000 volumes (open 2 hours a day; check with the porter), and **Jesus College** (✆ **01223/339-339**), founded in 1492 on the site of a convent. Its chapel has been enlivened with stained-glass windows designed by Edward Burne-Jones and a ceiling by William Morris; both were leaders in the Arts and Crafts Movement of the late 19th century. (You can admire the chapel during Evensong on Tues, Thurs, and Sat at 6:30pm.)

Nearby on Castle Street is **Kettle's Yard ★★** (✆ **01223/748-100;** www.kettlesyard.co.uk). Jim Ede was the curator at the Tate during the 1920s and 1930s, and he and his wife Helen acquired this collection of artworks, furniture, and decorative objects, which are displayed as he arranged them in his home. You'll find works by Ben Nicholson, Christopher Wood, and Alfred Wallis, and sculptures by Henry Moore, Henri Gaudier-Brzeska, Brancusi, and Barbara Hepworth. Around the corner is **Kettle's Yard Gallery,** with a respected collection of 20th-century contemporary art. It's open Tuesday to Sunday from 1:30 to 4:30pm (2–4pm in winter). Admission is free.

On Trumpington Street, **The Fitzwilliam Museum ★★** (✆ **01223/332-900;** www.fitzmuseum.cam.ac.uk) shows off a horde of Egyptian and Greek antiquities, Chinese jades and bronzes, pages from Books of Hours, and the first draft of Keats's "Ode to a Nightingale," as well as china, glass, majolica, silver,

### Picnic by the Cam

**If the weather's nice, go to Market Square for picnic food (see "Shopping," below), and then head to the Backs for an idyllic moment by the River Cam. Two of Cambridge's most famous landmarks—the Wren Library and King's Chapel—are especially impressive when viewed across the grassy expanse of the Backs.**

Punting on the River Cam in Autumn.



and clocks. Its treasure-trove of paintings ranges from medieval and Renaissance works to contemporary canvases and includes Titian's Tarquin and Lucretia, Rubens's The Death of Hippolytus, brilliant etchings by Van Dyck, rare Hogarths, and 25 Turners, as well as works by William Blake, the Impressionists, and the more recent artists Paul Nash and Sir Stanley Spencer. The museum is open Tuesday to Saturday 10am to 5pm and Sunday noon to 5pm; admission is free.

One of Cambridge's hidden gems of historical memorabilia is the **Polar Museum ★**, Lensfield Rd. (✆ **01223/336-540;** www.spri.cam.ac.uk), detailing the lives and work of adventurers such as Sir Robert Scott and Ernest Shackleton, who gave their lives trying to reach and explore the north and south poles. The gear, photos, and diaries of the doomed expedition are haunting and fascinating, and the information is so well-displayed you find yourself caught up in the excitement (open Tues–Sat 10am–4pm, with free admission).

## ORGANIZED TOURS

The **Cambridge Tourist Information Centre** offers interesting and thorough 2-hour walking tours of the city, from £8 to £14.50 for adults and up to £7 for children under 12. Times vary, and so stop in when you arrive to find out what's on.

**City Sightseeing** (www.city-sightseeing.com) offers an 80 minute open-top **bus tour** (£13 adults, £9 seniors and students, and £7 children aged 5–12). Buses depart daily from the train station starting at 9:45am and run every 15 to 20 minutes until 3 or 4pm, depending on the season.

## OUTDOOR ACTIVITIES

The smooth, wide expanse of the River Cam is perfect for boating, and the traditional method is "punting"—pushing a flat-bottom boat by means of a long pole. All you have to do is put the 16-ft (5-m) pole straight down into the shallow water until it finds the river bed, and then gently push and retrieve the pole in one deft, simple movement. It's simple once you get the hang of it, but watching

## Nearby

The **Imperial War Museum Duxford** (✆ **01223/835-000;** www.iwm.org.uk) is situated on the outskirts of Cambridge (exit 10 of the M11 motorway) and is well worth a visit. It houses the largest aviation museum in Europe and was a major air base during World War II. The museum is open in summer from 10am to 6pm and in winter 10am to 4pm. Admission is £16.50 adults, £13.20 students and seniors, and free for under-15s (there are also reduced rates of entry in Nov and Dec).

The cathedral city of **Ely** is 16 miles (26km) north of Cambridge. After a visit to the cathedral (image below) to see the views from the tower, pop into the **Ely Museum,** Market St. (✆ **01353/666-655;** www.elymuseum.org.uk), which is situated inside the old jail (or "gaol"). It's open daily in summer Monday, Wednesday to Saturday from 10:30am to 5pm and Sunday 1 to 4pm. Doors shut an hour earlier during winter and admission is £3.50 and free for up to four children under 16 with every paying adult. **Oliver Cromwell's House,** 29 St. Mary's St. (✆ **01353/662-062;** www.ely.org.uk), now the town's tourist information office, houses a museum dedicated to the controversial puritan who famously banned Christmas and suppressed Catholicism in the 17th century (open in summer daily 10am–5pm, winter Mon–Fri and Sun 11am–4pm, Sat 10am–5pm). Admission is £4.50 for adults and £3.10 for under-6s.

You might also want to stop by **Saffron Walden,** 14 miles (22km) northeast of Cambridge. It's a beautifully preserved medieval market town with aged, half-timbered buildings, many of them filled with antiques shops and galleries. There's also a ruined motte-and-bailey castle and an ancient turf maze.

inexperienced punters plunge head-first into the river is a popular form of local entertainment. On a sunny afternoon the river takes on a carnival atmosphere. But don't be afraid. Rent a boat from **Scudamore's Punting Company** at its

Magdalene Bridge or Mill Lane stations (✆ **01223/359750;** www.scudamores.com) and try it for yourself. Punts cost £18 per hour (maximum of six people per boat).

## Shopping

In Market Square, from Monday to Saturday, there's a **General Market ★** with fruit and vegetables, clothes, books, and jewelry, and on Sundays the **Arts and Crafts and Local Produce Market** takes over, selling homemade goods such as cakes, fresh bread, and organic food. On Saturdays, **All Saints Garden Art and Craft Market** off Trinity Street is also good for gifts and mementoes.

There are gift shops galore in **King's Parade ★★**, which runs into **Trinity Street** and then **St. John's Street.** There's been a bookshop since 1581 on the present site of the **Cambridge University Press book shop,** 1–2 Trinity St. (✆ **01223/333-333;** www.cambridge.org), although the bookshop **Heffers,** 20 Trinity St. (✆ **01223/568-568;** www.heffers.co.uk), is also a Cambridge institution. **Rose Crescent,** near the market, is pretty with smart clothes and cosmetics shops while the **Bene't St. Area,** or Arts Quarter, off King's Parade has fashion, ceramics, and jewelry shops.

## Where to Eat

A long-established pioneer of vegetarian eating, **Rainbow Vegetarian Café,** 9a King's Parade, across from King's College (✆ **01223/321551;** www.rainbowcafe.co.uk), offers vegan and gluten-free food and organic wine and cider. Spinach lasagna is the Rainbow's signature dish with most mains priced £7.95 to £9.95. There's also a children's menu and free organic jars of baby food.

The **Cambridge Blue,** 85–87 Gwydir St. (✆ **01223/471-680;** www.thecambridgeblue.co.uk) serves savory pies, hamburgers, and sandwiches (£7–£11), and has a sunny beer garden. Another pub option is **The Anchor,** Silver St. (✆ **01223/353-554**), which overlooks the river across from Queen's College. Expect hearty traditional pub food including lamb pies and fish and chips, as well as real ale. For afternoon tea and sandwiches, pop into **Auntie's ★**, 1 St. Mary's Passage off Market Square (✆ **01223/315-641**).

# OXFORD

This "sweet city with her dreaming spires" (to quote the poet Matthew Arnold) is best known as the seat of one of the world's most respected centers of learning. Many of its streets have barely changed since Oscar Wilde walked them as a student here, and the lovely green water meadows and sturdy school walls that inspired students including John Donne, C. S. Lewis, and J. R. R. Tolkien have endured through the centuries.

As you explore Oxford, you'll notice that town and gown converge on lively commercial streets. This city is not all about brainpower (though there's quite a bit of it in evidence): For every architectural masterpiece by Sir Christopher Wren and medieval cobbled lane, there's a snug pub or a lovely riverside walk to enjoy.

Most first-time visitors to Oxford have trouble working out exactly where Oxford University is located. This is because Oxford University is in fact made up of 39 autonomous colleges sprinkled throughout the center of town; there's no central campus. Students apply to and attend an individual college, and mixing between colleges is rare. Touring every college would be a formidable task, and so it's best to focus on just a handful.

You'll want to spend a full day in order to see all Oxford has to offer.

## Essentials

### VISITOR INFORMATION

The **Oxford Information Centre,** 15–16 Broad St. (✆ **01865/252-200;** www.visitoxford.org) can tell you when colleges are open, and point you in the right direction. It has a comprehensive range of maps, brochures, and souvenirs and is open Monday to Saturday 9:30am to 5pm (5:30pm in summer), Sunday and national holidays 10am to 4pm.

### SCHEDULING CONSIDERATIONS

Most colleges are open daily from 2 to 5pm, but it's wise to check with the university website or the Oxford Information Centre for hours and admission policies, because colleges are often closed during exams and at other times.

### GETTING THERE

#### By Train

First Great Western trains run from London Paddington to Oxford every 30 minutes. The journey takes around 1 hour with round-trip tickets starting from £27.

#### By Car

Oxford is 60 miles (97km) west of London. The quickest route from London is the M40, a trip that usually takes a little over an hour. Parking in the town center is incredibly expensive—many carparks charge £30 a day. The best places to park are the well-marked Park and Ride locations on the ring road at the main approaches to the city. Most are open daily until 11 or 11:30pm. You pay a £2.20 round-trip bus fare into the city center. Ask the driver to let you know when the bus reaches the Cornmarket stop—it makes a good place to start exploring the city.

#### By Bus

The **Oxford Tube** (✆ **01865/772-250;** www.oxfordtube.com) bus service leaves from Grosvenor Gardens—a block from London Victoria—for Oxford every 12 minutes during the day, and every 20 to 30 minutes at night. The journey takes 1½ hours and a round-trip ticket costs £16. **National Express** buses (✆ **08717/818-178;** www.nationalexpress.com) also leave from London's Victoria bus station for Oxford about every 30 minutes. The trip takes about 1 hour 20 minutes and round-trip tickets start at £19.

### GETTING AROUND

You can probably get anywhere you want to go in Oxford on foot. The train station is about a 10 minute walk west of the city center, off Park End Street, and the bus station is on the northwest side of the city center, off George Street on Gloucester Green. The two main shopping and business streets are Cornmarket Street, running north to south through the center, and High Street, running east to west through the center. There's a taxi rank outside the train station; if you want to reserve a taxi, call **001 Taxis** (✆ **01865/240-000**) or **City Taxis** (✆ **01865/794-000**).

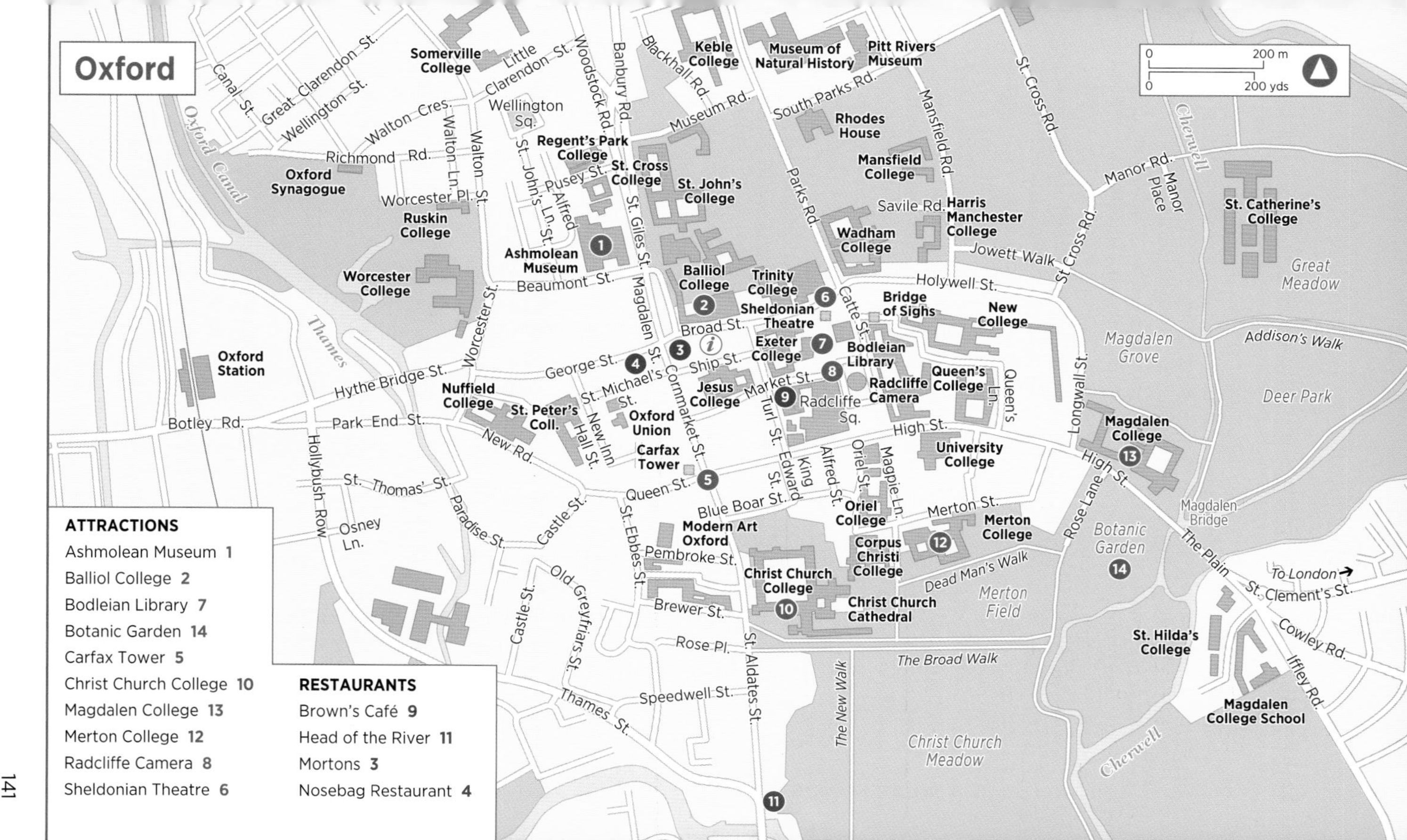
Oxford
0 200 m
0 200 yds
ATTRACTIONS
Ashmolean Museum 1
Balliol College 2
Bodleian Library 7
Botanic Garden 14
Carfax Tower 5
Christ Church College 10
Magdalen College 13
Merton College 12
Radcliffe Camera 8
Sheldonian Theatre 6
RESTAURANTS
Brown's Café 9
Head of the River 11
Mortons 3
Nosebag Restaurant 4
Somerville College
Keble College
Museum of Natural History
Pitt Rivers Museum
Rhodes House
Mansfield College
St. Catherine's College
Regent's Park College
St. Cross College
St. John's College
Oxford Synagogue
Ruskin College
Ashmolean Museum
Harris Manchester College
Wadham College
Worcester College
Balliol College
Trinity College
Sheldonian Theatre
Bridge of Sighs
New College
Exeter College
Bodleian Library
Oxford Station
Jesus College
Radcliffe Camera
Queen's College
Nuffield College
St. Peter's Coll.
Oxford Union
Carfax Tower
Magdalen College
University College
Modern Art Oxford
Oriel College
Merton College
Corpus Christi College
Christ Church College
Christ Church Cathedral
St. Hilda's College
Magdalen College School
Great Meadow
Magdalen Grove
Deer Park
Botanic Garden
Merton Field
Christ Church Meadow
Cherwell
Thames
Oxford Canal
To London

## A Day in Oxford

St. Aldate's Street leads you straight to grand **Christ Church College ★★** (✆ **01865/276-150;** www.chch.ox.ac.uk), and you can hardly miss its main entrance, topped by Christopher Wren's Tom Tower with its 18,000-pound (8160-kilogram) bell. Cardinal Wolsey, King Henry VIII's powerful associate, founded the college in 1525 and graced it with the largest quad in Oxford. Christ Church also claims a Norman church, 800-year-old **St. Frideswide** (better known as Oxford Cathedral), and a Picture Gallery graced with works by Sir Joshua Reynolds and William Gainsborough. William Penn and John Wesley studied at Christ Church, as did many British prime ministers; Lewis Carroll, better known for his Alice in Wonderland, taught mathematics here for many years. The college is open Monday to Saturday 9am to 5pm, Sunday 1 to 5pm. Admission is £8 for adults and £6.50 for seniors, students, and children.

Across Christ Church Meadow and adjoining Merton Field on the banks of the River Thames is **Merton College ★** (✆ **01865/276-310;** www.merton.ox.ac.uk). Dating to the 13th century, this is one of the earliest centers of learning in Oxford; its 14th century library houses Geoffrey Chaucer's astrolabe (a device used to locate the planets and stars). The Old Library is occasionally open by guided tour from July through September. There's no admission charge to the grounds, and the library tour costs £2.

Across Rose Lane, the **Botanic Garden ★** (✆ **01865/286-690;** www.botanic-garden.ox.ac.uk) was founded in 1621 for the study of medicinal plants—a rose garden commemorates the Oxford researchers whose work paved the way for the discovery of penicillin (open daily 9am–4:30pm; admission £4).

Crossing the river that flows in front of the gardens, a pretty stone bridge leads to **Magdalen College ★** (✆ **01865/276-000;** www.magd.ox.ac.uk).

Magdalen College.

Radcliffe Camera.

Oscar Wilde studied here, and the area is much now as it was then. The sprawling bucolic grounds include a deer park and water meadows sprinkled with wildflowers. Magdalen (pronounced "maud-len") is simply picturesque, with dazzling Gothic architecture, most notably the elegant **Magdalen Tower.** The tallest building in Oxford (at 140 ft/44m), the tower was completed in 1509. Visit the 15th-century chapel below it; the Magdalen choir sings ethereal Evensong here Tuesday to Sunday at 6pm. The college is open afternoons daily. Admission is £4.50 for adults, and £2.50 for seniors, students, and children.

If you follow High Street back toward the town center, and turn right (north) into Radcliffe Square you reach the **Bodleian Library ★★** (✆ **01865/277-224;** www.bodleian.ox.ac.uk), established in 1450 and the oldest library in Europe. More than 11 million volumes (many of them antiquarian, including a rare Gutenberg Bible) are tucked away on its 120 miles (190km) of shelving, and students using the library still take an oath "not to bring into the library or kindle therein any fire or flame." The library's main reading room is the iconic, domed **Radcliffe Camera.** You can enter the Exhibition Room and wander the quadrangles of these handsome structures for free, but to get a better understanding of their history, take a tour. Standard tours lasting an hour start with the university's oldest teaching and examination room, the **Divinity School** (completed 1488). Purchase tickets in the lodge on the right hand side of the Great Gate on Catte Street. The highly recommended extended 90 minute tours also include the Old Library and Radcliffe Camera. These tours normally run every Sunday at 11:15am and 1:15pm, at 10am on most Saturdays, and 9:30am on most Wednesdays. Book in advance online.

The ravishing, circular piece of Palladian architecture next door to the Bodleian on Broad Street is the **Sheldonian Theatre ★★** (✆ **01865/277-299;** www.ox.ac.uk/sheldonian), which was completed in 1668 to a design by Sir Christopher Wren. As well as admiring the immaculate interior and ceiling frescoes, you can climb up to the cupola and enjoy fine views over Oxford. It's open Monday to Saturday from 10am to 12:30pm and from 2 to 4:30pm (3:30pm in winter); the admission fee is £2.50 for adults and £1.50 for under-14s. Concerts and plays are regularly performed here; check the website before your visit to find out what's on.

Farther west on Broad Street at the intersection of St. Giles Street, **Balliol College ★** (✆ **01865/277-777;** www.balliol.ox.ac.uk) was founded in 1263. In the 16th century, bishops Latimer and Ridley and Archbishop Cranmer were burned at Balliol (pronounced "bay-ley-ill") College entrance for heresy on the orders of Mary Tudor (also known as Bloody Mary due to her rampage against Protestants); the huge gates still bear scorch marks. The three men are also commemorated with the **Martyrs Monument,** just across St. Giles Street.

From St. Giles Street, follow Beaumont Street to the **Ashmolean Museum ★★** (✆ **01865/278-000;** www.ashmolean.org). In a grand, Palladian building, this history and art museum contains some real gems, not least the **Alfred Jewel,** a rare Anglo-Saxon gold ornament dating from the 9th century adorned with the words "Alfred ordered me made" (in Anglo-Saxon). It contains classical paintings from the Italian Renaissance (Raphael and Michelangelo among them), a large collection of antiquities from ancient Egypt, and rare Asian ceramics and sculptures. The rooftop restaurant, the **Ashmolean Dining Room,** is a pleasant place to take tea on a sunny day, while the cafe in the vaulted crypt is perfect when it rains.

Finally, climb the 99 steps of the **Carfax Tower** situated at the crossroads of the town's busiest thoroughfares (Cornmarket, Queen, St. Aldate's, and High Streets). This Gothic church tower is distinguished by its clock and figures that strike on the quarter-hour. It's all that remains of St. Martin's Church, which stood on this site from 1032 until 1896, when most of it was demolished to make way for a wider road. The tower used to be higher, but after 1340 it was lowered, following complaints from the university to Edward III that townspeople threw stones and fired arrows at students. The tower is open daily 10am to 5pm; admission is £2.20 for adults and £1.10 for children.

## ORGANIZED TOURS

The entertaining 2-hour **walking tour** through the city and colleges from the Oxford Information Centre, 15–16 Broad St. (✆ **01865/252-200;** www.visitoxfordandoxfordshire.com) starts daily at 11am, 1pm, and 2pm. These cost £8 for adults and £4.50 for children 16 and younger. The Information Centre also offers a long list of themed tours, everything from "Magic, Murder & Mayhem" to "Pottering in Harry's Footsteps."

For something spooky, try **Bill Spectre's Oxford Ghost Trails ★** (✆ **0794/1041-811;** www.ghosttrail.org), on Friday and Saturday evenings at 6:30pm. Dressed as a Victorian undertaker, Bill illustrates his ghoulish walks with props and tricks, taking in all the most famous and gruesome Oxford ghost stories. He charges £7 for adults and £4 for children.

Alternatively, contact Felicity Tholstrup at **Hidden Oxford ★** (✆ **01865/512-650;** www.hiddenoxford.co.uk), who specializes in critically acclaimed tailor-made tours of the city. Finally, **Oxford River Cruises** (✆ **0845/2269-396;** www.oxfordrivercruises.com) runs several boat tours along the River Thames, from the tranquil 1-hour Afternoon River Experience (£15) to a sunset picnic trip for £45 per person.

## MORE THINGS TO SEE & DO

Though somewhat off the main tourist track, the **University Museum of Natural History ★** (✆ **01865/272-950;** www.oum.ox.ac.uk) and the **Pitt Rivers Museum ★** (✆ **01865/270-927;** www.prm.ox.ac.uk) on Parks Road have unexpected charm. The venerable Natural History Museum (open daily 10am–5pm) shows off a good collection of dinosaur skeletons and other curiosities in a marvelous glass-roofed Victorian hall. The Pitt Rivers Museum (open Tues–Sun 10am–4:30pm and Mon noon–4:30pm), entered from the Natural History museum, is worth poking your head into for its curiosity value. General Pitt Rivers gave his collection of ethnic artifacts to the university in 1884, and there are now more than half a million objects in old-fashioned cases crammed into a dimly lit room. Arranged by type, rather than geography or date, the exhibits demonstrate how different peoples tackled the same tasks. Most redolent of adventure are the 150 pieces collected during Captain Cook's second voyage, from 1773 to 1774. Both museums are free to enter.

Artefacts on display in glass cases at the Pitt Rivers Museum.

### OUTDOOR ACTIVITIES

You can enjoy Oxford's rivers from a boat, rented by the hour from the **Cherwell Boathouse,** Banbury Rd. (✆ **01865/515-978**); and from **Old Horse Ford,** off High St. under the Magdalen Bridge (✆ **01865/202-643**). Both are open from mid-March to mid-October and charge £12 to £14 an hour.

## Shopping

**Golden Cross** ★, an arcade of locally owned clothing and arts shops, lies between Cornmarket Street and the Covered Market. Parts of the colorful gallery date from the 12th century. **Alice's Shop,** 83 St. Aldate's (✆ **01865/723-793;** www.aliceinwonderlandshop.co.uk) is a souvenir shop for Lewis Carroll fans inside a 15th-century building where Alice Liddell, the inspiration for Alice in Wonderland, bought candy when Carroll was a professor at Christ Church. The **Bodleian Library Shop,** Old School's Quadrangle, Radcliffe Square, Broad St. (✆ **01865/277-091;** www.shop.bodley.ox.ac.uk), specializes in Oxford souvenirs from books and paperweights to Oxford banners and coffee mugs. Not too surprisingly, Oxford is well-endowed with bookstores. **Blackwell's,** 48–52 Broad St. (✆ **01865/792-792**), is the largest, with more than 200,000 new and rare books and more than 3 miles (5km) of shelving in its cavernous underground Norrington Room. **Oxford University Press Bookshop,** 116–117 High St. (✆ **01865/242-913**), sells dictionaries and a complete inventory of other books published by the university's famous press, founded in the 15th century.

## Where to Eat

You can stock up on provisions for a picnic or grab a quick bite in the **covered market** ★★ on Cornmarket Street, or get sandwiches and soup at **Mortons** ★ on Broad St. (✆ **01865/200-860**), and tea and scones or a well-priced hot lunch in the **Ashmolean Café** at the Ashmolean Museum. Other options are to crowd in with the students at the **Nosebag Restaurant,** 6 St. Michael's St. (✆ **01865/721-033**), for healthy vegetarian curries, soups, and casseroles, or try **Brown's Café** in the Covered Market (✆ **01865/243-436**) for home-cooked, hearty food (bacon, eggs and toast, sausage sandwiches, fish and chips). Alternatively, have a pub lunch at one of the city's many pubs—try the **Head of the River,** Folly Bridge, at the end of St. Aldate's St. (✆ **01865/721-600**), for lunch with a river view.

### Walking: Oxford

For a quick escape into bucolic settings, take a riverside walk: From St. Aldate's Street, you'll find entrances to **Christ Church Meadow** and a network of paths that follow the rivers Thames and Cherwell. From Walton Road, northwest of the center, you can enter Port Meadow, where you may be joined by grazing livestock. For a leisurely afternoon, follow the Thames-side path north from Port Meadow to two charming pubs: the **Perch** (✆ **01865/728-891**) and the nearby **Trout** (✆ **01865/302-071**); they are about a 2-mile (3.2-km) walk from the center of Oxford and have delightful riverside gardens. Pick up walking maps from the Oxford Information Centre before setting off.

### Nearby

In Woodstock, about 8 miles (13km) north of Oxford (on the A44), is the vainglorious 18th-century **Blenheim Palace** ★★★ (✆ **08700/602-080**; www.blenheimpalace.com), former childhood home to Sir Winston Churchill. One of the largest private houses in England, it's the only non-royal, non-religious house in the country to hold the title of "palace." Imposing and even a bit overwhelming, it was built in 1720 for the Duke of Marlborough, and is still home to his descendants. The building is packed with antiques, porcelain, oil paintings, and tapestries. It has carvings by Grinling Gibbons (in the Great Hall) and family portraits by Sir Joshua Reynolds and John Singer Sargent. The grounds, designed by the 18th-century British landscaper Capability Brown, are lavish and stretch across miles of formal gardens and lush, green countryside. The palace and gardens are open mid-February to mid-December daily 10:30am to 5:30pm (closed Mon–Tues Nov–Dec). Admission is £19 for adults, £15 seniors and students, and £11 children 5–15. The no. 20 bus from Oxford train station runs every 30 minutes (£5.50 round-trip).

# TUNBRIDGE WELLS

Tunbridge Wells, 30 miles (48km) outside London in the rolling Kent hills, first gained prominence in the 17th century when a mineral spring was discovered here. An ailing courtier to King James I drank from the waters, and after feeling revived, spread the word around London of his recovery; before long, the Royal family visited the town to sample the waters for themselves. As the town's popularity grew as a destination of the upper classes, a rush of new houses were built, and although some modern development has done the city no favors, the homes and parks those early health-seekers built make Tunbridge Wells the fine-looking place it is today.

The town's creamy wedding cake architecture is mostly 18th and early 19th century (until 1676, there were few permanent dwellings in the town and water seekers had to camp).

You can easily see all that Tunbridge Wells has to offer in a morning, leaving the afternoon free to explore one of the many great houses in the surrounding area (see p. 152).

## Essentials

### VISITOR INFORMATION

The **Tunbridge Wells Information Centre** (✆ **01892/515-675;** www.visittunbridgewells.com), in the Old Fish Market, is open Monday to Saturday from 9:30am to 5pm (until 6pm in the summer) and Sunday from 10am to 4pm.

### SCHEDULING CONSIDERATIONS

Tunbridge Wells is the shopping center for all the surrounding towns and villages, and so parking on Saturdays can be difficult. Aim to come during the week or on a Sunday for a more laidback visit.

### GETTING THERE

#### By Train

Southeastern trains run about every 30 minutes from London Charing Cross to Tunbridge Wells, talking around 1 hour. A round-trip costs £17. Tunbridge Wells station is on the busy A26, but it's just a 10 minute walk to the Pantiles walkway.

**The Pantiles.**

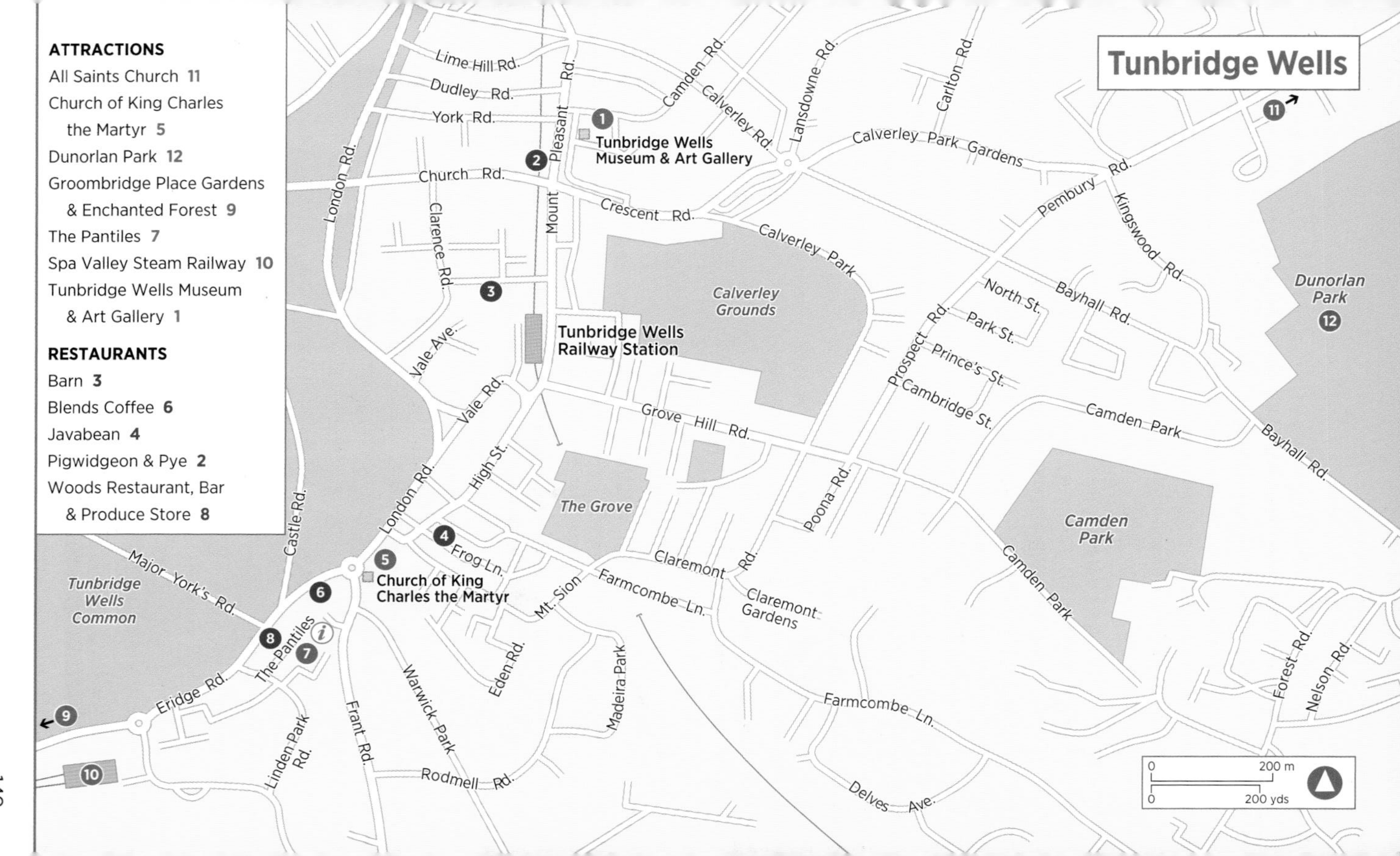

Tunbridge Wells
ATTRACTIONS
All Saints Church 11
Church of King Charles the Martyr 5
Dunorlan Park 12
Groombridge Place Gardens & Enchanted Forest 9
The Pantiles 7
Spa Valley Steam Railway 10
Tunbridge Wells Museum & Art Gallery 1
RESTAURANTS
Barn 3
Blends Coffee 6
Javabean 4
Pigwidgeon & Pye 2
Woods Restaurant, Bar & Produce Store 8
Tunbridge Wells Museum & Art Gallery
Tunbridge Wells Railway Station
Church of King Charles the Martyr
Calverley Grounds
The Grove
Camden Park
Dunorlan Park
Tunbridge Wells Common
Lime Hill Rd.
Dudley Rd.
York Rd.
Pleasant Rd.
Camden Rd.
Calverley Rd.
Lansdowne Rd.
Carlton Rd.
Calverley Park Gardens
Pembury Rd.
Kingswood Rd.
Church Rd.
Mount
London Rd.
Clarence Rd.
Crescent Rd.
Calverley Park
North St.
Bayhall Rd.
Park St.
Prospect Rd.
Prince's St.
Cambridge St.
Camden Park
Vale Ave.
Vale Rd.
Grove Hill Rd.
High St.
Poona Rd.
Castle Rd.
Frog Ln.
Claremont Rd.
Claremont Gardens
Mt. Sion
Farmcombe Ln.
Major York's Rd.
The Pantiles
Eridge Rd.
Linden Park Rd.
Frant Rd.
Warwick Park
Eden Rd.
Madeira Park
Rodmell Rd.
Delves Ave.
Forest Rd.
Nelson Rd.
0
200 m
200 yds

### By Car

Tunbridge Wells is 30 miles (48km) southeast of London. Take the M25 to the A21 and follow the exit signs. The journey takes just over an hour.

### By Bus

**National Express** buses leave London Victoria's bus station for Tunbridge Wells several times a day. The journey takes about 90 minutes and costs around £10 for a round-trip.

### GETTING AROUND

Tunbridge Wells is a sprawling place, but the historic section in the center is easy to explore on foot with the main sights contained within a 10 minute walk of the train station.

## A Day in Tunbridge Wells

Any visit to Tunbridge Wells is likely to start in the colonnaded walkways of **The Pantiles ★**. This area off Nevill Street and Linden Park Road was a favorite of the town's royal visitors and their wealthy friends, who came in the 1600s to drink the mineral water pouring from the Chalybeate Spring, and to shop and socialize. The white buildings and wide lanes haven't changed a great deal in 300 years; they're still lined with upscale shops and coffeehouses. There's a dipper above the spring in summer, and you can help yourself to some of the bitter, sulfurous brew.

Across the road from The Pantiles, on Chapel Place, is the **Church of King Charles the Martyr ★★** (✆ **01892/511-745**). Built in 1678, its creamy, swirly ceiling is the result of plasterwork by Christopher Wren's favorite plasterer, Henry Doogood. Admission is free from Monday to Saturday from 11am to 3pm (closed Sun). The nearby **High Street,** with its 17th- and 18th-century buildings, has mainly shops, restaurants, and pubs.

Church of King Charles the Martyr.

Dunorlan Park.

On Mount Pleasant Road, the **Tunbridge Wells Museum & Art Gallery** (✆ **01892/554-171;** www.tunbridgewellsmuseum.org) has an eclectic but absorbing array of artworks, antique toys, and artifacts. It also has a display on the local woodwork known as Tunbridge Ware (inlaid wood made into jewelry cases and furniture). It's open on Monday through Saturday from 9:30am to 5pm, and Sunday 10am to 4pm, with free admission.

Just up the steep hill at the edge of the town center on Pembury Road, **Dunorlan Park** (✆ **07901/513-287**) is a perfect place to have a picnic or just explore. Once the grounds of a grand manor house, it's now a beautifully landscaped public park (the house was demolished years ago). You can wander the smooth lawns, rent a boat and paddle across the lake, or climb the slopes and take in views that stretch for miles. Open daily, admission free.

Half a mile from the current train station, the town's old rail station, Tunbridge Wells West, still operates, albeit with just one service, the **Spa Valley Steam Railway** ★ (✆ **01892/537-715;** www.spavalleyrailway.co.uk). This restored antique steam train chugs through a short timetable of stops in the villages of High Rocks, Groombridge, and Eridge. Round-trip tickets cost £9 for adults and £4.50 for children.

If you hop off in Groombridge, it's a 10 minute walk from the station to **Groombridge Place Gardens & Enchanted Forest** ★★ ☺ (✆ **01892/861-444;** www.groombridge.co.uk), a combination of formal gardens (designed and established in the 17th century), a forest filled with exotic animals, and playgrounds for children (open daily Mar–Oct 10am–5:30pm; admission £10 adults, £8.45 for seniors and children 3–12).

Just outside Tunbridge Wells in the suburban village of Tudeley, **All Saints Church** (on B2017; ✆ **01732/808-277**) is a modest church built over the 13th and 14th centuries. It is best known for its 12 extraordinary stained-glass windows designed by the artist Marc Chagall. Open daily 9am to 6pm, admission free.

### Nearby

Tunbridge Wells is virtually surrounded by old manor houses. Within 15 miles (24km) of the town are Anne Boleyn's childhood home, **Hever Castle** (see p. 105), the grand house and garden at **Knole** (see p. 86), along with **Leeds Castle** (see p. 111) and **Sissinghurst** (see p. 94).

In addition, 6 miles (10km) away from Tunbridge Wells, **Penshurst Place ★** (✆ **01892/870-307;** www.penshurstplace.com) is a spectacular example of a complete 14th-century manor house, with an extensive collection of tapestry, art, and armor (open Apr–Oct daily 10:30am–6pm; admission £9.80 for adults and £6.20 children 5–16).

Ten miles (16km) away from Tunbridge Wells is **Ightham Mote ★** (✆ **01732/811-145;** www.nationaltrust.org.uk), a lovely medieval manor house dating from 1320. The rooms in this well-maintained house exude warmth, especially the Great Hall and Tudor chapel with its painted ceiling. Ightham Mote is located in Ivy Hatch, 6 miles (10km) east of Sevenoaks on the A227. It's open from early March through October Monday, Thursday to Sunday 11am to 5pm (June–late Aug also on Wed, reduced hours in Nov–Dec). Admission is £11 for adults and £5.50 for children 5 to 15.

### ORGANIZED TOURS

The Information Centre offers absorbing guided 1-hour walking tours of Tunbridge Wells, which take place every Thursday and Saturday morning from March through December, starting at 11:30am and costing £4.

## Shopping

The Pantiles is packed with shops, although particularly note-worthy are **Pantiles Books and Papertole,** 13 The Pantiles (✆ **01892/618-191;** www.pantilespapertole.com), which specializes in craft supplies for decoupage as well as used books, and **Fairfax Gallery,** 23 The Pantiles (✆ **01892/525-525;** www.fairfaxgallery.com), where you can spend a few moments browsing a contemporary art exhibition. On High Street, **Miss Magpie,** 72 High St. (✆ **01825/790-817;** www.missmagpie.com), sells affordable, often sparkly, jewelry, bracelet charms, and accessories. **Mark Maynard ★**, 26 High St. (✆ **01892/617-000;** www.markmaynard.co.uk), sells restored antique furniture and small gifts for the home at reasonable prices, with an emphasis on shabby chic style.

## Where to Eat

**Woods Restaurant, Bar & Produce Store ★★**, 62 The Pantiles (✆ **01892/614-411;** www.woodsrestaurant.co.uk), is a warm, bright eatery, serving meals and afternoon teas throughout the day. The brunches are especially good: Try the eggs Benedict royale with smoked salmon (£7.95). Stop in for coffee and a muffin at **Blends Coffee,** 20 The Pantiles or at **Javabean,** 67 High St. (✆ **01892/511-121**). The casual and friendly **Barn ★**, 1 Lonsdale Gardens (✆ **01892/510-424;** www.barn-pub-rest.co.uk), is a pub-restaurant that claims to have the best steaks in town (mains £8.75–£14.45). Finally, **Pigwidgeon & Pye ★**, 71 Mount Pleasant Rd. (✆ **01892/615-495;** www.pigwidgeonandpye.com), is a fanciful cafe-bar that uses fresh, local meats, bread, and produce to make delicious sandwiches and cakes, with most things under £5.

# 7

# SUN, SAND & SEA BREEZES

The traditional seaside will remain a fond memory in the minds of any visitor to the English coast: nothing can quite compare to the breezy seafront promenades, the jingle of fishing boats or the allure of the neon festooned amusement pier. The brightest offering within an hour's reach from London is Brighton, fashionable and quirky with a myriad of lanes offering everything from cozy pubs to secondhand garb and vegetarian cafes. The beach and pier attract huge crowds on sunny days, whilst the Royal Pavilion provides a delightful taste of 19th century decadence.

---

The Spinnaker Tower on Portsmouth's Gunwharf Quay celebrates a city steeped in naval history. The historic dockyard is home to legendary ships including Admiral Nelson's HMS Victory and the Mary Rose. Neighboring Southsea has a sweeping pebble beach, two amusement piers and seafront parkland popular for summer festivals and picnics.

On the Essex coast, Leigh-on-Sea bestows a salty air with artsy shops, quaint fishermen's cottages and fresh 'off-the-boat' seafood. The trendy Whitstable, a Kentish harbor town famed for its oysters, sits not far from the lively Broadstairs, a colorful Victorian resort and favorite haunt of Charles Dickens, which remains as popular today with families.

# BRIGHTON

On the Sussex coast, a mere 50 miles (80km) south of London on the English Channel, Brighton is England's most famous and popular seaside town. The town was a small fishing village until the prince regent, a fun-loving dandy who reigned as George IV from 1820 to 1830, became enamored of the place and had the Royal Pavilion built. Where royalty moves, fashion follows, and Brighton eventually became one of Europe's most popular towns. The long terraces of Regency town houses you see everywhere in Brighton date from that period. Later in the 19th century, when doctors prescribed breathing sea air as a cure-all, the Victorians descended en masse, as did the world-weary simply looking for a little fun—and they still do.

Today, Brighton draws artists and musicians and all that they bring with them: laidback coffee shops, vibrant nightlife, and a host of cosmopolitan restaurants. Its arty shops are well worth your time—you're unlikely to go home empty-handed.

Reaching Brighton from London is so easy that you can easily nip down for an afternoon to hang out on the beach or wander around The Lanes, although a whole day could easily be spent here too.

PREVIOUS PAGE: **HMS Warrior 1860, the Historic Harbor, Portsmouth.**

## Essentials

### VISITOR INFORMATION

Brighton's **Visitor Information Centre,** Royal Pavilion Shop, 4–5 Pavilion Buildings (✆ **0906/711-2255;** www.visitbrighton.com), is next to the Royal Pavilion shop, about a 10 minute walk toward the sea from the train station. The center is open daily from 10am to 5pm (until 4pm Sun).

### SCHEDULING CONSIDERATIONS

The Brighton Pavilion.

Brighton is most in its element in the summer, when the sun glints off the sea, but also at its most crowded on summer weekends. You may want to schedule your visit in May, when the **Brighton Festival** (✆ **01273/709-709;** www.brightonfestival.org) fills the city with drama, literature, art, dance, and music for three weeks. Brighton and adjoining Hove are the settings for one of Europe's largest **Gay Pride** celebrations, with a big parade and lively street parties (✆ **01273/775-939;** www.brightonpride.org).

### GETTING THERE

#### By Train

Southern and First Capital Connect trains leave London Victoria and London Bridge stations for Brighton roughly every 15 minutes; the journey takes about an hour. Expect to pay £16 to £22 for the round-trip.

#### By Bus

**National Express** (✆ **08717/818-178;** www.nationalexpress.com) buses run hourly from London Victoria's bus station to Brighton. The journey takes about 2 hours (around £13 round-trip).

#### By Car

The M23 from central London leads to the A23, which takes you to Brighton. The drive should take about 1 hour. Once you're in town, look out for the blue signs leading you to parking areas. Parking can cost up to £25 a day, and so be careful. Parking at the train station costs £11 per day. You can also park for free at the park and ride lot at Withdean Stadium on the north side of town. Buses into town run every 15 minutes and cost £3.70 round-trip.

### GETTING AROUND

Brighton is fairly compact, so the easiest way to get around is on foot. Heading down from the station, the Royal Pavilion is about 10 minutes' walk downhill to the left; the shopping lanes are about 5 minutes' walk downhill to the right. Taxis are usually available at the train station, or you can call **Streamline** (✆ **01273/747-474**) to book one.

## A Day in Brighton

Start your explorations at Brighton's one must-see attraction, the **Royal Pavilion ★★★** (✆ **01273/290-900;** www.royalpavilion.org.uk). Bounded

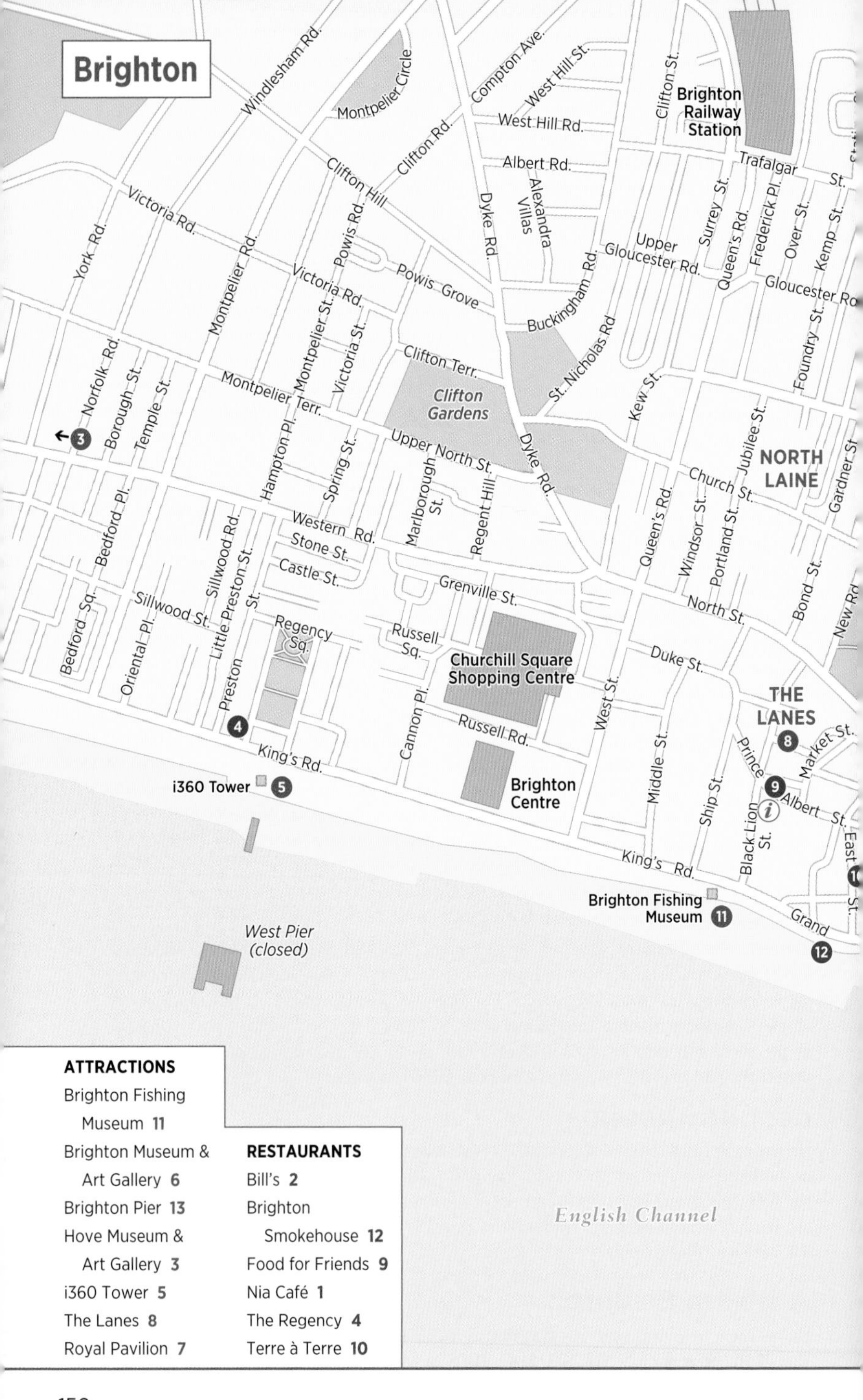
Brighton
Windlesham Rd.
Montpelier Circle
Compton Ave.
West Hill St.
West Hill Rd.
Albert Rd.
Clifton St.
Brighton Railway Station
Trafalgar St.
Clifton Rd.
Clifton Hill
Victoria Rd.
York Rd.
Montpelier Rd.
Powis Rd.
Dyke Rd.
Alexandra Villas
Upper Gloucester Rd.
Surrey St.
Queen's Rd.
Frederick Pl.
Over St.
Kemp St.
Gloucester Rd.
Powis Grove
Buckingham Rd.
Montpelier St.
Victoria St.
Norfolk Rd.
Borough St.
Temple St.
Clifton Terr.
St. Nicholas Rd.
Foundry St.
Montpelier Terr.
Clifton Gardens
Kew St.
Jubilee St.
Hampton Pl.
Spring St.
Upper North St.
NORTH LAINE
Marlborough St.
Regent Hill
Church St.
Gardner St.
Bedford Pl.
Western Rd.
Stone St.
Castle St.
Windsor St.
Portland St.
Sillwood Rd.
Little Preston St.
Preston St.
Grenville St.
North St.
Bond St.
New Rd.
Sillwood St.
Bedford Sq.
Oriental Pl.
Regency Sq.
Russell Sq.
Churchill Square Shopping Centre
Duke St.
West St.
THE LANES
Russell Rd.
Cannon Pl.
King's Rd.
Middle St.
Prince Albert St.
Market St.
i360 Tower
Brighton Centre
Ship St.
Black Lion St.
East St.
Brighton Fishing Museum
Grand
West Pier (closed)
English Channel
ATTRACTIONS
Brighton Fishing Museum 11
Brighton Museum & Art Gallery 6
Brighton Pier 13
Hove Museum & Art Gallery 3
i360 Tower 5
The Lanes 8
Royal Pavilion 7
RESTAURANTS
Bill's 2
Brighton Smokehouse 12
Food for Friends 9
Nia Café 1
The Regency 4
Terre à Terre 10

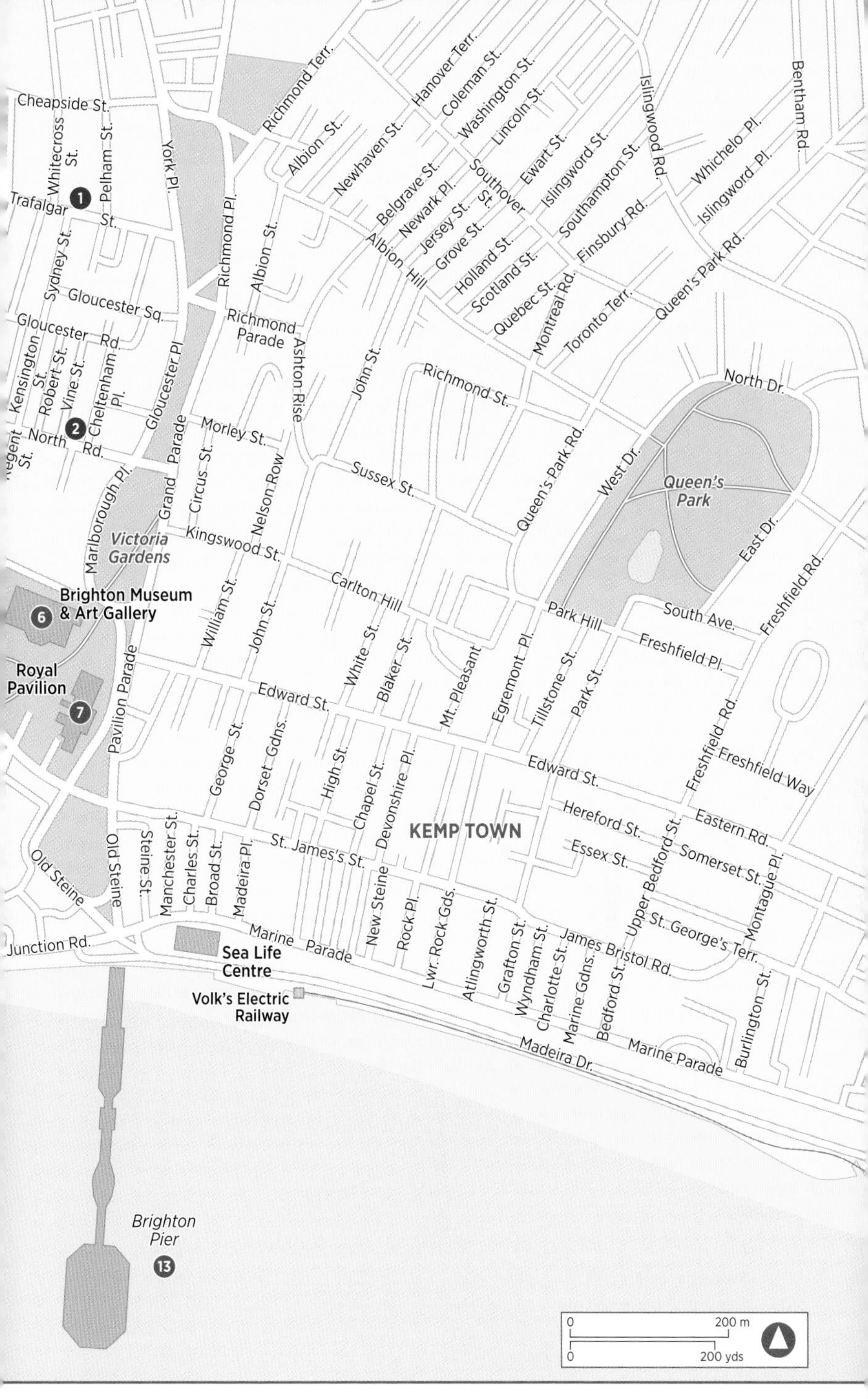
Cheapside St.
Whitecross St.
Pelham St.
York Pl.
Trafalgar St.
Sydney St.
Gloucester Sq.
Gloucester Rd.
Kensington St.
Robert St.
Vine St.
Cheltenham Pl.
Gloucester Pl.
Regent St.
North Rd.
Richmond Terr.
Albion St.
Newhaven St.
Hanover Terr.
Coleman St.
Washington St.
Lincoln St.
Belgrave St.
Newark Pl.
Jersey St.
Southover St.
Grove St.
Albion Hill
Ewart St.
Islingword St.
Southampton St.
Islingwood Rd.
Bentham Rd.
Whichelo Pl.
Islingword Pl.
Finsbury Rd.
Holland St.
Scotland St.
Quebec St.
Montreal Rd.
Toronto Terr.
Queen's Park Rd.
Richmond Pl.
Richmond Parade
Ashton Rise
John St.
Richmond St.
North Dr.
Morley St.
Grand Parade
Circus St.
Nelson Row
Marlborough Pl.
Sussex St.
Queen's Park Rd.
West Dr.
Queen's Park
Victoria Gardens
Kingswood St.
East Dr.
Freshfield Rd.
Brighton Museum & Art Gallery
6
William St.
John St.
Carlton Hill
Park Hill
South Ave.
Freshfield Pl.
Royal Pavilion
7
Pavilion Parade
Edward St.
White St.
Blaker St.
Mt. Pleasant
Egremont Pl.
Tillstone St.
Park St.
George St.
Dorset Gdns.
High St.
Chapel St.
Devonshire Pl.
Edward St.
Freshfield Rd.
Freshfield Way
Hereford St.
Eastern Rd.
KEMP TOWN
Essex St.
Upper Bedford St.
Somerset St.
Montague Pl.
Old Steine
Steine St.
Manchester St.
Charles St.
Broad St.
Madeira Pl.
St. James's St.
New Steine
Rock Pl.
Lwr. Rock Gds.
Atlingworth St.
Grafton St.
Wyndham St.
Charlotte St.
Marine Gdns.
Bedford St.
St. James Bristol Rd.
St. George's Terr.
Burlington St.
Old Steine
Junction Rd.
Marine Parade
Sea Life Centre
Volk's Electric Railway
Madeira Dr.
Marine Parade
Brighton Pier
13
1
2
0
200 m
0
200 yds

Music Room in the Brighton Pavilion.

by North Street, Church Street, Olde Steine, and New Road, the Pavilion is a fanciful mélange of ivory domes, swirls, and columns, set within a small, leafy garden. The prominent early-19th-century architect John Nash re-designed the original farmhouse and villa on this site into an Indian fantasy of turrets and minarets for George IV (when the king was still prince regent). The fun and food-loving George (from whom the Regency era got its name) lived here with his mistress, Lady Conyngham, until 1827, and filled the rooms, festooned with carvings of dragons and other whimsical creatures, with the elaborate furnishings and ornaments typical of the period. The Music Room is especially ornate, with a domed ceiling encrusted with seashells and red walls filled with Chinese scenes.

The king's brother, William IV, and their niece, Queen Victoria, also used the pavilion, though Victoria found the place vulgar and later sold it to the city of Brighton for £1 in 1850. Give yourself about an hour for a leisurely walk-through tour of the sumptuous and fantastically extravagant interior. The **Long Gallery** has a color scheme of bright blues and pinks; the **Music Room** has a domed ceiling of gilded, scallop-shaped shells; and the **king's private apartments** on the upper floors epitomize the Regency lifestyle of the rich and royal. The **Queen Adelaide Tea Room** is a nice spot for a light lunch or afternoon tea (open daily 10am to 5:45pm (5:15pm in winter)). Admission is £9.80 for adults, £7.80 for students and seniors, and £5.60 for children.

### Catcreeping Through Brighton

**Exploring Brighton's "catcreeps" and "twittens" takes you into a secretive, hidden side of this otherwise flamboyant seaside town. Catcreeps are flights of steps connecting two roads at different levels on a hillside, and a twitten is a Sussex word used to describe a narrow path between walls or hedges.**

On the west side of the Royal Pavilion's gardens, on Church Street, you find the **Brighton Museum & Art Gallery** (✆ **01273/290-900**). Admission is free to this small museum's interesting collection of Art Nouveau and Art Deco furniture, glass, and ceramics. There's also a fashion gallery. The museum is open Tuesday from 10am to 7pm, Wednesday through Saturday from 10am to 5pm, and Sunday from 2 to 5pm.

From the museum, head south on New Road, turning left onto North Street, and follow the signs to **The Lanes** ★. This warren of narrow streets was once Brighton's original fishing village, and is now filled with small, mainly independent shops and cafes (see "Shopping" below).

Follow East Street down to **the seafront** ★★ and the pebbly public beach. You can walk two ways: on a wide path along King's Road above the level of the beach, or on the beachfront below, awash with bars and shellfish stalls. The beach stretches for miles, with businesses occupying arches under the road. The elaborate, Victorian pier is **Brighton Pier** ★ ☺, built in the 19th century. It's still a highlight for families, packed with sweet stands, arcade games, and rollercoasters. It's open from 10am to midnight and admission is free. Another seafront star is the free **Brighton Fishing Museum** (✆ **01273/723-064;** www.brightonfishingmuseum.org.uk), with fishing boats, memorabilia, and old photos of Brighton. Look out for the **Brighton Smokehouse** (see "Where to Eat"), where fish are smoked in a beach hut and you can buy a hot kipper sandwich for £2.80. Along the way music pours out of bars, bands play on the beach, and rollerbladers whizz by as surfers paddle out into the blue.

Heading west down the seafront, the tall tower across from the Hilton Metropole is the new **i360 Tower** (scheduled to open in summer 2012, see www.brightoni360.co.uk). The slim tower's circular, spaceship-like viewing deck

Brighton beach and pier.

carries crowds up 492ft. (150m) to the top for unmatchable views. It will be Britain's highest viewing tower.

If you have time to spare, you could walk or catch a bus to **Hove,** the town that adjoins Brighton to the west. The **Hove Museum & Art Gallery,** 19 New Church St. (✆ **03000/290-900**), is housed in an impressive Victorian villa and contains a good collection of 20th-century paintings and drawings, 18th-century furniture and decorative art, and the "Hove to Hollywood" film collection featuring footage of the town in 1900 shot by local moviemakers. (The British film industry started in Hove.) The museum is a 20-minute bus ride from North St. (bus no. 1, 1A, 6, 6A, or 49), and is open Monday, Tuesday, Thursday to Saturday from 10am to 5pm and Sunday 2 to 5pm. Admission is free.



### ORGANIZED TOURS

**City Sightseeing Bus Tours** (✆ **01273/886-200;** www.city-sightseeing.com) offers 50-minute, historical hop-on/hop-off tours of the city in open-top, double-decker buses. Tours leave Brighton Pier at 10am and run every half-hour until 6pm. The cost is £8 for adults, £7 for students, £6 for seniors, and £3 for children 5 to 15.

### OUTDOOR ACTIVITIES

The beach is perfect for sunbathing and swimming, and on warm sunny days it's absolutely packed. Be warned, though, that even on the hottest days the English Channel is chilly, and you need swim-shoes because, although the pebbles are smooth, they hurt bare feet. The seafront is perfect for jogging, rollerblading, and biking. Rent a bike at **Brighton Cycle Hire,** right underneath the station (£6.50 per day; ✆ **01273/571-555;** www.brightoncyclehire.com).

## Shopping

**The Lanes ★★★** is a must-visit warren of alleyways and narrow streets behind North Street and its big-name shops. It's full of boutiques, cafes, and alternative stores of all kinds. Those in the know slide farther north to **North Laine ★★**—between the Lanes and the train station—which is a hive of retro and second-hand shops (www.northlaine.co.uk). A good hour or so can be spent in **Snooper's Paradise** (7–8 Kensington Gardens), an indoor market with 90 plus stalls of vintage goods with affordable price tags. Innumerable antique shops in the Lanes carry old books and jewelry; check out the clothing boutiques in converted backyards on Duke Lane just off Ship Street.

At the heart of the Lanes is **Brighton Square,** which is ideal for relaxing or people-watching near

Shops and cafes around the North Laine.

## Nearby

Two miles (3km) north of Brighton resides the handsome **Preston Manor** (✆ 03000/290-900), a perfect example of the upper-class Edwardian lifestyle, with rooms laid out in all their finery. Easily reached by train, it's only one stop from Brighton to Preston Park station, or you could even walk it in around 30 minutes. It's open April through September Tuesday to Saturday 10am to 5pm and Sunday 2 to 5pm. Admission is £5.50 for adults, £4.50 for seniors and students, and £3.10 for under-16s.

Just 8 miles (13km) north of Brighton, **Lewes** is a quiet, historic town, once the rural epicenter of Virginia Woolf's Bloomsbury Group. There you can visit a castle, the home of one of Henry VIII's wives, Anne of Cleves, as well as **Monk's House**, where Woolf lived and wrote, and **Charleston**, where her sister Vanessa Bell painted the walls, doors, and furniture into extraordinary artworks. See p. 31.

Just outside of Lewes is **Glyndebourne** (✆ **01273/813-813;** www.glyndebourne.com), a world-famous opera house tucked away in the Sussex countryside. See p. 36. The small city of **Chichester** is 30 miles (48km) east along the A27 and easily reached by trains along the coast in around 50 minutes. See p. 58.

the fountain on one of the benches or from a cafe-bar. **Regent Arcade,** between East Street, Bartholomew Square, and Market Street, sells artwork, jewelry, and other gift items, as well as high-fashion clothing. Bargain-hunters head for the **Kemp Town Flea Market,** Upper James Street, held Monday to Saturday 9:30am to 5:30pm and Sunday 10:30am to 5pm. A flea market is also held in the train station carpark, but only on Sunday from 6am to 2pm.

## Where to Eat

If you have one meal in Brighton, make it fish and ships from **The Regency ★★**, 131 King's Rd. (✆ **01273/325-014;** www.theregencyrestaurant.co.uk), the town's best seafood place. The mood is casual and a filling lunch will only set you back £10. For big breakfasts and light lunches, head to **Bill's ★**, 100 North St. (✆ **01273/692-894;** www.billsproducestore.co.uk)—a deli-cum-restaurant and local institution that serves terrific salads, great quiches, and a constantly changing list of hot meals, including burgers and steaks, all for less than £10. On the beach, **Brighton Smokehouse ★★**, 176 King's Arches, provides fresh and cheap sustenance.

Head to North Laine to try the leaf teas, great coffee, sandwiches, and goats cheese tarts at **Nia Café,** 87 Trafalgar St. (✆ **01273/671-371;** www.niabrighton.co.uk). Sit by the huge windows to take in the street action as you sample the steaming hot soup of the day or a cool salad. Vegetarians will feel spoilt for choice around this area: **Food for Friends ★★,** 17–18 Prince Albert St. (✆ **01273/202-310;** www.foodforfriends.com), and **Terre à Terre** (✆ **01273/729-051;** www.terreaterre.co.uk), are sure bets for a tasty and inventive meal without meat.

# LEIGH-ON-SEA

The promises of salty sea air, fresh-off-the-boat seafood, and the hungry call of seagulls circling the day's catch, offer a perfect reason to visit this area, as do the often unique and arty shops that line both the main street and the fishing cottages in Old Leigh.

Just 38 miles (23.6km) from central London, where the Thames flows out into the Channel, Leigh-on-Sea feels like an overgrown fishing village, which is more or less what it is. A fishing town has existed here since at least the 11th century and in the Domesday Book it's recorded as "Legra." These days the town is split into two areas of old and new, a comfortable mix of artsy seaside getaway, traditional fishing community, and a trendy, mostly independent-led shopping destination.

Over the years, Leigh's borders have blurred with busy, neighboring Southend-on-Sea, but the two are very different in terms of ambiance, with Leigh offering a much quieter, laidback alternative to Southend's busy shopping area and boisterous seafront arcades and pleasure park.

It takes less than half a day to see all that Leigh has to offer, but you can combine this trip with a jaunt along the historic Southend Pier, the longest in the world; it even has a train to help you make the 1.33-mile (2-km) distance.

## Essentials

### VISITOR INFORMATION

There's no official tourism office, but the **Heritage Centre,** on High Street in Old Leigh (✆ **01702/470-834;** www.leighsociety.co.uk), has plenty of information about the town and can answer any questions you might have. At the entrance of **Southend Pier** on the Western Esplanade, the Visitor Information Centre for the Southend area is open daily 8.15am to 8pm (✆ **01702/618-747;** www.southend.gov.uk).

### SCHEDULING CONSIDERATIONS

Leigh is rarely overrun with visitors except during the **Folk Festival** (www.leighfolkfestival.co.uk) and **Leigh Art Trail** (www.leigharttrail.co.uk), which both happen in June. The town is heaving during the **September Regatta,** though, which fills the sea with sails.

### GETTING THERE

#### By Train

Trains run from London's Fenchurch Street station to Leigh-on-Sea every 15 minutes throughout the day; the journey takes around 45 minutes. Expect to pay £15 for the round-trip. The station is down by the shore, easy walking distance to both the main town center and Old Leigh.

#### By Bus

National Express buses run twice a day to Leigh-on-Sea, the journey taking around 1¾ hours and costing £19 or so.

#### By Car

Leigh-on-Sea is 38 miles (23.6km) east of London. To get there, take the A13 and follow signs. You can park on the street in Leigh, but places can be hard to find. There are public carparks all over the town, though, including on North Street, Elm Road, and at the train station. Expect to pay around £5.

### GETTING AROUND

Leigh is small and you can explore the entire area on foot, but the streets leading down to the sea are very steep indeed, and so comfortable shoes are recommended.

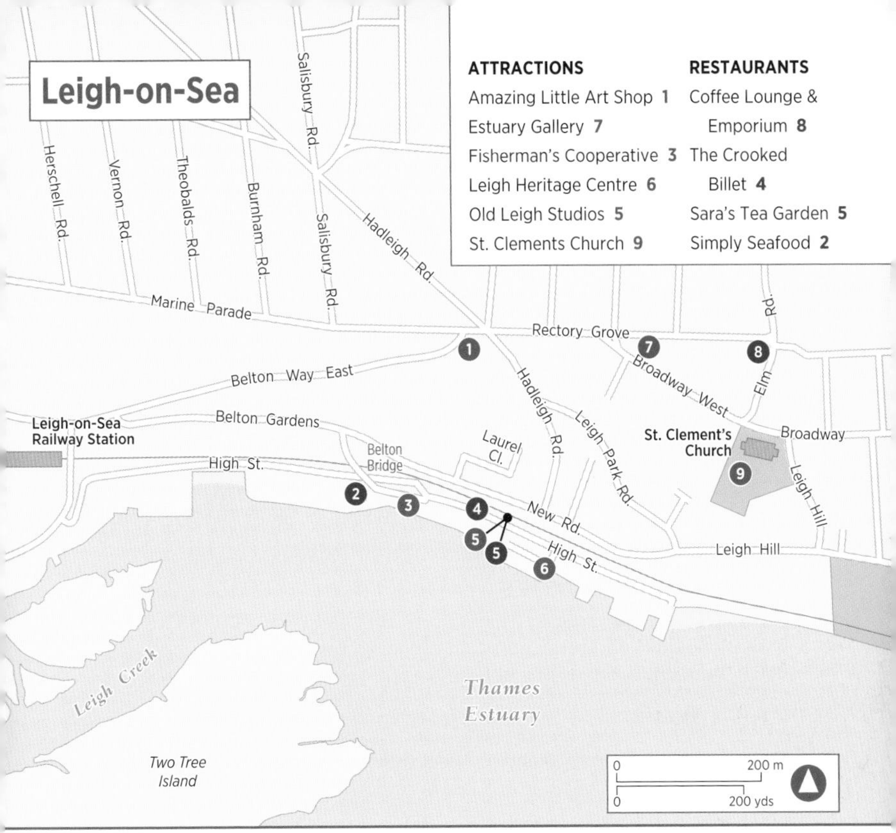

**Leigh-on-Sea**

**ATTRACTIONS**
- Amazing Little Art Shop **1**
- Estuary Gallery **7**
- Fisherman's Cooperative **3**
- Leigh Heritage Centre **6**
- Old Leigh Studios **5**
- St. Clements Church **9**

**RESTAURANTS**
- Coffee Lounge & Emporium **8**
- The Crooked Billet **4**
- Sara's Tea Garden **5**
- Simply Seafood **2**

Herschell Rd.
Vernon Rd.
Theobalds Rd.
Burnham Rd.
Salisbury Rd.
Hadleigh Rd.
Marine Parade
Rectory Grove
Belton Way East
Belton Gardens
Leigh-on-Sea Railway Station
High St.
Belton Bridge
Laurel Cl.
Broadway West
Elm Rd.
Leigh Park Rd.
New Rd.
St. Clement's Church
Broadway
Leigh Hill
Leigh Creek
Thames Estuary
Two Tree Island
0 200 m
0 200 yds

## A Day in Leigh-on-Sea

Start your exploration at the train station, which sits at the edge of the shoreline where the land falls away to the sea, and fishing and pleasure boats are anchored by the dozen just offshore.

Fishing boats in Old Leigh.

High Street runs between the sea and the train tracks, and you can follow it straight to the little neighborhood of **Old Leigh,** where warehouses and cockle sheds line the narrow street, along with pubs, restaurants, and artists' studios. **Old Leigh Studios ★**, 61 High St. (www.richardbaxter.com), is where the potter Richard Baxter, and artist Sheila Appleton work and sell their art. A block or so away at 16 High St., the **Leigh Heritage Centre** is based inside the old blacksmiths' shop and has a small exhibition on the history of Leigh as a fishing town. It is entirely run by volunteers, and so opening times can vary but generally it's daily 11am to 2pm, with later closing quite possible on weekends. Across the street, the **Fisherman's Cooperative ★** at Bell Wharf is inside a boatshed where the day's catch is sold fresh off the boats.

Walk to the end of High Street in Old Leigh, crossing over the railway bridge by the Ye Olde Smack pub. Once on Leigh Hill, climb the steep stairway leading up on your right to the historic **St. Clement's Church,** 80 Leigh Hill (✆ **01702/475-967**), dating back to the 15th century. The ceiling in the north aisle famously looks like the hull of a ship; lore has it that it was built by local boat builders.

Farther up the hill from St Clement's, **Broadway** is Leigh's main shopping street, lined for more than a mile with mainly independent shops and cafes. Nearby, on Rectory Grove, the **Estuary Gallery,** at no. 73 (✆ **07768/871-875**) features fine art photography and pottery by local artists. A short walk away, at 2 Belton Corner, the **Amazing Little Art Shop ★** (✆ **01702/435-566**) sells quality contemporary art by international artists.

### OUTDOOR ACTIVITIES

**Perfect Day Watersports,** Mike's Boatyard, Old Leigh (✆ **07887/890-389;** www.perfect.uk.com) runs courses in canoeing, kayaking, windsurfing, and sailing. A 1-day course starts at £100.

## Shopping

Broadway is Leigh's main shopping street with many locally owned stores. Just off Broadway at 109 Rectory Grove, **Ursula and Odette** (www.ursulaodette.co.uk)

Old Leigh Studios.

St.Clements Church.

Natural Edge.

is a beautifully designed fashion boutique selling clothes, jewelry, and accessories. At 47 Broadway, **Natural Edge** (✆ **01702/712-919**) is a cavernous gift shop with shabby chic home accessories, quality toiletries, greetings cards, and a large range of Cath Kidston accessories. A few shops down at 49 Broadway West, **The Book Inn** ★ ☺ (✆ **01702/716-614**) is a family-owned bookstore with polished pine floors, big windows, and a wide selection of books for children and adults. Back down in Old Leigh, at 66 High St., **Lynn Tait Gallery** ★★ (✆ **01702/471-737**) is an old foundry converted into a gift, art, and souvenir shop—you can also pick up your seaside bucket and spade here!

### Where to Eat

Some of the best places to eat are in Old Leigh. **Sara's Tea Garden,** 64 High St. (✆ **01702/477-315;** www.sarasteagarden.co.uk) is a charming, and rather tiny restaurant with a few tables inside and out, where you can opt for ploughman's lunches, sandwiches, or jacket potatoes, with most lunches priced reasonably from £4.25 to £5.95. Nearby, at 51 High St., **The Crooked Billet** ★★ (✆ **01702/480-289**) is a comfortable old pub serving sausages and mash, an array of sandwiches and salads, and fresh seafood. **Simply Seafood** ★★, at The Cockle Shed, off High St. (✆ **01702/716-645;** www.simplyseafood.co.uk) serves-up steaming, fresh plates of fish, direct from boats of local fishermen (small plates start from around £6).

A large number of eateries occupy the area around St. Clement's Church and the Broadway; the retro-themed **Coffee Lounge & Emporium,** 39–41 Elm Rd. (✆ **01702/480-408;** www.thecoffeebeancompany.com), sells superior coffee (and beans to buy for home).

## PORTSMOUTH & SOUTHSEA

The city of Portsmouth is 64 miles (103km) southwest from London and holds an important place in Great Britain's naval heritage. It has existed as a home to the British Royal Navy for the past 500 years and the historic dockyard is home to a few of the most famous vessels in history including the remains of Henry VIII's ship the Mary Rose and Admiral Nelson's Victory.

Much of Portsmouth's old architecture was destroyed during German bombing raids in World War II, and what you see today is starkly modern in comparison. However, the recently developed Gunwharf Quay has transformed part of the city, creating a vibrant leisure destination with designer shopping outlets, a cinema, restaurants, and quayside bars. Perhaps the most distinctive sight here is the Spinnaker Tower that rises 558ft. (170m) over the harbor, providing panoramic views that reach over 23 miles (37km).

### Walking Around Leigh-on-Sea

High up above Leigh, the ruins of 13th-century **Hadleigh Castle** (www.hadleighcountrypark.co.uk) guard the entrance to the Thames as they've done for centuries. All that remains is part of the keep and a section of stone wall, but it's in an evocative setting surrounded by a sprawling park. You can obtain walking maps with varying degrees of difficulty at the castle, but it's best to download one off the website before heading out as there's unlikely to be anybody on duty when you arrive at the castle. To get to the castle park, take London Road to Castle Road and follow signs.

Nearby, Southsea's seafront parade overlooks a vast pebble beach and has two piers, including a large amusement park.

A whole day could easily be spent between Portsmouth and Southsea, covering some of the historic dockyard and some traditional seaside fun.

## Essentials

### VISITOR INFORMATION

The **Visitor Information Service,** the Hard, Portsmouth (✆ **02392/826-722;** www.visitportsmouth.co.uk), is down near the Historic Dockyard (open daily 9:30am–5:15pm). There's also a **Southsea** information office, on Clarence Esplanade, open March to October daily during the same hours; between November and February, hours are Wednesday to Sunday 9:30am to 4:30pm.

### SCHEDULING CONSIDERATIONS

In the last weekend in November, the **Christmas Festival** fills the town with visitors drawn by a huge market, hundreds of people dressed in Victorian costumes, open shops, mulled wine, and music. The event is held at the Historic Dockyard: tickets cost £13 adults, £11.70 children and seniors.

### GETTING THERE

#### By Train

Southwest trains from London Waterloo run every 30 minutes to both local stations—Portsmouth & Southsea (for the town) and Portsmouth Harbour (for the Historic Dockyard). The trip takes 1½ hours. There's also an hourly train from Victoria, but that journey takes 2 hours. Expect to pay around £31 round-trip.

#### By Bus

**National Express buses** travel from London's Victoria bus station to Portsmouth every couple of hours. Tickets start at £18 round-trip, and the journey takes around 2 hours.

#### By Car

From London, head south on the M3 and then turn east on the M27 and follow signs for Portsmouth. The journey should take about 2 hours.

Portsmouth & Southsea
COPNOR
M275
Charles Dickens Birthplace Museum
9
Fratton Rd.
Military Rd.
Lake Rd.
Victoria Rd.
1
Mary Rose Museum
HMNB Portsmouth
HMS Victory
2
PORTSEA
Market Way
Commercial Rd.
Holbrook Rd.
FRATTON
National Museum of the Royal Navy
4
3
Queen St.
Arundel St.
Historic Dockyard
Victoria Park
Anglesea Rd.
Porthsmouth & Southsea Station
HMS Warrior
Kent St.
Portsmouth Harbour Station
Greetham St.
Fratton Station
Gunwharf Quays
6
Park Rd.
United Services Cricket Club
Burnaby Rd.
Spinnaker Tower
5
Winston
Churchill Rd.
Cambridge Rd.
7
Aspex Gallery
Gunwharf Rd.
St. George's Rd.
Ravelin Park
Hants Terr
St. Paul's Rd.
St. James Rd.
Somers Rd.
St. Andrew's Rd.
Victoria Rd. North
Fawcett Rd.
8
Broad St.
OLD PORTSMOUTH
Museum Rd.
High St.
King's Rd.
King's Terr
Elm Grove
Castle Rd.
Penny St.
Pembroke Rd.
Southsea Terr.
Grove Rd.
Lawrence Rd.
Nelson Rd.
Victoria Rd. South
Albert Rd.
Kent Rd.
Hovercraft Terminal
Pier Rd.
Duisburg Way
Clarence Pier
10
Osborne Rd.
11
Clarence Parade
SOUTHSEA
Waverley Rd.
Southsea Common
Clarence Esplanade
Granada Rd.
Blue Reef Aquarium
South Parade
12
Pyramids Centre
13
Southsea Castle
South Parade Pier
The Solent
To Ryde (I. of Wight)
ENGLISH CHANNEL
ATTRACTIONS
Aspex Gallery 7
Charles Dickens Birthplace Museum 9
Clarence Pier 10
Historic Dockyard 3
HMS Victory 2
Mary Rose Museum 1
National Museum of the Royal Navy 4
South Parade Pier 13
Southsea Castle 12
Spinnaker Tower 6
RESTAURANTS
Fin's 11
Old Customs House 5
Still & West 8
0
1/4 mi
0
1/4 km

### Visiting the Dockyard

Your ticket to the **Portsmouth Historic Dockyard** admits you to numerous attractions including HMS Victory, the Mary Rose, and the National Museum of the Royal Navy. Tickets cost £20 for adults, £17 for seniors, and £14:50 for children 5 to 15. The ticket includes a boat trip around the harbor (summer months only). The ships and the Royal Navy Museum are all open April to October daily 10am to 4:30pm; November to March daily 10am to 3:45pm.

### GETTING AROUND

Portsmouth is a sprawling metropolis, so to see all its sights you either need a car or have to rely on public transportation. The local bus company is **First Group,** and you can get bus route maps off the local government website (www.portsmouth.gov.uk). You'll find taxis at the train stations, or you can call **City Wide Taxis** (✆ **02392/833-333**) or **Pompey Cars** (✆ **02392/877-822**).

## A Day Around Portsmouth

Towering over the Portsmouth Harbour train station is the sail-shaped edifice of the **Spinnaker Tower ★**, Gunwharf Quays (✆ **02392/857-520;** www.spinnakertower.co.uk). A glass lift sweeps you to the top, where on a clear day you can see miles in all directions—including across the Solent to the Isle of Wight. In the crow's nest you can "walk on air," on the largest glass floor in Europe or take a break in the Tower Café & Bar. The tower opens daily 10am to 6pm (Aug Sun–Thurs until 7:30pm). Admission costs £7.55 for adults, £6.75 students and seniors, and £5.95 for children 3 to 15.

Spinnaker Tower.

The **Historic Dockyard ★★★**, at Victory Gate (✆ **02392/839-766;** www.historicdockyard.co.uk), includes several places of interest within it, but perhaps the main highlight for many will be the **HMS Victory ★★★**, the oldest commissioned warship in the world. The tall, masted vessel was launched in 1765 and earned its fame in the Battle of Trafalgar. The **Mary Rose Museum ★** (✆ **02392/812-931;** www.maryrose.org) houses the remains of Henry VIII's ship that sank in the Solent in 1545 with 400 men on board, as the king watched from shore. The ship was recovered 450 years later, and on display is an array of weaponry including cannons, daggers, swords,

HMS Victory, Historic Dockyard.

and longbows and arrows, some still in shooting order. In early 2012, a new boat-shaped museum, built as part of a multi-million heritage project, will open to house the hull of the boat including a reconstruction of the missing side.

Also at the Dockyard is the **National Museum of the Royal Navy,** which is filled with enormous displays on battles and heroes of the seas. Among these is one on the "real" Horatio Nelson, the naval hero who lost an eye at the Siege of Calvi in 1794, an arm at the Battle of Tenerife in 1797, and his life at Trafalgar in 1805. The dockyard complex is open daily from 10am to 6pm (with slightly earlier closing at 5:30pm Nov–Mar). Admission is in the form of a multi-use ticket that can be re-used for some of the attractions for up to one year from purchase. The HMS Victory, Mary Rose Museum, and Harbour Tours can be entered only once, but the HMS Warrior 1860, National Museum of the Royal Navy, and Action Stations are open to as many visits as you wish. Prices for the ticket start at £21.50 for adults, £18.35 for seniors and students, and £15.80 for children.

Nearby on Gunwharf Quays, the **Aspex Gallery** (✆ **0239/277-8080,** www.aspex.org.uk) is a respected contemporary art gallery specializing in new

Naval hero Admiral Horatio Nelson.

Drop by the multi-functional Aspex Gallery.

Southsea seafront.

works by young artists. It also has a cafe, hosts events, film screenings and talks, and is open daily from 11am to 4pm. Admission is free.

From the dockyard, make your way to **Old Portsmouth ★**— whether you're walking or driving the way is well-signposted east along the seafront from the train station (the main street is High Street and it continues along the seafront on East and West Streets). Sadly, even here modern development encroaches but it's the only place in the city where you get a glimpse of how the town once looked.

Before leaving Portsmouth for Southsea, literary buffs may be interested in the **Charles Dickens Birthplace Museum,** 393 Old Commercial Rd. (✆ **02392/827-261;** www.charlesdickensbirthplace.co.uk), where the author was born February 7, 1812. The parlor, dining room, and bedroom are decked out in the Regency style with various paraphernalia and furniture to evoke the times. A few of Dickens's possessions are displayed—a snuff box and inkwell—and rather morbidly the couch on which he died in 1870, originally from his home Gads Hill Place in Kent.

### Walking in Portsmouth

Ask in Portsmouth's Visitor Information Service (see p. 166) about the **Millennium Promenade Walk,** an attractive marked 2-mile (3-km) waterfront walking route linking the Hard by Portsmouth Harbour with atmospheric **Old Portsmouth** and **Southsea.** The path is well-marked, and has distinctive blue streetlights along the route. Stop off for a pint of real ale at the historic **Still & West pub ★**, Bath Square (✆ **02392/821-567**).

## PLAY UP pompey

Portsmouth's football (soccer) club, known by fans as "Pompey," has always received the keen affection of local residents and many consider it an important aspect of their town's heritage. In the days before the club's official foundation in 1898, the author Sir Arthur Conan Doyle played as goal keeper; Conan Doyle was a local resident and penned his first tale of detective Sherlock Holmes while living in Southsea.

The club enjoyed its heyday in the 1930s and 1940s, during which time they won the FA Cup (retaining the trophy for a record five years due to the competition's suspension during World War II). During this time Portsmouth's most respected player, Jimmy Dickinson, began his career at the club, one which was to garner a record 764 league appearances. Dubbed "Gentleman Jim" due to his good behavior on the pitch (he was never sent off, or even booked for misconduct during play, in a total of 845 games), he was later awarded an MBE before going on to manage the team.

If you're interested in catching a game, tickets are priced from £20 and can be purchased as e-tickets from the website (www.portsmouthfc.co.uk). Saturday matches start at 3pm. Fratton station is 5 minutes' walk from the stadium and is on the main rail line (it also serves trains from London Waterloo and London Victoria).



The area on the waterfront at the southern end of Portsea Island in Portsmouth is known as **Southsea ★**. A pleasant, largely Victorian neighborhood lined with traditional terrace houses, it trips down to the beach where two piers (**South Parade Pier** and **Clarence Pier**) hold amusement arcades. There's a permanent carnival next to Clarence Pier. The **beach ★** at Southsea is broad and sweeping, and covered in smooth pebbles. In the water offshore, four large **forts** were created in the 1860s as further invasion protection. Never used, they're known as Palmerston's Folly, after the prime minister who ordered them built.

At the tip of Southsea, the low-slung, gray-stone, straight-edged building is **Southsea Castle ★** (✆ **02392/827-261;** www.southseacastle.co.uk), built in 1544 on the orders of Henry VIII to protect the port from French invaders. Funded by money seized in the dissolution of the country's monasteries, the castle was heavily fortified and bristled with weapons. Centuries later, when the French became less of a threat, the castle was used as a prison. These days it's a museum, and you can climb its sturdy walls and see displays inside on Tudor England warfare. Open from May 14 to the end of October only, Tuesday to Sunday 10am to 5pm; admission is free.

The park around the castle is regularly used for concerts, festivals, and firework shows, and is an ideal spot for a picnic.

### ORGANIZED TOURS

You can learn more about Admiral Lord Nelson on a Nelson walking tour provided by local guides from the Visitor Information Service. The hour-long tour starts every day at 2:30pm and costs £3. Contact the visitor center for more information (see p. 166). Interesting and creative tours are frequently held at the Historic Dockyards—check the website to see what's on while you're in town.

### Nearby

A trip to the **Isle of Wight ★★** (www.iwight.com) is like stepping back in time. This diamond-shaped island a few miles offshore of Portsmouth measures just 13 miles (21km) from Cowes in the north to St. Catherine's Point in the south. Known for its family-friendly, sandy beaches and marinas favored by the yachting set, its Victorian streets make it a wonderfully old-fashioned place to explore. **Hovertravel Ferries** (✆ **01983/811-000;** www.hovertravel.co.uk) run between Southsea and the island, and **Wightlink Ferries** (✆ **0871/376-1000;** www.wightlink.co.uk) run to the island from Portsmouth Harbour. The crossing takes 10 to 20 minutes. On the island, Cowes is a yachting town with a castle, but Yarmouth is prettier, and is a starting point for many scenic walks.

Portsmouth is also 17 miles (27km) from the arty cathedral city of **Chichester,** with its galleries and charming shops. See p. 58.

## Shopping

Southsea is the neighborhood to find antique stores and small eclectic shops. **A. Fleming ★** in the Clock Tower, Castle Rd. (✆ **02392/822-034;** www.flemingantiques.co.uk), sells a good mix of fine and affordable antiques in a lovely old building. **Barbara Tipple ★** sells gorgeous, handmade jewelry from an elegant shop at 15 Marmion Rd. (✆ **02392/753-025;** www.barbaratipple.co.uk). Find a mix of quality antiques and reproductions at **Victoriana ★★**, 76 Marmion Rd. (✆ **02392/812-835;** www.victoriansouthsea.co.uk).

## Where to Eat

The **Old Customs House ★**, Gunwharf Quays (✆ **02392/832-333;** www.theoldcustomshouse.com), serves pies and other pub classics in a grand 19th-century building. In **Gunwarf Quays outlet mall,** Portsmouth Harbour (✆ **02392/836-700;** www.gunwharf-quays.com), there are a number of affordable chain restaurants, including Japanese-style noodle bar Wagamama, pizzeria Zizzi, and family-friendly Giraffe. Nearby, in Old Portsmouth, on the waterfront, the **Still & West ★★** pub, Bath Square (✆ **02392/821-567**), serves an eclectic and creative gastro menu featuring freshly caught fish and local meats. In Southsea, **Fin's,** 106 Palmerston Rd. (✆ **02392/362-970;** www.finsbar.co.uk), is a light and lively cafe in a handy location, with great coffee, homemade soup, and baguettes.

# WHITSTABLE & BROADSTAIRS

The Kent Coast is only a hop from London, and you can be taking in the lovely coastal views and holding an ice cream in less than a few hours. The coastline presents a diverse range of attractions, from Dover Castle and the White Cliffs (p. 103) to blue-flag beaches, the coastal resorts of Ramsgate and Margate, and the Viking Coastal Trail that weaves around the Thanet Peninsula. There's a lot to take in, so for now we focus on two of the smaller towns, Whitstable and Broadstairs, both of which provide ideal days out from London.

Overflowing with bohemian charm, the ancient town of Whitstable centers on a small harbor and is famed for its oysters, celebrated annually at a festival held in July. A perfect place to stroll, Harbour Street provides visitors with plenty of restaurants, galleries, and local independent shops to browse.

A few miles away across the headland, Broadstairs was a popular seaside escape for the Victorians, including Charles Dickens, who rested at Bleak House and wrote several of his novels here; the character Betsey Trotwood (from David Copperfield), was based on a resident of a cottage on the main parade, which today houses the Dickens House Museum. In the warmer months, this is still a popular town with day trippers heading onto the crowded Viking Bay, although it only takes a short amble along the coast to find a more peaceful spot. A visit to this traditional seaside town would be incomplete without a trip to the famous Morelli's ice-cream shop and a round of miniature golf.

You could easily spend a whole day in Whitstable or Broadstairs, relaxing on the beaches or just ambling around the shops and museums.

## Essentials

### VISITOR INFORMATION

Whitstable has a touchscreen **Tourist Information Point** at the harbor office (✆ **01227/378-100;** www.canterbury.co.uk). The main **Visitor Information**

**Centre** for **Thanet** is in Margate, The Droit House (✆ **01843/577-577;** www.visitthanet.co.uk). The local websites **www.visitbroadstairs.co.uk** and **www.seewhitstable.com** are also informative.

## SCHEDULING CONSIDERATIONS

Given the location on the seafront, it's no surprise that Whitstable and Broadstairs can both be very busy on summer weekends. Brave the weekend crowds and you'll find a market atmosphere with stalls selling all manner of crafts and bric-a-brac. Whitstable's annual **May Day** celebration—on the Saturday closest to May 1—is a lively event with Morris dancers, bands, and a market. Broadstairs holds a host of festivals; the **Folk Festival** is very much a family-friendly affair held every August (www.broadstairsfolkweek.org.uk), while the **Dickens Festival** in June sees fans of the author descend upon the town dressed in Victoriana (✆ **01843/861-827;** www.broadstairsdickensfestival.co.uk). Up-to-date information can be found on the town website (www.visitbroadstairs.co.uk).

## GETTING THERE

### By Train

Southeastern Trains run from London Victoria to Whitstable and Broadstairs every 30 minutes. You can also catch trains at London St. Pancras, but on those you must change at Rochester. Either way, the journey takes around 1½ hours. Expect to pay £25 for the round-trip. Trains run between Whitstable and Broadstairs every 30 minutes.

### By Bus

National Express runs several buses a day between London's Victoria bus station and Whitstable. The journey takes around 2 hours and costs about £20.

Harbour Street, Whitstable.

### By Car

Whitstable is 60 miles (96km) southeast of London. To get there, take the A2 east; it becomes the M2 once you're outside the conurbation. When the motorway ends, turn onto the A299 heading east and look out for signs. For Broadstairs, turn onto the A256 and again follow the signs. The journey from London takes around 1½ hours.

## GETTING AROUND

Both Whitstable and Broadstairs are small towns and easily explored on foot.

## A Day around Whitstable

**Whitstable ★★★** is the kind of place you wander around, rather than a town packed with specific sights. Its streets are lined with art galleries, coffee bars, boutiques, and crafts shops—exploring them is the joy of this place.

As you walk towards the **harbor ★★**, notice the tiny alleys with names such as "The Old Favourite," and "Squeezegut Alley." Most of this harbor area was built in the early 19th century by the Canterbury and Whitstable Railway Company as part of its work creating the **Crab and Winkle Line** (p. 57), which ran from London through Canterbury to the sea. The main thoroughfare **Harbour Street ★** is full of quirky shops, good restaurants, and coffee bars.

The shingle beach at Whitstable.

Follow the seafront to the left and you pass quaint cottages, then beach huts, and as the harbor curls around, the village of **Seasalter ★★**, with colorful, compact houses and fishing boats. Head the opposite way and you reach the quayside with its black-painted fishing sheds (where fish-boat owners leave nets to dry), and the **Fish Market ★★**, where people are selling the day's catch, or cooking it and serving it up outside. Walk around the quay to **East Quay** to find a quiet stretch of shingle beach.

On Tower Hill, the gray towers and walls of **Whitstable Castle ★** are hard to miss (**✆ 01227/281-726;** www.whitstablecastle.co.uk). More of an 18th-century family home than castle, it's presently used as the unofficial town hall, and the scene of local events and celebrations including the May Day festival. The building isn't open to the public, but you can wander the grounds and take in the sweeping view of the harbor and town below.

Twenty miles (32km) east of Whitstable, the Victorian seaside town of **Broadstairs** has a very different ambiance but is just as enticing. The colorful,

Dickens House Museum, Broadstairs.

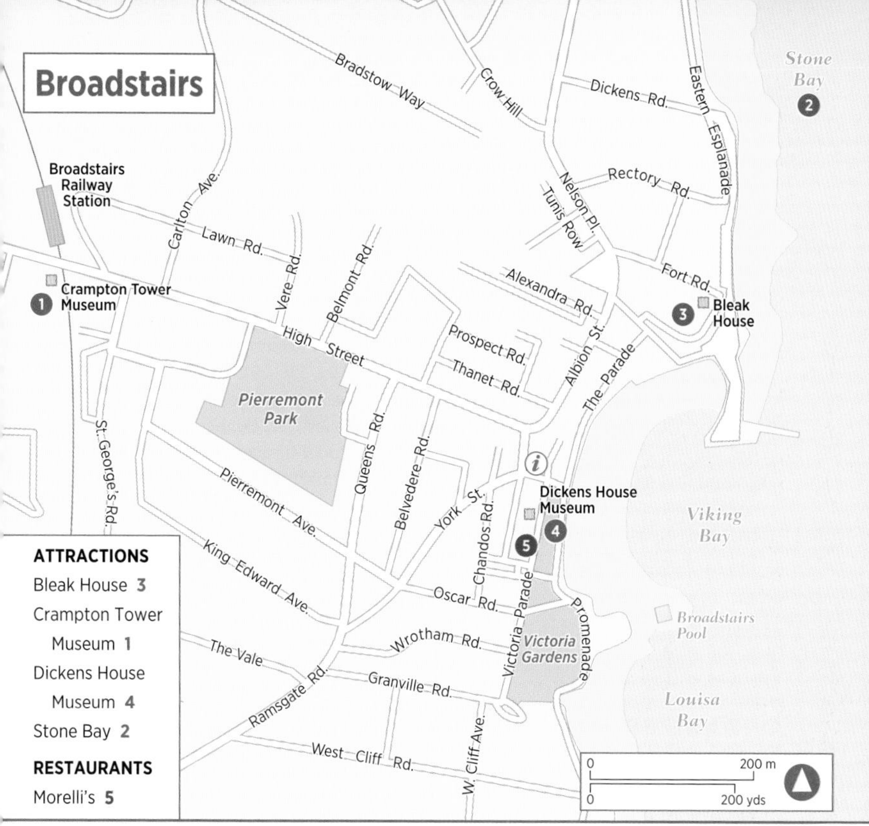


flower-bedecked promenade and bandstand is close by the **Dickens House Museum ★**, 2 Victoria Parade (✆ **01843/861-232**), once home to Miss Mary Pearson who's thought to be the inspiration behind the fictional character Betsey Trotwood. The museum's open April to October daily 2 to 5pm; admission £3.50. On Fort Road, **Bleak House ★**, where Charles Dickens wrote the novel of the same name, is closed to the public but it's easy to see where its gloomy moniker came from. Follow the coastal path left out of the main bustle of town until you reach the beach huts of **Stone Bay.**

If you have time and are interested in trains, don't miss the **Crampton Tower Museum** (www.cramptontower.co.uk). Close to the town's station

### The Kent Coast

**The Kent coastline offers some breathtaking views and several coastal walks are well set out and easy to follow on foot or by bicycle. The Viking Coastal Trail follows the path around the Thanet Peninsula. The trail is divided into several different themed sections, including one called "Historic Broadstairs." To download a map, go to www.visitthanet.co.uk.**

### Nearby

Whitstable is some 6 miles (10km) from the cathedral city of **Canterbury**, with its winding medieval streets. See p. 51.

A 17-mile (27-km) journey takes you to the sleepy seaside town of **Margate,** home to the **Turner Contemporary Art Gallery ★ (✆ 01843/233-000;** www.turnercontemporary.org) and beautiful beaches. J. M. W. Turner frequently painted in this area, inspired by the light, and 100 of his works are displayed here. For less artistic pleasures, the seafront **Dreamland Amusement Park** (www.dreamlandmargate.com) is a "heritage" fun park, with antique rides including a scenic railway wooden rollercoaster, which was here when the park opened in 1921.

Those seeking more historic sites can head to **Portchester Castle,** only 6 miles (10km) from Portsmouth. This Roman fort dating to the 3rd century has an intact Norman keep (**✆ 02392/378-291;** www.english-heritage.org.uk). Opening hours are April through September 10am to 6pm and October through March 10am to 4pm. Admission is £4.80 for adults and £2.90 for children.

and situated in an old flint water tower, the museum is dedicated to the life of Thomas Russel Crampton (1816–88), best-known as an engineer and designer of locomotives.

### ORGANIZED TOURS

Learn more about Broadstairs' history in a free, 90-minute walking tour (**✆ 01843/871-133**) that takes in all the town's highlights. Tours take place Saturdays at 2pm, weather permitting. Meet outside Suzanne's Gift Shop on Victoria Parade.

## Shopping

Whitstable is the place to go for unusual art, crafts, and other goodies. At 30 Harbour St., **Mosaic ★** (**✆ 01227/276-779**) sells imaginative gifts, jewelry, and homemade items from the UK and around the world, all ethically sourced. On Oxford St., **The Walker-Platt Gallery ★★** (**✆ 01227/276-718**) sells contemporary arts and crafts by British artists in a bright, airy space. Nearby, the **Fish Slab Gallery ★**, 11 Oxford St. (www.fish-slabgallery.com), showcases the work of local artists. At 44 Oxford St., **L'Image** has a good selection of antiques and reproductions in shabby chic style (**✆ 01227/366-288**).

## Where to Eat

Whitstable is an oyster-fishing port and the fresh local seafood is served everywhere in town. The best-known eatery is the **Whitstable Oyster Company ★★**, The Horsebridge (**✆ 01227/276-856;** www.whitstableoystercompany.com), a pleasingly informal restaurant easily identified by the piles of oyster shells outside. Half a dozen local oysters start at £9. But if you're looking for oysters, you don't have to look far—the quayside is awash with stalls selling the little mollusks (you can get half a dozen shucked for £4.40 from **Wheelers Oyster Bar ★**, 8 High

Morelli's Italian gelato parlor.

St. (✆ **01227/273-311**)). If you prefer your seafood cooked, head to the **Fish Market** on the harbor, where the day's catch is fried up and served outside; or go upstairs to the **Crab and Winkle ★** restaurant (✆ **01227/779-377;** www.crabandwinklerestaurant.co.uk) for a wider-ranging menu.

While visiting Broadstairs, it's imperative to pop into **Morelli's ★★** Italian gelato parlor (www.morellisgelato.com) in Victoria Parade, an institution that has been dishing out delicious ice cream from this spot since 1932.

# 8

# SUGGESTIONS FOR LONGER DAY TRIPS

There are a few places just a little farther away from London that can be visited in a day if you set off early in the morning, although we have suggested some accommodation options if you decide that two days would provide a more relaxing timescale to see everything they have to offer. The historic city walls of York surround a magnificent Gothic cathedral, the winding half-timbered 'Shambles' and an attractive city centre, with several impressive museums, plenty of shopping opportunities, riverside pubs and the legendary Betty's Tearooms. A 14th-century castle and another impressive cathedral with the largest cloister in Europe can be found in Norwich, a city rich in medieval architecture and only a short distance to the waterways of the Norfolk Broads, which an extended stay would allow you to discover.

---

Shakespeare fans should find time for a visit to Stratford-upon-Avon, the town in which the Tudor playwright was born and later retired as a wealthy man. If everyone else appears to have had the same idea when you arrive, you can always escape the crowds with a gentle row along the River Avon, although catching a performance at the Royal Shakespeare Theatre shouldn't be missed.



## NORWICH

The British author George Borrow described Norwich as "a fine old city," and you'll probably agree as you see this beautiful assemblage of many medieval buildings, crowned by a castle and clustered on narrow lanes beneath the spires of a magnificent cathedral and 32 churches from the Middle Ages. By the late 11th century, the small Saxon settlement on the River Wensum had grown into one of the largest and most important cities in England, making its fortunes from wool. Today, remnants of its former glory are plentiful: sections of the old city walls remain, although the city has long since sprawled beyond them, and the medieval quarter is filled with tiny, winding lanes and beautifully preserved medieval buildings.

Given the distance from London, you'll want to devote a full day to Norwich. If you decide to extend the trip any farther, however, the countryside nearby is full of hidden gems, from the breathtakingly lovely, reed-covered waterways of the Norfolk Broads, to the queen's summer residence, Sandringham Palace (see p. 90).

FACING PAGE: **Detail of Norwich cathedral cloister.**

### The Norwich 12

No, this isn't the name of an infamous gang, but of a collection of stunning landmarks from Norwich's colorful past. Many of the buildings are included in our recommendations for a day in Norwich. Others include the Assembly House, built as an entertainment venue for Georgian gentry in 1755; St. James Mill, a yarn mill from the Industrial Revolution in the 1830s that transformed England (it's now an office complex); and the Art Deco City Hall, built in the 1930s and called the "foremost English public building of between the wars." For more information about visiting the Norwich 12, ask for a free booklet at the Tourist Information Centre (see above), housed in the stunning Forum complex, itself one of the "12."

## Essentials

### VISITOR INFORMATION

The **Tourist Information Centre,** The Forum, Millennium Plain (✆ **01603/ 213-999;** www.visitnorwich.co.uk), is well-stocked with maps and information. The center is open Monday to Saturday from 9:30am to 6pm (Nov–Mar to 5:30pm) and, in summer, Sundays as well, from 10:30am to 3pm. The shiny, modern Forum building also houses a digital art gallery (free admission).

### SCHEDULING CONSIDERATIONS

Try and time your visit to Norwich to coincide with one of the excellent, and free, guided tours of the cathedral (see "A Day in Norwich," below).

### GETTING THERE

#### By Train

Trains from London Liverpool St. take just under 2 hours. During the day they leave every 30 minutes; from 6pm to midnight they return every hour. Expect to pay around £45 round-trip on the day; however, the cost drops to £15 if you book just a couple of days ahead. (And sometimes just a few pounds more for a first-class ticket, too).

#### By Bus

**National Express** buses (✆ **08717/818-178;** www.nationalexpress.com) leave every hour for the 3-hour ride to Norwich. Expect to pay around £30 on the day of travel.

#### By Car

From London, head north toward Cambridge on the M11, and turn northeast at the junction with the A11, which takes you into Norwich. Much of the old city is closed to traffic, and so you'll want to use one of the carparks at the edge of the city center.

### GETTING AROUND

The central area of Norwich is easy to navigate on foot. Prince of Wales Road leads to Elm Hill and the cathedral, and the castle is just to the west. There are usually taxis waiting at the train station, or you can try **Five Star** (✆ **01603/ 455-555**).

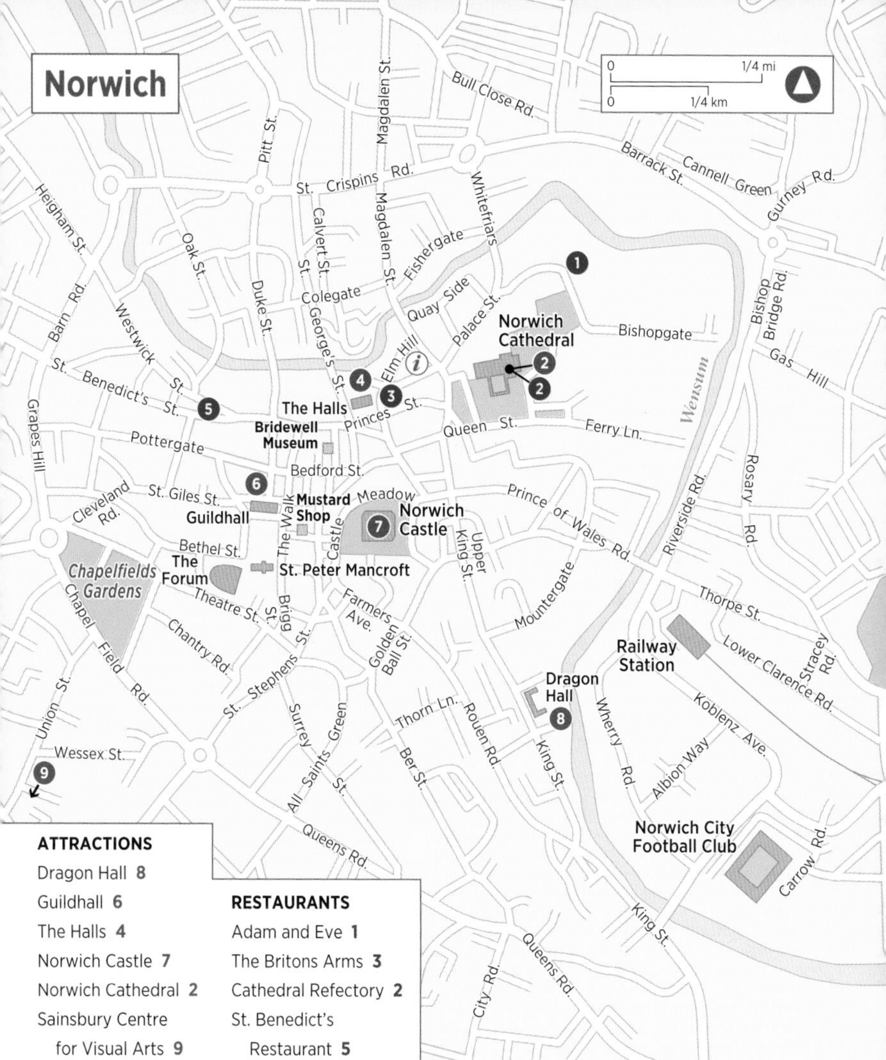


## A Day in Norwich

By far the city's most impressive sight, and certainly its most visible, is **Norwich Cathedral ★★★** (**✆ 01603/218-300;** www.cathedral.org.uk), which is considered one of the great engineering achievements of the Middle Ages. The 315-ft. (96-m) spire stretches, finger-like, above the rooftops of central Norwich. Rows of graceful columns support a high vaulted ceiling and rows of arcades, all of it light and airy, and a Romanesque masterpiece. Mirrors placed throughout the nave make it easier to view the 300 bosses of carved stone that are placed at joints in the fan-vaulted ceiling and depict biblical scenes. An enormous cloister, the largest in Europe, was once the province of the more than 250 Benedictine

monks for whom the cathedral was the center of a community devoted to worship, hospitality, and learning.

Just outside the east end of the church is the simple grave of Edith Clavell, a Norfolk nurse who was arrested and shot in Belgium during World War II for helping Allied soldiers escape, and from there a path continues past the refectory and other monastic buildings to the banks of the River Wensum. Among these medieval buildings is the **Great Hospital,** founded in 1247 to house paupers, care for the sickly poor (treatments included bloodletting and bone-setting), and dispense a dole of bread and soup. The cathedral is open daily 7:30am to 6:30pm. Guided tours are held on the hour from 11am to 3pm, every day except Sunday. Admission and tours are free, though donations are requested.

TOP: **Norwich Cathedral;** RIGHT: **The cloister of the cathedral.**

Many of Norwich's medieval houses and monuments are clustered around the cathedral on **Elm Hill.** Some of the most impressive landmarks on the hill are the **Halls ★** (✆ **01603/628-477;** www.standrewshall.co.uk), a medieval friary complex built between 1307 and 1470. In keeping with the Dominican vow of poverty, the flint stone buildings are simple and unadorned and include chapels and halls that, over the centuries, have been used as a granary, a workhouse, and a mint. There's an antiques market here every Wednesday, and book and record markets on Saturdays. The Halls are open Monday to Saturday, 9am to 5pm (but call ahead—they are often booked for private events). Admission is free.

Medieval buildings line Elm Hill.

The 14th-century **Norwich Castle ★** (✆ **01603/493-625;** www.norwich12.co.uk) may be a shadow of its former self—all that remains today is the central stone keep, or fortification—but it's found a latter-day lease of life as a museum and art gallery. Among the highlights of its collection are items from the so-called Snettisham Hoard of gold and other precious objects, believed in effect to be the crown jewels of the Iceni tribe, who fought the Romans for control of East Anglia 2,000 years ago. The castle is open Monday to Saturday from 10am to 4:30pm and Sunday from 1 to 4:30pm. Admission costs £6.20 adults, £5.30 seniors and students, and £4.40 children.

Two examples of the secular might of medieval Norwich sit beneath the castle. The elaborate, castellated **Guildhall** (✆ **01603/666-071**) reflects Norwich's prominence as England's second-largest medieval city. Most of the building isn't open to the public, but tours can be booked through the Tourist Information Centre (see above). The Mayor's Court, with its stained-glass windows and elaborate Renaissance woodwork, is particularly worth seeing. The 600 year-old **Dragon Hall ★**, on King Street (✆ **01603/663-922;** www.dragonhall.org), is an extremely rare example of a medieval trading hall—possibly the last in

## Stay the Night

If you choose to stay the night in Norwich, you might try the **DeVere Dunston Hall ★★** (Ipswich Rd., ✆ **01508/4704444,** www.devere-hotels.co.uk) at the edge of town, which is a 19th-century mansion with modern comforts. It makes good use of a historic building, and has a fabulous spa (from £120 double). Another more historic option, the **Maids Head Hotel ★** (Tombland, ✆ **01603/209955,** www.maidshead hotel.co.uk) has been in business since 1272—Elizabeth I is said to have stayed here. The beamed, low-ceilinged hotel is filled with 15th-century detail, with comfortable rooms and the choice of a convenient nightcap in the pub downstairs (from £90 double). As a budget option, consider the **Premier** Inn in the town center (Duke St., ✆ **0871/5278840,** www.premierinn.com). It has big, comfortable rooms and everything you need right in the middle of the action. (Doubles from £60.)

Reflection on the Sainsbury Centre for Visual Arts.

Europe. The building takes its name from the 14 carved, wooden dragons that adorned the massive oak beams that span the width of the Great Hall, though only one survives today. It's open Monday to Friday 10am to 4pm, Sunday noon to 4pm; admission costs £4.50 adults, £4 children, seniors, and students.

The Norman Foster-designed **Sainsbury Centre for Visual Arts ★★** (✆ **01603/593-199;** www.scva.org.uk) displays paintings by Francis Bacon, Henry Moore, Alberto Giacometti, and others. The collection also includes Art Nouveau works, and pottery and other artifacts from the ancient Mediterranean. The gallery is at the University of East Anglia, on the west side of Norwich, and can be reached using buses nos. 22, 25, and 35. It's open Tuesday to Sunday, 10am to 5pm (8pm Wed). Admission is free.

## Shopping

The backstreets and alleys of the **Norwich Lanes,** including Elm Hill and Timberhill, contain a host of intriguing independent stores, selling vintage clothing, gifts, homewares, and books. The **Royal Arcade** is a picturesque shopping area: Among its offerings is The **Colman's Mustard Shop,** 15 Royal Arcade (✆ **01603/627-889;** www.colmansmustardshop.com), selling nostalgic knick-knacks relating to the distinctive local mustard, made here since the 19th century. Opposite the cathedral, the **Tombland Antiques Centre,** 14 Tombland (✆ **01603/619-129**), houses 60 antique dealers across three floors. Popular, high-street stores

Vintage tin in the Colman's Mustard Shop.

## Nearby

Norwich lies at the western edge of the **Norfolk Broads ★★★**, a vast wetland of marshes and woods that comprise some of the most uniquely beautiful scenery in England. They can be explored by boat, bike, or on foot. Begin at the tourism office at **Wroxham,** 7 miles (11km) northeast of Norwich (✆ **01603-782-281;** open daily Easter to Oct, 9am–1pm and 2–5pm). For a boat tour, contact **Norfolk Broads Direct** (✆ **01603/782-281;** www.broads.co.uk); a half-day costs about £8 for adults and £6 for children.

Fourteen miles (23km) north of Norwich, the grand 17th-century **Blickling Hall ★★** (✆ **01603/493-625;** www.nationatrust.org.uk) claims to be Britain's most haunted house. According to lore, Anne Boleyn crosses the grounds in a horse-drawn carriage, severed head in hand. Blickling's more earthly highlights include the cavernous Long Gallery and extraordinary historic library. It's open March to October, Wednesday to Sunday, from 11am to 5pm (also Mon in midsummer). Admission is £8.85 for adults and £4.40 for children.

The waterside at Wroxham.

Blickling Hall.

can be found in two large shopping centers: **The Mall,** in the city center on Castle Mall, and **Chapelfield,** next to the bus station on St. Stephen's Street. In the town center on Gentlemans Walk near City hall, **Norwich Market** (✆ **01603/213537**) is a large bustling covered market with nearly 200 sellers peddling everything from food to secondhand goods and clothes. The market has been in operation for centuries – there's even mention of a market in Norwich in the 1086 Domesday book. Open Monday to Saturday 9am to 5pm.

## Where to Eat

Housed in a thatched cottage that started life as a medieval women's refuge, **The Britons Arms,** 9 Elm Hill (✆ **01603/623-367**), serves freshly prepared light meals and cakes. The equally venerable **Adam and Eve** (✆ **01603/667-423**), thought to have been an inn since the 13th century, serves basic but tasty bar food, including homemade pies. **St. Benedict's Restaurant,** 9 St. Benedict's St. (✆ **01603/765-377;** www.stbenedictsrestaurant.co.uk), has a delicious but affordable set menu featuring salmon crabcakes and vegetable moussaka (two courses £9.95). After wandering around the cathedral, the **Cathedral Refectory,** in an airily beamed stone building on the grounds, is a decent venue for a coffee break or small meal. Light lunches such as mixed salads or fajitas are priced from £5.50 to £7.00.

Norwich market.

# STRATFORD-UPON-AVON

This market town on the River Avon, 91 miles (146km) northwest of London, is a shrine to the world's greatest playwright, William Shakespeare, who was born, lived much of his life, and is buried here. Stratford boasts many fine and beautifully preserved Tudor, Elizabethan, and Jacobean buildings, but it's not really a quaint village anymore. If you arrive by train, your first glimpse is of a vast carpark across from the station. Don't let this put you off. The charms of Stratford's formerly bucolic setting haven't been completely lost, and you'll find plenty of quaint corners as you explore. If the weather is cooperative, you can escape the crowds and float along the River Avon in the company of swans. Besides the literary pilgrimage sights, the top draw in Stratford is the Royal Shakespeare Theatre, where Britain's foremost actors perform.

There's so much to see here that, though it's possible to do it all in a long day, many people prefer to stay overnight so they can take their time.

## Essentials

### VISITOR INFORMATION

Stratford's **Tourist Information Centre,** Bridgefoot (✆ **0870/160-7930;** www.shakespeare-country.co.uk), provides information and maps of the town and its principal sights. It also has a currency exchange and a room-booking service (open Apr–Sept Mon–Sat 9am–5:30pm, Sun 10am–4pm; Oct–Mar Mon–Sat 9am–5pm, Sun 10am–3pm).

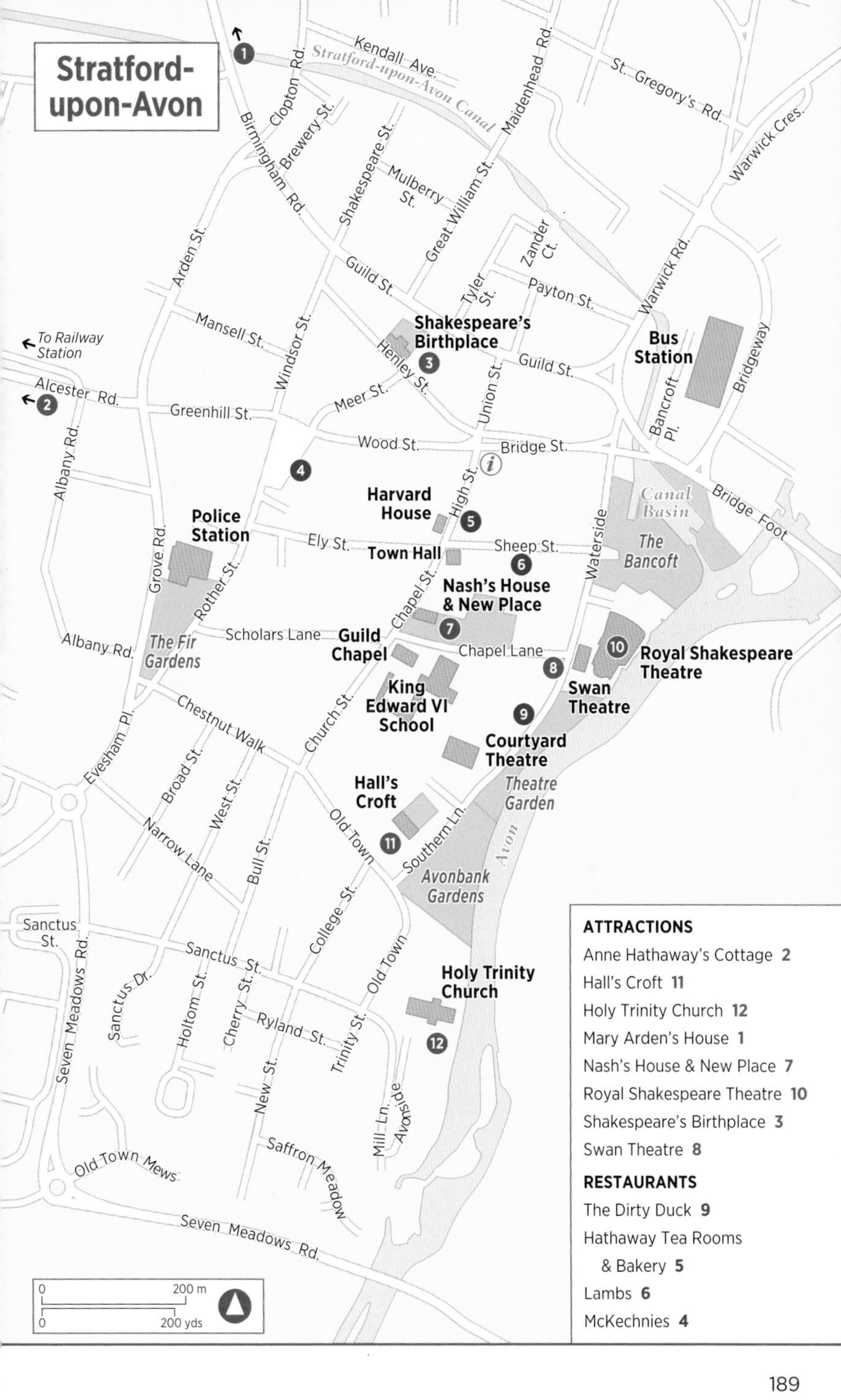

Stratford-upon-Avon
Stratford-upon-Avon Canal
Kendall Ave.
St. Gregory's Rd.
Warwick Cres.
Clopton Rd.
Brewery St.
Birmingham Rd.
Maidenhead Rd.
Shakespeare St.
Mulberry St.
Great William St.
Arden St.
Zander Ct.
Tyler St.
Guild St.
Payton St.
Warwick Rd.
Mansell St.
Windsor St.
Shakespeare's Birthplace
Henley St.
Guild St.
Bus Station
Bridgeway
To Railway Station
Alcester Rd.
Greenhill St.
Meer St.
Union St.
Bancroft Pl.
Wood St.
Bridge St.
Albany Rd.
Harvard House
High St.
Canal Basin
Bridge Foot
Police Station
Ely St.
Town Hall
Sheep St.
Waterside
The Bancroft
Grove Rd.
Rother St.
Chapel St.
Nash's House & New Place
Scholars Lane
Guild Chapel
Chapel Lane
Royal Shakespeare Theatre
Albany Rd.
The Fir Gardens
Swan Theatre
King Edward VI School
Chestnut Walk
Church St.
Courtyard Theatre
Evesham Pl.
Broad St.
Theatre Garden
Hall's Croft
West St.
Narrow Lane
Old Town
Southern Ln.
Avon
Bull St.
Avonbank Gardens
College St.
Sanctus St.
Seven Meadows Rd.
Sanctus St.
Old Town
Holy Trinity Church
Sanctus Dr.
Holtom St.
Cherry St.
Ryland St.
Trinity St.
New St.
Mill Ln.
Avonside
Saffron Meadow
Old Town Mews
Seven Meadows Rd.
0 200 m
0 200 yds
ATTRACTIONS
Anne Hathaway's Cottage 2
Hall's Croft 11
Holy Trinity Church 12
Mary Arden's House 1
Nash's House & New Place 7
Royal Shakespeare Theatre 10
Shakespeare's Birthplace 3
Swan Theatre 8
RESTAURANTS
The Dirty Duck 9
Hathaway Tea Rooms & Bakery 5
Lambs 6
McKechnies 4

> **Enjoying a Shakespeare Combo**
>
> There are five properties in Stratford connected with Shakespeare and if you plan to visit a few, if not all of them, a combination ticket saves you money. It's priced at £19.50 for adults, £17.50 for seniors and students, and £12 for children. You can purchase the ticket at any Shakespeare property (✆ **01789/204-016;** www.shakespeare.org.uk).

## SCHEDULING CONSIDERATIONS

All of the Shakespeare properties keep basically the same hours, opening daily between 10 and 11am and closing at 5pm. They open slightly earlier in the summer and close an hour earlier in the winter. The town can be very crowded on summer weekends. Crowds are heaviest from June through mid-September; if you're visiting during those times, you'll find the town less congested on weekdays. If you want to see a play at the **Royal Shakespeare Theatre,** book ahead. The theater is closed during October.

## GETTING THERE

### By Train

There are two or three direct trains a day from London Marylebone station to Stratford-upon-Avon, but you can travel anytime changing at Birmingham. The journey takes about 2½ hours and tickets start at around £40 for the round-trip. Note that on this route, tickets are significantly cheaper if purchased in advance. You can buy online and collect your tickets at the station.

### By Bus

**National Express** (✆ **08717/818-178;** www.nationalexpress.com) offers a daily express bus service from London Victoria bus station; the trip takes just under 4 hours and costs about £25 round-trip.

### By Car

By car from London, take the M40 toward Oxford and then onto Stratford-upon-Avon, leaving at exit 15. Allow 3 hours for the trip.

## GETTING AROUND

Stratford is compact and can be explored easily on foot. The train and bus stations are less than a 15 minute walk from the town center. Pop into the Tourist Information Centre to pick up a map. Some of Stratford's sights are at the edge of town, though, and for these you may need transportation (if you don't like long walks). Try **Main Taxis** (✆ **01789/414-514**) or **Elite Taxis** (✆ **01789/296-666**). **City Sightseeing** (see under "Organized Tours," below) runs a convenient hop-on/hop-off bus service to all the Shakespeare properties.

# A Day in Stratford-upon-Avon

The obvious place to begin your exploration of Stratford is the sprawling, half-timbered building called simply **Shakespeare's Birthplace ★★★**. It's very hard to miss on busy Henley Street (✆ **01789/204-016;** www.shakespeare.org.uk) due to the crowds usually around it. This is where the writer, son of a glover and wool merchant, was born in 1564. You enter through the modern **Shakespeare Centre ☺,** where exhibits illustrate his life and times. It's geared primarily at children, though, and you would be forgiven for hurrying on into the house. The house, filled with Shakespeare memorabilia, is actually composed of two 16th-century half-timbered houses joined together. You can visit the bedroom where Shakespeare was born, the living room, and a fully restored Tudor-style kitchen. Opening hours are generally April through October daily 10am to 5pm (closing 6pm in July and Aug only) and November through March daily 11am to 4pm. Admission is £12.50 for adults, £8 for children 5 to 16.

Shakespeare's Birthplace.

On Chapel Street, a lush walled garden is virtually all that remains of **New Place** (✆ **01789/204-016;** www.shakespeare.org.uk), where a prosperous Shakespeare retired in 1610 and died in 1616. The Bard bought the house for the then-astronomical sum of £60. The Reverend Francis Gastrill, who owned it in the 18th century, allegedly tore the house down rather than continue paying taxes on it. He said he couldn't live in it because of the hordes of Shakespeare fans. You enter the garden through **Nash's House,** which belonged to Thomas Nash, husband of Shakespeare's granddaughter. The house contains 16th-century period rooms and an exhibit illustrating the history of Stratford. Hours are daily April through October 10am to 5pm, and November through March 11am to 4pm.

A bedroom inside Hall's Croft.

Shakespeare's tomb, Holy Trinity Church.

Anne Hathaway's Cottage.

A 5-minute walk away in Old Town, **Hall's Croft ★★** is the magnificent Tudor house where Shakespeare's daughter Susanna and her husband, Dr. John Hall, lived. The house is furnished in the style of a middle-class 17th-century home and has an absorbing exhibit on medicine of that time. It has the same opening hours as New Place/Nash's House.

From Hall's Croft, it's a short walk down Southern Lane, which runs beside the river, to Trinity Street and the footpath to **Holy Trinity Church ★** (✆ **01789/266-316**), where Shakespeare is buried. He died on his birthday, April 23, 1616, at age 52. His tomb lies in the chancel in front of the altar. Alongside his grave are those of his wife, Anne, and other members of his family. On the north wall a bust of Shakespeare overlooks the room: it was erected 7 years after his death—within the lifetime of his family and friends—and is believed to be a true likeness. The church is open April through September Monday to Saturday 8:30am to 6pm (9am–4pm in winter), and Sunday year-round from 12:30 to 5pm. The church is free, but to see the grave costs £2.

About a mile south of the town center, **Anne Hathaway's Cottage ★★★** is the childhood home of Shakespeare's long-suffering wife. (When Shakespeare died, his will included nothing for his wife except his "second best bed.") Of all the Shakespeare properties, this one is most evocative of the Tudor period; a pretty thatched wattle-and-daub cottage surrounded by gardens. The Hathaway family were yeoman farmers, and their descendants lived in the cottage until 1892. As a result, it was never renovated and provides a rare insight into family life in the 16th century. Many original furnishings, including kitchen utensils and the courting settle (the bench on which Shakespeare is said to have wooed Anne), are still there. Before leaving, be sure to stroll through the beautiful garden and orchard. The house is on Cottage Lane in the village of Shottery about 1 mile (1.6km) south of Stratford. To get there, walk along the well-marked country path from Evesham Place or hop on a bus from Bridge Street. It has the same opening hours as New Place and Hall's Croft.

## All the World's a Stage

If you want to catch a performance at the **Royal Shakespeare Theatre,** advance booking is recommended. For **ticket reservations** book online or call ✆ **0844/800-1110.** A small number of tickets are always held for sale on the day of a performance, but it may be too late to get a good seat if you wait until you arrive in Stratford. The box office is open Monday to Saturday 9am to 8pm. Seats range in price from £5 to £35.

The last Shakespeare property is **Mary Arden's House & the Shakespeare Countryside Museum ★** in Wilmcote, about 3.5 miles (5.5km) north of Stratford on the A34. The redbrick house where Shakespeare's mother, Mary Arden, grew up has hardly changed. Dating from 1514, the house contains country furniture and domestic utensils; the extensive collection of farm implements in the barns and outbuildings illustrate life and work in the local countryside from Shakespeare's time to the present. To reach the house, follow signs to Wilmcote or take the City Sightseeing bus (see "Organized Tours," below).

Completely refurbished in 2010, the **Royal Shakespeare Theatre,** Waterside (✆ **01789/403-403;** www.rsc.org.uk), is a major showcase for the acclaimed Royal Shakespeare Company (RSC), with a season that runs from April to November, and typically features five Shakespeare plays. The RSC also stages productions in the smaller **Swan Theatre** next door. Even if you're not seeing a performance, you can take a guided **Theatre Tour.** It lasts an hour and

Mary Arden's House & the Shakespeare Countryside Museum.

takes you behind the scenes. Tours run every two hours from 9:15am (Mon–Sat) and from 10:15am (Sunday). Tickets cost £6.50 for adults and £3 for under-18s.

Royal Shakespeare Theatre.

## ORGANIZED TOURS

The **Stratford Town Walk** ★ (✆ **01789/292-478;** www.stratfordtownwalk.co.uk) is a lively and absorbing 2-hour insider's tour of Shakespeare's Stratford. It departs daily (Mon–Wed at 11am, Thurs–Sun at 2pm) from the Swan Fountain near the Royal Shakespeare Theatre. No need to book a place; just show up: £5 for adults, £4 for seniors and students, and £2 for children 15 and under.

**City Sightseeing,** 14 Rother St. (✆ **01708/866-000;** www.city-sightseeing.com), is a hop-on/hop-off guided tour of Stratford that leaves from outside the tourist office. Open-top, double-decker buses depart every 15 to 30 minutes daily between 9:30am and 5:30pm (until 3:30pm in winter). You can hop off at all five Shakespeare properties, including Mary Arden's House in Wilmcote, although your bus ticket isn't admission to the houses. The bus tour costs £11.75 for adults, £9.75 for seniors and students, and £6 for children 11 and under. You can buy your ticket on the bus.

## OUTDOOR ACTIVITIES

**Avon Boating** (✆ **01789/267-073**) offers 30-minute cruises on the River Avon in traditional Edwardian launches, with regular departures Easter through October (10am–dusk) from Swan's Nest Boatyard near the Royal Shakespeare

### Stay the Night

Close to the train station, **Penryn House ★,** 126 Alcester Rd. (✆ **01789/293-718;** www.penrynguesthouse.co.uk), is convenient and affordable. Rooms are small, but well furnished, and breakfasts are made with local eggs and bacon. Double rooms cost from £60 to £70.

In Stratford's oldest building, the **White Swan ★,** Rother St. (✆ **01789/297-022;** www.white-swan-stratford.co.uk), is atmospheric and romantic. Rooms are comfortable if not big or modern, but this place is all about history and ambiance. The walls are decorated with art 500 years old. A standard double or twin room costs £85.

**The Stratford,** Arden St., (✆ **01789/271-001;** www.qhotels.co.uk), is definitely not one of the atmospheric inns of Stratford-upon-Avon. But if you prefer a modern hotel with up-to-date conveniences when paying your call to the Bard, this hotel is for you. Bedrooms are spacious and elegant, some come with four-poster beds, and doubles are priced from £79 to £114.

## Nearby

Eight miles (13km) northeast of Stratford, **Warwick Castle ★** (image above) (✆ **0870/442-2000** for recorded information; www.warwick-castle.co.uk) stands nobly above the River Avon as it has since A.D. 914. Much of the enormous castle was built in the 14th century and it's thoroughly medieval, with chunky towers, crenellated battlements, and a moat surrounded by gardens, lawns, and woodland. Scattered through the castle apartments (restored to the way they appeared in the late 19th century) are lifelike wax figures, created by Madame Tussauds, to represent famous figures who visited the castle and the servants who kept the place running. There's a scary dungeon, battlements to walk on, and towers to explore, as well as playgrounds for kids. It's all good, touristy fun. It's open daily 10am to 6pm, closing at 5pm from early October to March. Admission costs £18.60 for adults, £15 for students, and £13.80 seniors and children 4 to 16. To get there, **Chiltern Railways** (✆ **08705/165-165;** www.chilternrailways.co.uk) runs direct trains to Warwick from Stratford-upon-Avon; the trip takes 20 to 30 minutes. By car from Stratford, take the A439 and the A46 to the M40 and then follow Stratford Road and the Warwick signs for 2 miles (3km). Bus tours of Warwick Castle from Stratford-upon-Avon are available through City Sightseeing (see above).



Theatre. The cost is £4 for adults, £3 for seniors, £2.50 for children. Rowboats, punts, and canoes can be rented for £3 per hour.

## Shopping

Stratford's weekly **Market,** held every Friday on Rother Street, dates back more than 800 years. The **Shakespeare Bookshop ★**, in the Shakespeare Centre, Henley St. (✆ **01789/201-819**), is the region's best bookshop for Shakespeare-related material. The nearby **Pickwick Gallery ★**, 32 Henley St. (✆ **01789/294-861**), carries a wide variety of old and new engravings. **Elaine Rippon Craft Gallery ★★**, Shakespeare Craft Yard off Henley St. (✆ **01789/415-481**), designs, creates, and sells sumptuous silk and velvet accessories and carries fine British crafts.

## Where to Eat

Stop in for afternoon tea and cakes at the **Hathaway Tea Rooms & Bakery ★**, 19 High St. (✆ **01789/292-404**). The scones are light and airy, and it's all served up in a building that dates to 1610. For more substantial cuisine, **Lambs ★★,** 12 Sheep St. (✆ **01789/292-554;** www.lambsrestaurant.co.uk), serves meaty English classics, priced from £10.95 to £16.50, at a location near the Royal Shakespeare Theatre. **McKechnies,** 37 Rother St. (✆ **01789/299-575;** www.mckechniescafe.talktalk.net), is a cozy cafe near the market on Rother Street priding itself on locally sourced food. Its toasted sandwiches and zesty soups make a perfect lunch for about £5. **The Dirty Duck ★★** on Waterside near the theater (✆ **01789/297-312;** www.dirtyduck-pub-stratford-upon-avon.co.uk) has been a traditional hangout for actors from the RSC since the 18th century. It serves real ale and classic pub lunches, including a range of burgers (mains £7.50–£10.50).

Hathaway Tea Rooms & Bakery.



# YORK

Surrounded by ancient city walls and dominated by a huge cathedral, York is one of the most historic cities in England and one of the best-preserved medieval cities in Europe. York began life as a Roman fort and settlement known as Eboracum, and then became the Saxon Eofowic, capital of Northumbria, and then a thriving Viking settlement called Jorvik. Finally, after the Norman Conquest under William the Conqueror, the city became known as York, a thriving port and trade center. For thousands of years it acted as a guardian of the north with Romans, Saxons, Vikings, and Normans all using it as a fortress to protect their hold on the region. After the cathedral was built here in the 12th century though, the city's role changed, and it became a religious center and market town. You can still see elements of the past everywhere you go—this is a piece of history you can walk through. But York is a thriving modern city, too, and its workaday life coexists smoothly with the tourism hubbub.

The enormous York Minster, the largest Gothic structure north of the Alps, dominates the city, along with the ancient city walls and fortified gateways, dating in part to Roman times. You can soak up the city's history while exploring its maze of ancient streets and winding hidden walkways, known as "snickelways."

Most of York's attractions can be visited in a day, but there's plenty here to induce an overnight stay.

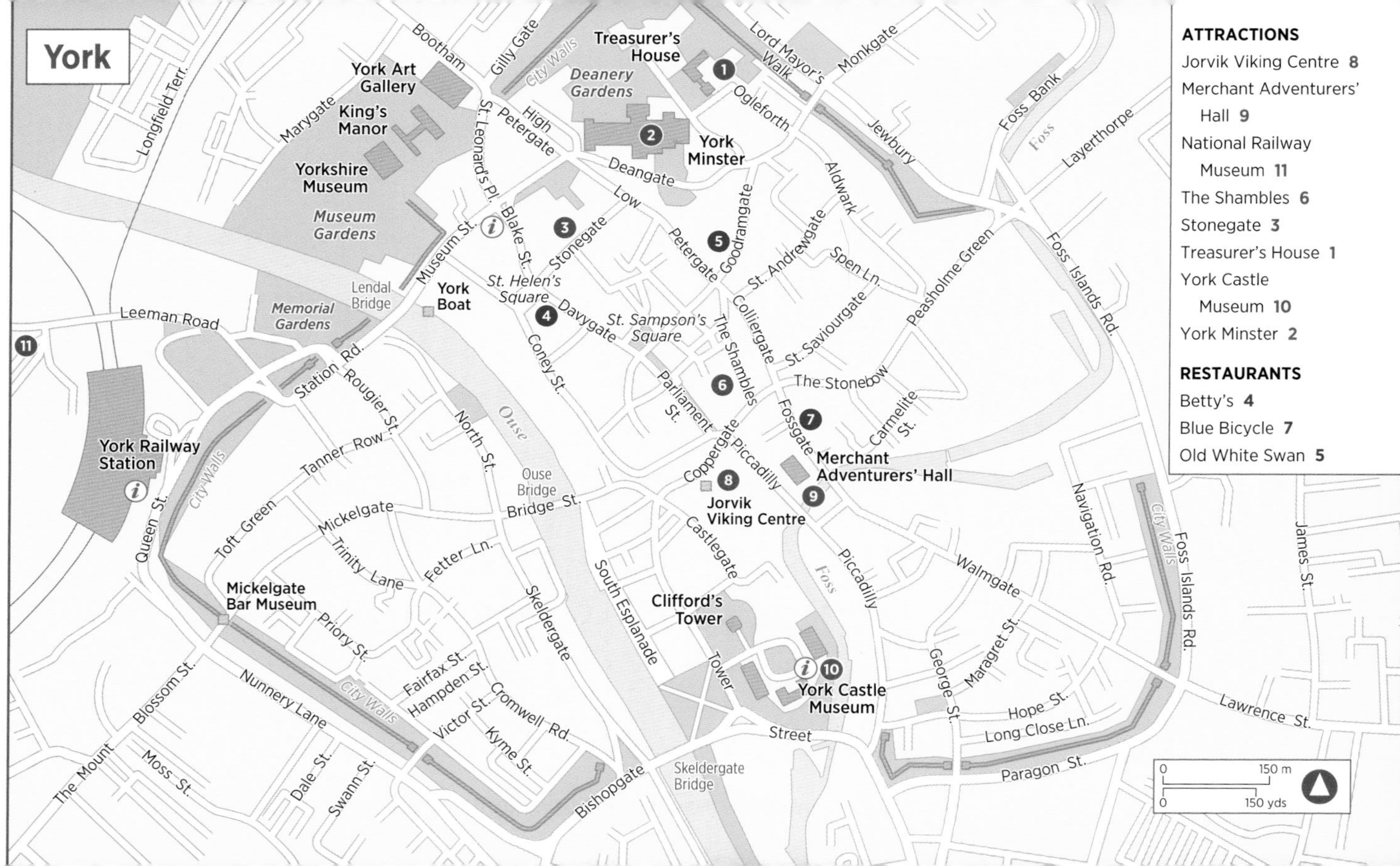
York
ATTRACTIONS
Jorvik Viking Centre 8
Merchant Adventurers' Hall 9
National Railway Museum 11
The Shambles 6
Stonegate 3
Treasurer's House 1
York Castle Museum 10
York Minster 2
RESTAURANTS
Betty's 4
Blue Bicycle 7
Old White Swan 5
0 150 m
0 150 yds
Longfield Terr.
Bootham
Gilly Gate
City Walls
Treasurer's House
Deanery Gardens
York Art Gallery
King's Manor
Marygate
Lord Mayor's Walk
Monkgate
Ogleforth
High Petergate
St. Leonard's Pl.
York Minster
Jewbury
Foss Bank
Foss
Layerthorpe
Yorkshire Museum
Museum Gardens
Deangate
Low
Aldwark
Blake St.
Stonegate
Goodramgate
Petergate
St. Andrewgate
Spen Ln.
Peasholme Green
Foss Islands Rd.
Museum St.
Lendal Bridge
York Boat
St. Helen's Square
Davygate
St. Sampson's Square
Colliergate
The Shambles
St. Saviourgate
Memorial Gardens
Leeman Road
Station Rd.
Rougier St.
Coney St.
Parliament St.
The Stonebow
Carmelite St.
Fossgate
York Railway Station
Tanner Row
North St.
Ouse
Coppergate
Piccadilly
Merchant Adventurers' Hall
Ouse Bridge
Bridge St.
Jorvik Viking Centre
Navigation Rd.
James St.
Toft Green
Mickelgate
Queen St.
Trinity Lane
Fetter Ln.
Castlegate
Walmgate
Skeldergate
South Esplanade
Mickelgate Bar Museum
Clifford's Tower
Priory St.
Margaret St.
George St.
Tower
York Castle Museum
Hope St.
Lawrence St.
Blossom St.
Nunnery Lane
Fairfax St.
Hampden St.
Victor St.
Cromwell Rd.
Kyme St.
Street
Long Close Ln.
Paragon St.
The Mount
Moss St.
Dale St.
Swann St.
Bishopgate
Skeldergate Bridge

 York Pass

The York Pass, available online at **www.yorkpass.com** or at either of the city's tourist information centers, grants you free admission to 30 attractions, public transport around the city, and discounts on dining. It includes admission to York Minster, the Merchant Adventurers' Hall, Treasurer's House, York Castle Museum, and nearby Castle Howard. A one-day pass is £34 for adults and £18 for children.



## Essentials

### VISITOR INFORMATION

A convenient branch of the **Tourist Information Centre** is in the train station so you can pick up a map at the very start. The main **Tourist Information Centre** on Museum Street (✆ **01904/550-099;** www.visityork.org), near York Minster, is also helpful. Both branches are open Monday through Saturday from 9am to 5pm (to 6pm in summer), and Sunday from 10am to 4pm (to 5pm in summer).

### SCHEDULING CONSIDERATIONS

York is a popular place and draws visitors year-round, especially on weekends and from Easter through the summer months. If you want the city more to yourself, visit from mid-October to mid-March, but be aware of reduced hours at many attractions.

### GETTING THERE

#### By Train

East Coast trains leave every 30 minutes from King's Cross for the 2-hour trip to York. Advance-purchase round-trip tickets cost about £65, but tickets will cost much more if purchased on the day of travel. York station is a 5-minute walk into the city center, across the river—head left from the station, follow the road down the hill, and to the right.

#### By Bus

**National Express** buses (✆ **08717/818-178;** www.nationalexpress.com) travel from London's Victoria bus station to York several times a day. Tickets start at £23, but the journey takes around 5½ hours.

#### By Car

If you're driving from London, take the M1 expressway north to exit 45, east of Leeds, and from there continue northeast on the A64 to York. The drive takes 3½ to 4 hours. Park in one of the carparks outside the city walls and walk into the city; there's no driving or parking in the center.

### GETTING AROUND

The train station is a 5-minute walk from York's pedestrian-friendly historic city center, which is where you'll want to spend your time and is easily traversed on foot. If you need a taxi, contact **Station Taxis** (✆ **01904/623-332**).

## A Day in York

Begin your day at **York Minster ★★★**, Minster Yard (✆ **01904/557-216**). The largest Gothic cathedral in Northern Europe was begun in 1220, when Archbishop Walter de Grey set out to build a cathedral to rival the one in Canterbury. Before entering, walk around the exterior to take in the massive size of the structure—534 ft. (160m) long, 249 ft. (75m) at its widest point, 90 ft. (27m) high. Light in the cavernous interior is diffused by the medieval stained glass (the cathedral contains fully half of all the stained glass in England); the Great West Window, with stained glass dating from 1338, is called the "Heart of Yorkshire." A 15th-century choir screen decorated with statues of 15 kings of England, from William I (the Conqueror) to Henry VI, separates the nave from the choir. In the south transept, you can descend into the undercroft, where excavations have revealed the Roman basilica that stood here nearly 2,000 years ago, as well as portions of a Roman street and an earlier Norman cathedral. From the nave, a separate entrance leads to the 13th-century octagonal chapter house, filled with superlative stone carvings and medieval glass. You can ascend the mighty tower for a fabulous view of York and the surrounding countryside. The minster is open Monday to Saturday from 9am to 6:30pm

RIGHT: **Medieval stained glass windows;** BOTTOM: **York Minster.**

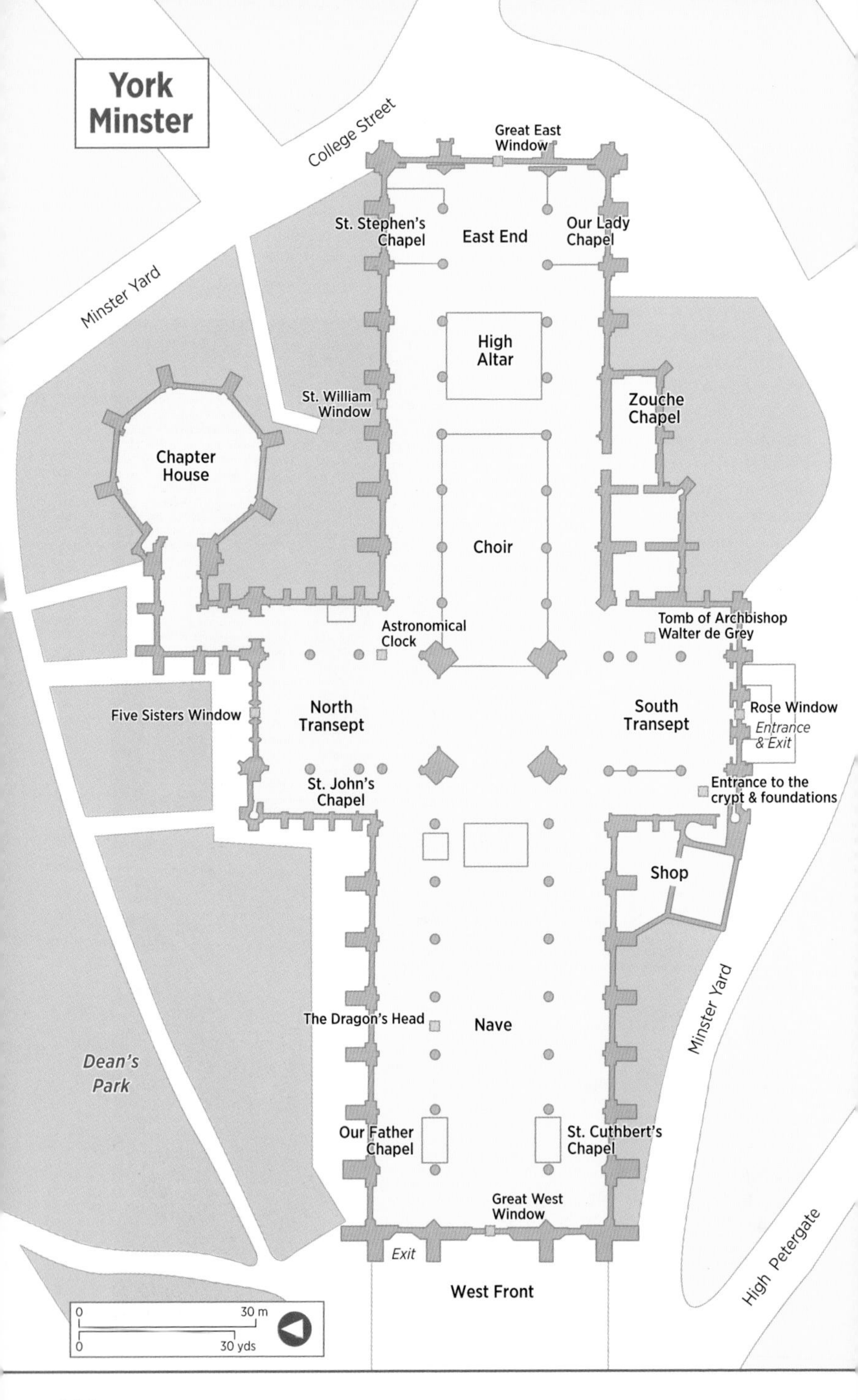
York Minster
College Street
Minster Yard
Great East Window
St. Stephen's Chapel
East End
Our Lady Chapel
High Altar
St. William Window
Zouche Chapel
Chapter House
Choir
Astronomical Clock
Tomb of Archbishop Walter de Grey
Five Sisters Window
North Transept
South Transept
Rose Window
Entrance & Exit
St. John's Chapel
Entrance to the crypt & foundations
Shop
Minster Yard
The Dragon's Head
Nave
Dean's Park
Our Father Chapel
St. Cuthbert's Chapel
Great West Window
Exit
West Front
High Petergate
0
30 m
0
30 yds

(5:30 in winter), and Sunday noon to 4pm. Admission is £9 for adults, £8 for seniors, free for children 16 and under.

Next to the cathedral, in Minster Yard, stands an elegant stone house known as **Treasurer's House ★** (✆ **01904/624-247**). Built in 1620 to house the treasurers of York Minster, the house and its gardens were extensively remodeled during the Victorian era by an eccentric collector. Inside are beautiful period rooms with collections of 17th- and 18th-century furniture, glass, and china. It's open mid-March through November, Saturday through Thursday from 11am to 4:30pm (until 3pm in Nov). Admission is £5.90 for adults, £3 for children 5 to 15. The peaceful walled garden is free to visit.

The Shambles.

Virtually in front of the Minster, **Stonegate ★★** is a wide, pedestrian street heading toward the river and lined on both sides by shop fronts from as far back as Tudor times. The tiny statues perched above shop windows acted as business signs in an age when most people couldn't read. Keep an eye out for the red devil, this figure once represented a printers shop, a common symbol in those days for this trade. The apprentices that worked here were known as the 'printers devils.'

Heading off Stonegate into the tangle of medieval streets around the Minster, Petergate leads you to **The Shambles ★**. Up until 150 years ago, the Shambles was a street where butchers displayed their finest cuts in open windows on wide shelves called *shammels*. Today this narrow, winding lane where the half-timbered buildings are so close together they nearly shut out the light is filled with a combination of touristy gift shops and specialty stores, but the old butchers hooks still hang from many walls.

A short walk away on Piccadilly, the 14th-century stone and half-timbered structure is the **Merchant Adventurers' Hall ★** (✆ **01904/654-818;** www.theyorkcompany.co.uk). With a great hall on the main floor and a hospital and a chapel below, it served York's most powerful guild, the Merchant Adventurers. (Adventurers, in this context, means investors, and members profited from trade into and out of the city.) It's open Monday through Thursday 9am to 5pm (Nov–Feb only until 4pm), Friday and Saturday 9am to 4pm (until 3:30 in winter), and Sunday 11am to 4pm (closed Sun in winter). Admission is £6 for adults, £5 for seniors and students, and free for children 16 and under.

Backtrack on Piccadilly to Coppergate, where you turn south and then turn east on Castlegate to the **Jorvik Viking Centre** ☺ (✆ **01904/643-211;** www.jorvik.co.uk). There you can hop into a "time car" and be transported back to A.D. 948, when Eric Bloodaxe was king and York was Jorvik, a thriving Viking port and trading town. The scenes you pass—of village life, market stalls, crowded houses, and the wharf—are re-creations based on archaeological finds in this area; open

Jorvik Viking Centre.

daily from 10am to 5pm (Nov–Mar only until 4pm). Admission is £9.25 for adults, £7.25 for seniors and students, and £6.25 for children 5 to 15.

Continue on Castlegate to **York Castle Museum ★** (© **01904/653-611;** www.yorkcastlemuseum.org.uk), housed in a former castle and debtors prison and today the most popular folk museum in the country. Using a treasure-trove of now-vanished everyday objects, the exhibitions re-create slices of life from the last 400 years. A highlight of the museum is the recently re-vamped Kirkgate Street, re-creating shops, a school, and even a padded cell, all as they would have looked and felt in the Victorian period. The museum is open daily 9:30am to 5pm. Admission is £8.50 for adults and free for under-16s. The ticket is valid for one year, covering as many visits as you wish.

Nearby, the station on Leeman Rd., the **National Railway Museum ★** (© **01904/621-261;** www.nrm.org.uk), is packed with working vintage locomotives and antique railway cars, the earliest dating from the 1840s. Peek into the windows of private royal trains, including Queen Victoria's plush 1869 coach (open daily from 10am–6pm, admission is free).

## Climbing the Walls

**Some 3 miles (5km) of stone walls surround York city center and a walk along the top of them takes you along 2,000 years of history. The Romans raised the first walls around the city, and these were rebuilt and strengthened by Vikings and Normans. The walls are crossed by fortified medieval gates, called "bars." One, Monk's Bar, still has its portcullis. Micklegate Bar is the most elaborately decorated, because this was the entrance used by the royal family. Staircases can be found near each bar, and you can walk along the walls to the lookout towers for free.**

## ORGANIZED TOURS

The **York Association of Voluntary Guides** (© **01904/640-780**) offers free, 2-hour guided tours of the city. The tours depart daily, year-round, at 10:15am from the front of the York Art Gallery in Exhibition Square. Additional tours are offered at 6:45pm from June to August. You don't need a reservation; just show up.

**Yorkwalk** (© **01904/622-303;** www.yorkwalk.co.uk) leads 2-hour guided walks that focus on Roman York, hidden alleyways (snickelways), the walls, and other elements of the city. Guides are extremely well-informed and provide fascinating commentary; cost is £5.50 for adults, £5 for seniors and students, £4 for children. Call or check the website to find out what tours are on offer while you're in town.

TOP: **National Railway Museum;** RIGHT: **The Roman walls of York.**

Allegedly the most haunted city in Britain, York is hugely popular with ghost hunters and those who believe in a spectral world. There are many ghost tour options—the tourism office can bury you in information. A good one to try is the **Original Ghost Walk** (© **01947/603-159;** www.theoriginalghostwalkofyork.co.uk). It's a thorough and knowledgeable look at the city's most famous ghosts. Tours start at 8pm in front of the King's Arms Pub on Ouse Bridge, and cost £4.50 for adults and £3 for students, seniors and children under 15.

## Shopping

High-end shops, including designer clothes boutiques and fine jewelry, are found on **Swinegate ★**. The area around **Stonegate** has a balanced mix of independent shops and chain boutiques. **Newgate Market,** between Parliament Street and the Shambles, is York's biggest open-air market, open daily with stalls selling crafts, clothes, candles, you name it. Appropriately for such a historic city, York has lots of antiques and antique jewelry stores. Try **Red House Antiques Centre ★★**, 1 Duncombe Pl. (just south of York Minster; ✆ **01904/637-000**), where 60 dealers sell quality merchandise. The **York Antiques Centre ★**, 2 Lendal St. (✆ **01904/641-445**), has 25 small dealers selling antique jewelry, clothes, and furniture.

Assorted pastries and cakes at Betty's.

## Where to Eat

The most famous eatery in York is the tea shop at the end of Stonegate, **Betty's** (✆ **01904/659-142;** www.bettys.co.uk), where pots of tea and warm scones studded with raisins have been served since 1912. The sunny dining room is an ideal place to take an afternoon break, but it's so popular there's almost always a wait for a table. The **Old White Swan ★★★**, Goodramgate (✆ **01904/540-911;** www.nicholsonspubs.co.uk), is a fine pub in a sprawling medieval building,

### Stay the Night

If you choose to stay the night in York, there are plenty of options. **The Hazelwood ★**, 24–25 Portland St. (✆ **01904/626-548;** www.thehazelwoodyork.com), is a 19th-century home on a quiet lane inside the city walls. Rooms are well furnished (doubles cost £85–£120) and breakfasts are enormous. If you want to splurge a bit, the **Hotel du Vin ★★**, 89 The Mount (✆ **01094/557-350;** www.hotelduvin.com), just outside the city walls, is a lovely option, with exposed brick walls, roll-top tubs, and hugely comfortable beds. Expect to pay £200 to £300 for a double room. If you'd like to spend a night in a haunted inn, The **Black Swan,** Peasholme Green (✆ **01904/686-911;** www.blackswanyork.com), is in a 16th-century building with comfortable guestrooms (doubles £110) filled with antiques, and a good dinner menu downstairs.

## Nearby

Fifteen miles (24km) east of York, **Castle Howard ★★ (✆ 01653/648-333;** www.castlehoward.co.uk) is the largest house in Yorkshire and has been the home of the Howard family since the 17th century. The facade showcases elegant architectural details, including statues, long arched windows, and a beautiful cupola crowning the center of the house. The marble entrance hall, lit by the dome, is particularly impressive, as is the Long Gallery, but the house has many superb rooms, all filled with fine furniture, statues, and china. The collection of paintings includes works by Rubens, Tintoretto, Van Dyck, Canaletto, and Reynolds, as well as a famous portrait of Henry VIII by Hans Holbein. There's a tea shop overlooked by strutting peacocks, and a playground for kids. To reach Castle Howard by train from York, take the local Scarborough line to Malton and then a taxi. If you're driving, take the A64 north from York. Castle Howard is open late March through October and late November to mid-December daily from 11am to 4pm (the grounds open at 10am). Admission is £13 for adults, £11 seniors and students, and £7.50 for children 5 to 16 (under-5s are admitted free).

apparently haunted, with excellent food and local ale on tap. Light lunches of sandwiches, scampi, or salads are priced from £5.95 to £6.75. If you stay in town for dinner, the **Blue Bicycle ★★**, 34 Fossgate (**✆ 01904/673-990;** www.thebluebicycle.com), is an elegant restaurant set inside a former 19th-century brothel. The seasonal menu often has exceptional seafood and beef dishes and makes good use of locally sourced produce, with main lunch courses priced from £4.50 to £8.50.

# 9

# PLANNING YOUR DAY TRIP

The range of day-trip options out of London is considerable, and sorting out the places you want to go and the logistics of traveling to them takes both planning and patience. Each chapter of this book has information about how to get to each destination, and so here we concentrate on general useful information about traveling around, and provide a few tips that might help you save some money. To help you focus on day trips that will appeal most to you, we also include a chart listing various attractions and the activities available at each destination (see "Day Trips at a Glance").

---

Once you've chosen some trips you think you'd like to make, have a read through the relevant chapters and do some homework. Pay special attention to how long it takes to reach the various destinations and our advice on the minimum time to allot to a place; some spots can easily be tackled as half-day excursions, whereas others need a whole day.

In each of our themed chapters, we also give you specific information to help you get to your chosen destination by train, bus, or car. In this chapter, you can find more general information about each of these transportation options, as well as info on how to get around London and reach the various departure stations. Don't feel daunted by the many options available to you as a day-tripper from London: When you start planning, you'll discover that one of the great pleasures of being in the capital is the ease with which you can get out of town!

# WHEN TO GO: DAY TRIPS FOR ALL SEASONS

## Spring

English gardens are at their peak in late spring. This is the time to enjoy the amazing garden "rooms" at **Sissinghurst Castle Garden** as well as the gardens at **Hever** and **Leeds** castles.

It's also a good time to go to places that tend to be overcrowded in the height of summer—**Salisbury** and **Stonehenge, Windsor,** and **Stratford-upon-Avon,** for example.

## Summer

All of England seems to move outdoors in summer, and picnics are perfect for a warm day on the grounds of great houses such as **Knole, Monk's House** and **Sandringham,** and **Leeds Castle.** The decent weather also enables you to get the most out of a visit to **Rye, Lewes,** and **Leigh on Sea,** and other places

FACING PAGE: **White cliffs coastal path, Dover.**

## Day Trips at a Glance

| | Biking | Boating/River Excursions | Country Walks | Castle or Palace | Church or Cathedral | Historical/Archaeological Sites | Gardens | Charming Town or Village | Families | Literary Sites | Museums | See page |
|---|---|---|---|---|---|---|---|---|---|---|---|---|
| Bath | ✓ | ✓ | | | ✓ | ✓ | ✓ | ✓ | ✓ | ✓ | ✓ | p. 124 |
| Bradford on Avon | ✓ | ✓ | ✓ | | ✓ | ✓ | | ✓ | | | | p. 17 |
| Brighton | | | | ✓ | | ✓ | | ✓ | ✓ | | ✓ | p. 154 |
| Broadstairs | ✓ | | | | | | | | ✓ | ✓ | ✓ | p. 172 |
| Cambridge | ✓ | ✓ | | | ✓ | ✓ | | | ✓ | | ✓ | p. 132 |
| Canterbury | ✓ | ✓ | | | ✓ | ✓ | | | ✓ | ✓ | ✓ | p. 51 |
| Chichester | ✓ | | ✓ | | ✓ | ✓ | | ✓ | | | ✓ | p. 58 |
| Dover Castle | | | ✓ | ✓ | | ✓ | | | ✓ | | | p. 99 |
| East Bergholt | ✓ | | ✓ | | ✓ | | ✓ | | ✓ | | ✓ | p. 23 |
| Hampton Court | | ✓ | ✓ | ✓ | | ✓ | ✓ | | ✓ | | ✓ | p. 80 |
| Hever Castle | | | ✓ | ✓ | | ✓ | ✓ | ✓ | ✓ | | | p. 105 |
| Knole | | | ✓ | ✓ | | | ✓ | | ✓ | | | p. 86 |
| Lavenham | ✓ | | ✓ | | ✓ | | | ✓ | | | ✓ | p. 27 |
| Leeds Castle | | | | ✓ | | | ✓ | | ✓ | | | p. 111 |
| Leigh-on-Sea | | ✓ | | | ✓ | | | ✓ | | | ✓ | p. 161 |
| Lewes | ✓ | | ✓ | ✓ | | ✓ | | ✓ | | ✓ | ✓ | p. 31 |
| Norwich | | | ✓ | | ✓ | ✓ | ✓ | | | | ✓ | p. 181 |
| Oxford | ✓ | ✓ | ✓ | | | | ✓ | | ✓ | ✓ | ✓ | p. 139 |
| Portsmouth & Southsea | | | | ✓ | | ✓ | | | ✓ | ✓ | ✓ | p. 165 |
| Rye | ✓ | | ✓ | | ✓ | ✓ | | ✓ | | ✓ | | p. 36 |
| Salisbury & Stonehenge | | | ✓ | | ✓ | ✓ | | | ✓ | | ✓ | p. 63 |
| Sandringham Palace | | | ✓ | ✓ | | | ✓ | | | | | p. 90 |
| Sissinghurst Castle Garden | | | | ✓ | | | ✓ | | | ✓ | | p. 94 |
| Stratford-upon-Avon | | ✓ | ✓ | ✓ | | ✓ | ✓ | | | ✓ | ✓ | p. 188 |
| Tunbridge Wells | | | | | ✓ | | ✓ | ✓ | ✓ | | ✓ | p. 147 |
| Whitstable | ✓ | | | ✓ | | | | ✓ | | | | p. 172 |
| Winchester | | | ✓ | | ✓ | ✓ | | ✓ | | | ✓ | p. 72 |
| Windsor & Eton | ✓ | ✓ | ✓ | ✓ | | ✓ | ✓ | | ✓ | | | p. 116 |
| Woodbridge | ✓ | ✓ | ✓ | | ✓ | ✓ | | ✓ | | | ✓ | p. 43 |
| York | | ✓ | ✓ | | ✓ | ✓ | | | ✓ | | ✓ | p. 196 |

where you'll spend a good portion of your time out-of-doors. Many destinations, **Brighton** and **Broadstairs** among them, host lively summer festivals, with the backdrop of a seaside resort.

You can also include a long walk and other outdoor activities on your day-trip schedules—walk along the White Cliffs after visiting **Dover Castle,** punt along the River Cam in **Cambridge,** or bicycle along the canal in **Bradford-upon-Avon.**

## Autumn

The parks and gardens at great houses such as **Knole, Hever Castle, Leeds Castle,** and **Windsor** are alluring at this time of year, when the air is crisp and forested hillsides are a carpet of color. As in spring, crowds thin out in busier places, making it easier to enjoy such popular spots as **Bath, Canterbury, Stratford-upon-Avon,** and **York.**

## Winter

English towns are especially welcoming in the winter. With cobbled lanes and cozy inns, **Rye** and **Lewes** are both appealing places to spend a winter's day. **York** is a most Christmassy city as well, with its historic shopfronts all aglow—and the country town of Woodbridge holds a festive market at the start of the month which takes over the main high street, with homemade gifts and food stalls.

At this time of year, you'll want to go someplace with plenty of indoor activities to get you out of the winter chill—the museums and chapels of **Cambridge** and **Oxford** are good examples, as are castles that give you the run of the place, such as **Hampton Court** and **Dover.**

## Calendar of Events

If your visit to London coincides with one of the following events in our day-trip destinations, you may well want to go out of your way to take part in the festivities. For more about events throughout England, go to www.visitbritain.com.

### FEBRUARY

**Jorvik Festival, York.** Two weeks from mid- to late-February, Vikings re-take the city, with costumed parades, mock battles, storytelling, song fests, food fairs, and more. For more information, contact ✆ **01904/643-211** or jorvik@yorkarchaeology.co.uk. See **York,** p. 196.

### MARCH

**Bath Literature Festival, Bath.** In early March some of the world's most acclaimed authors are on hand for readings and discussions of their works (✆ **01225/463-231;** www.bathfestivals.org.uk). See **Bath,** p. 124.

### APRIL

**The Shakespeare Season, Stratford-upon-Avon.** The Royal Shakespeare Company (RSC) opens its season in April, which then runs through to October, presenting works by the Bard on the stages of the Swan Theatre, Royal Shakespeare Theatre, and Courtyard Theatre. Contact the **RSC** (✆ **01789/403-444;** www.rsc.org.uk) for information and schedules. See **Stratford-upon-Avon,** p. 188.

**St. George's Day, Salisbury.** A traditional medieval celebration of the city's patron saint with mummers, juggling, acrobats, and fireworks (✆ **01722/334-956;** www.visitwiltshire.co.uk/salisbury). See **Salisbury,** p. 63.

### MAY

**Brighton Festival.** During May, the largest performing arts festival in Britain stages more than 400 events, bringing theater, dance, classical music, opera, film, and other programs to venues around the city (✆ **01273/709-709;** www.brightonfestival.org). See **Brighton,** p. 154.

**Glyndebourne Festival, Lewes.** May through August, this acclaimed opera festival stages six productions, attracting international voices and legions of ardent fans to a stunning hall (✆ **01273/813-813;** www.glyndebourne.com). See **Lewes,** p. 31.

**Bath International Music Festival.** During May and early June classical musicians from around the world perform in theaters and churches throughout this elegant and historic city (✆ **01225/462-231;** www.bathmusicfest.org.uk). See **Bath,** p. 124.

**Leigh-on-Sea Art Trail.** Each June, the many artists in this seaside town open their studios to visitors, galleries hold open nights, and music fills the streets (www.leigharttrail.co.uk). See **Leigh-on-Sea,** p. 161.

**Salisbury International Arts Festival.** From late May to early June, classical music, theater, jazz, films, and other events enliven the city for two weeks (✆ **01722/332-977;** www.salisburyfestival.co.uk). See **Salisbury,** p. 63.

## JUNE

**Dickens Festival, Broadstairs.** Every June, fans descend upon this traditional seaside town dressed in Victoriana (✆ **01843/861-827;** www.broadstairsdickensfestival.co.uk). See **Broadstairs,** p. 172.

**Chichester Arts Festival.** Over June and early July, events covering theater and the arts take center-stage in the city (✆ **01243/795-718;** www.chifest.org.uk). See **Chichester,** p. 58.

## JULY

**Hampton Court Flower Show.** The world's largest horticultural show features magnificent floral displays and show gardens. For information, contact the **Royal Horticultural Society** (✆ **0870/9063-791;** www.rhs.org.uk). See **Hampton Court Palace,** p. 80.

**Winchester Festival.** Choral concerts in the city's famous cathedral, plays at the Theatre Royal, and other musical and theatrical events are on tap the first two weeks of the month (✆ **01962/877-977;** www.musicatwinchester.co.uk). See **Winchester,** p. 72.

**Southern Cathedrals Festival, Chichester, Salisbury, and Winchester.** Held on alternating years, in the second part of July, choirs from the cathedrals of these three cities gather for concerts, candlelight recitals, and other events; the site alternates between the three cities. For an up-to-date schedule and festival information, call ✆ **01722/555-125** or check www.southerncathedralsfestival.org.uk. See **Chichester,** p. 58, **Salisbury,** p. 63, and **Winchester,** p. 72.

**Cambridge Folk Festival.** One of Europe's largest and most acclaimed celebrations of folk music brings together performers from around the world (✆ **01223/357-851;** www.cambridgefolkfestival.co.uk). See **Cambridge,** p. 132.

**Cambridge Shakespeare Festival.** Spread over July and August, this festival celebrating the bard includes open-air Shakespeare performances in the grounds of several colleges (✆ **07955/218-824;** www.cambridgeshakespeare.com). See **Cambridge,** p. 132.

**Sandringham Flower Show.** Toward the end of July, garden-lovers descend on the queen's favorite house for this horticultural show (✆ **01485/545-400;** www.sandringhamflowershow.org.uk). See **Sandringham Palace,** p. 90.

## AUGUST

**Pride in Brighton and Hove.** Brighton and adjoining Hove are the settings for one of Europe's largest gay-pride celebrations, with a big parade and lively street parties (✆ **01273/775-939;** www.brightonpride.org). See **Brighton,** p. 154.

### SEPTEMBER

**Balloon Festival, Leeds Castle.** Scores of hot-air balloons lift off from the castle grounds and fill the skies over Kent. For information on this event, contact the castle (✆ **01622/871-117;** www.leeds-castle.com). See **Leeds Castle,** p. 111.

**Rye Arts Festival.** Every September the festival invigorates the town with a program of concerts, lectures, and performances (✆ **01797/224-442;** www.ryefestival.co.uk). See **Rye,** p. 36.

### NOVEMBER

**Guy Fawkes Night, Lewes, Rye, and elsewhere on November 5.** Commemorating the day in 1605 when Guy Fawkes tried to blow up Parliament in retaliation for anti-Catholic legislation, towns everywhere celebrate with fireworks and bonfires. Lewes has the best event, but Rye's is very good as well. Check online for scheduling and planned activities. See **Lewes,** p. 31, and **Rye,** p. 36.

**London to Brighton Veteran Car Run, Brighton.** On the first Sunday in November, Brighton is the finish line of a 50-mile (80-km) drive from London, and the streets fill with the vintage entries (✆ **01580/893-413;** www.vccofgb.co.uk/lontobri). See **Brighton,** p. 154.

**Portsmouth Christmas Festival.** With hundreds of people in Victorian costumes, music, gifts and crafts markets, food, and mulled wine, Christmas kicks off in the last week of November in Portsmouth (✆ **0239/283-9766;** www.christmasfestival.co.uk). See **Portsmouth,** p. 165.

### DECEMBER

**Christmas Concert, Oxford.** Christ Church Cathedral is the setting for a concert, in which the Cathedral Singers are joined by other choirs and soloists from around the world (✆ **01865/305-305;** www.cathedralsingers.org.uk). See **Oxford,** p. 139.

**Festival of Nine Lessons and Carols, Cambridge.** This Christmas Eve service is broadcast around the world, and features the voices of the King's Chapel Choir (✆ **01223/331-313;** www.kings.cam.ac.uk). See **Cambridge,** p. 132.

**Ice-Skating at Hampton Court.** From the beginning of December through mid-January, you can skate on the banks of the Thames in the shadow of Henry VIII's palace (✆ **020/8241-9818;** www.hamptoncourtpalaceicerink.com). See **Hampton Court Palace,** p. 80.

## GETTING AROUND LONDON

Although this guidebook isn't about London, you may still be traveling across the city to get to a train or bus station for the start of your trip. For general London travel information, contact **Transport for London** (✆ **020/7222-1234;** www.tfl.gov.uk).

The first London word that any visitor needs to learn is "Oyster." The **Oyster Card** is a plastic smartcard that's your gateway to pretty much every form of London public transport, from the Underground (the "Tube") and the buses to surface rail networks. You can still pay to use all these services with cash, but an Oyster offers substantial savings on just about every journey (see "Saving with Travelcards & the Oyster" below for more information).

## The London Underground

Eleven Underground lines criss-cross the city and intersect at various stations where you can change trains. On Underground maps, every line is color-coded. All you need to know are the name of your stop, the Underground lines that go there, and the direction you're heading. After you figure out which line(s) to take, look on the Underground map for the name of the last stop in the direction you need to go. The name of that last stop on the line is marked on the front of the train and often on electronic signboards that display the name of the arriving train and when it's expected to arrive.

### THE VALUE OF THE BRITISH POUND VERSUS OTHER POPULAR CURRENCIES

| UK£ | US$ | Can$ | Euro (€) | Aus$ | NZ$ |
|---|---|---|---|---|---|
| £1 | $1.65 | C$1.60 | €1.10 | A$1.55 | NZ$2.00 |

The Underground system operates with automated entry and exit gates. You feed your ticket into the slot, the ticket disappears and pops up again, the gate bangs open, and you remove your ticket and pass through. Or, you touch your Oyster card (see "Saving with Travelcards & the Oyster" below) to panels at the entry and exit gates. At the other end of your journey, you do the same to get out. If you're using a ticket, the machine keeps the ticket (unless your ticket is good for more than one trip, in which case it's returned).

Underground service stops around midnight (a little earlier on less-used lines); keep that in mind if you plan on arriving back in London on a late train.

You'll also encounter many service disruptions and temporary closures, especially on weekends, as major improvements are fairly constantly underway on Underground lines.

### BUYING UNDERGROUND TICKETS

You can purchase Underground tickets at the ticket window in the station or from one of the automated machines found in most stations. (Machines can change £5, £10, and £20 notes, and some take credit and debit cards.) Tickets are valid for use on the day of issue only.

#### Money in England

Britain's decimal monetary system is based on the pound (£), which is made up of 100 pence (written as "p"). At press time, the exchange rate was £1 = US$1.65 (or US$1 = 60p), though fluctuations are constant. Currency-exchange services can be found in railway stations, at most post offices, and in many tourist information centers. Note, however, that you'll almost always get the best exchange rate by withdrawing funds from an ATM (automated teller machine) or using a debit card, although both of those can result in additional charges. It is best to avoid carrying large amounts of cash when traveling.

For fare purposes, the city is divided into six zones. **Zone 1** covers all of central London. **Zone 6** extends as far as Heathrow to the west and Upminster to the east. Make sure your ticket covers all the zones you're traveling through, or you may have to pay a £20 penalty fare.

At press time, a **one-way ticket** within one zone cost a whopping £4. Yes, that's exorbitant and no, you don't have to pay it every time you hop on the Underground. Instead, buy a multiuse Travelcard or Oyster card and save a bundle.

## SAVING WITH TRAVELCARDS & THE OYSTER

Paying a full-price one-way fare every time you use the Underground is needlessly costly. To save money, consider buying a Travelcard, which allows unlimited travel by Underground and bus, or an **Oyster card,** about the size of a credit card and easy to use—you just preload it with a set amount of money (usually £20) and swipe it over an electronic pad when entering and leaving the Underground or a bus. Both of these options result in you paying significantly less for each journey than if you buy a ticket every time you travel.

You can purchase **Travelcards** at any Underground station ticket window, or from vending machines that take credit cards. At press time, the following Travelcards are available:

- A 1-Day Travelcard for **Zones 1** and **2** (everything in central London) costs £8 for an adult and £4 for children 5 to 15. A card valid only during **off-peak** hours (after 9:30am Mon–Fri, all day Sat–Sun, and public holidays) costs £6.60 for adults, £3 for children.
- A 1-Day Travelcard for **all zones** costs £15 for adults and £7.50 for children. The **off-peak** versions cost £8 for adults and £3 for children.
- The 7-Day Travelcard for **Zones 1** and **2,** which is issued as an Oyster, is valid at all times and costs £27.60 for adults and £13.80 for children.
- A 7-day Travelcard for travel in **all zones,** also issued in Oyster form, is £50.40 for adults and £25.20 for children.

An Oyster card automatically gives you substantial discounts every time you travel. The cost of a trip in central London on the Underground, for instance, drops from £4 to £1.90, and a bus fare from £2.50 to £1.20. In addition to providing substantial discounts for each trip, the price for a day's worth of travel is capped—you never pay more than £8 for a day's worth of travel around central London, no matter how many trips you make in that day. You can purchase an Oyster at Underground stations and other outlets. The **Visitor Oyster,** issued only to international visitors, comes preloaded with £10, £20, £30, £40, or £50. Aside from being able to purchase the Visitor Oyster before you leave home, there aren't really many advantages over the regular Oyster. Plus, the system for purchasing a Visitor Oyster is fairly convoluted, and the cards are available only at such diverse and limited outlets as the Gatwick Express train office, National Express bus stations, on board Eurostar trains, and from Visit Britain offices overseas. The card costs £2, and so a card with a £10 balance costs £12. You can add credit to the cards at any Underground station.

### Using Your All-Zone Travelcard for Day Trips

We've discovered that, with some careful planning, it's often cheaper to buy an All-Zone Travelcard and pay supplemental rail fares to day-trip destinations than to buy a multiday BritRail pass. Show your All-Zone Travelcard at the ticket window of a London train station and tell the clerk you want to pay the "supplemental fare" to your destination. This way, your fare doesn't begin until you reach the end of Zone 6. You can often get to places such as Knole, Hever Castle, Windsor, Dover, Lewes, and Brighton for less than £15 round-trip this way, and the costs of some longer-distance day trips may also be reduced.

# DAY-TRIPPING BY TRAIN & BUS

## Tripping by Train

When all goes well, traveling by train is fun and convenient. In cities outside of London, the train stations are never more than a few minutes' walk or a short bus ride from the town center. Although all our information, including fares, was correct at press time, train information and fares change often and so check before you travel:

- Always **call National Rail Enquiries** (✆ **08457/484-950**) the night before your train trip to verify departure times and departure stations. Ask about any possible interruptions in service and how to avoid delays. For example, track work might delay trains to Dover from Victoria, though trains from Charing Cross might be running on time.
- Whenever possible, **choose a direct train** over one that requires a change along the way. In some cases, trains can get you to the same destination from more than one London station, but trains from one station may be much faster. It's always wise to ask National Rail Enquiries or ticket agents at the railway stations for the quickest and most direct routes.
- **Arrive at the station several minutes early**—at least 30 minutes early if you need to buy a ticket or have your BritRail pass (see "Using BritRail Passes" below) validated.
- At the station, the departures board will tell you when your train is leaving and from what track or platform. Each track has an electronic sign listing the train's destination—double-check these signs before boarding the train to make sure it's the right one.
- On some lines, Sunday is now one of the worst days to travel because there are fewer trains and they tend to be slow. Repair work is often undertaken on Sunday, sometimes causing long delays or requiring you to complete part of your journey on a bus on some occasions.

### TRAIN TYPES

Privately owned train companies run the train lines in England. The sleek, high-speed, long-distance trains are the most dependable and comfortable. These fast trains now go to York, Stratford-upon-Avon, and Bath. For shorter trips, such as to Brighton, Oxford, Leigh-on-Sea, and Cambridge, you often take regional **commuter trains.** In some cases you may need to transfer to an even smaller **local train** to reach your destination.

Smoking isn't permitted on trains or anywhere in any train station.

## SCHEDULING YOUR DAY TRIP

For the most current train schedules and fares, call **National Rail Enquiries** at ✆ **08457/484-950** in the United Kingdom. You can also find timetable information and fare schedules online at **www.nationalrail.co.uk**.

You can purchase tickets on this site, and with most day trips it's a good idea to buy well in advance—for destinations such as York, Stratford-upon-Avon, and Bath, tickets are cheaper if purchased a few weeks, or even just days, before you travel.

## BUYING YOUR TRAIN TICKET

You can buy your ticket online in advance or on the day of travel. If you buy in advance, you have the option to choose "collection," which means you collect your tickets from a machine at the station or at the ticket desk any time before your journey. You need to bring with you the credit card you used to purchase the ticket.

If you have a BritRail pass (see "Using BritRail Passes," below), you must have it validated at a ticket window before your first journey. After that, you don't have to bother with buying tickets; just board the train. At the platform barrier, you sometimes have to feed your ticket through a turnstile or show your BritRail pass in order to enter.

In England, a one-way train ticket is called a **"single,"** and a round-trip ticket is a **"return."** If you go on a day trip and are coming back the same day, ask for a **day return.** After 9:30am you can often, but not always, get a discounted ticket called a **cheap day return.** When purchasing your tickets, be sure to ask if any time restrictions might affect your plans.

When you buy your ticket, you must choose between **first** and **standard (second) class.** First-class tickets cost about one-third more than standard class. The first-class cars have roomier seats, but you can travel quite comfortably in standard class, and some commuter trains have no first-class cars. If you want a first-class ticket, you must request one—otherwise the agent will assume you want a standard-class ticket.

First-class service on some long-distance train routes includes free coffee, tea, beverages, and snacks, plus a free newspaper. Standard-class passengers can buy sandwiches and drinks in a cafe car. On some lines, an employee comes through with a food and beverage trolley.

## USING BRITRAIL PASSES

If you're from outside the UK and you plan to travel around England extensively by train, consider purchasing a BritRail pass. These must be purchased before you arrive in England. BritRail passes are convenient because you don't have to stand in line to buy train tickets; if a train is in the station, you can just hop on. BritRail passes can be ordered through a travel agent or by contacting **BritRail** (✆ **866/BRIT-RAIL** [274-8724]; www.britrail.com). The BritRail passes most pertinent to day-trippers are:

**BRITRAIL LONDON PLUS PASS** This pass is good for 2, 4, and 7 days of travel and covers a large area around London. It gets you to Bath, Brighton, Cambridge, Canterbury, Dover, Oxford, Salisbury, Stratford-upon-Avon, Winchester, and everywhere in between—so, it will get you to many of the day trips in this book. Whether or not it's a cost saver depends on how many trips you plan to make.

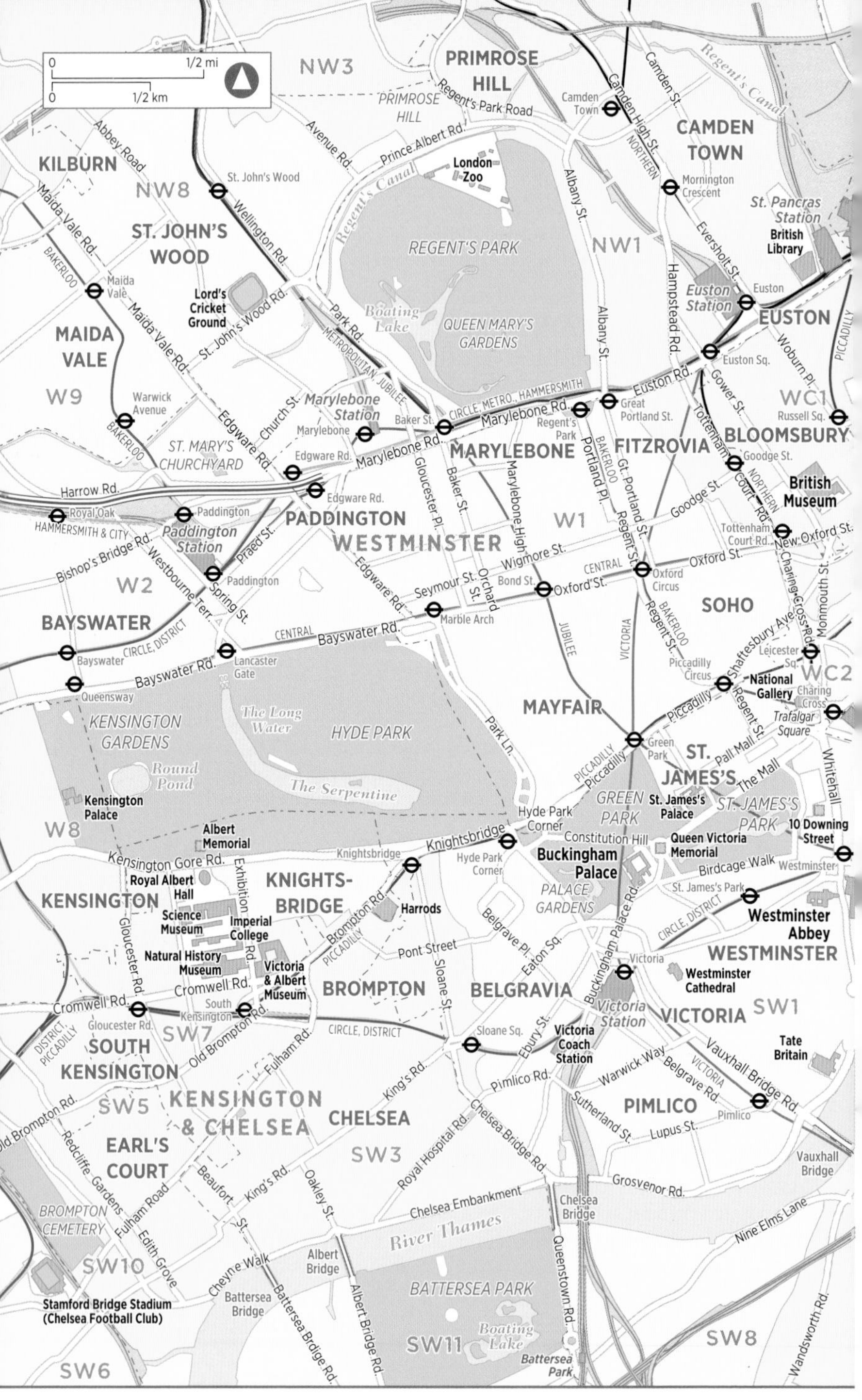

0
1/2 mi
0
1/2 km
NW3
PRIMROSE HILL
PRIMROSE HILL
Regent's Park Road
Camden Town
Camden High St.
NORTHERN
Camden St.
Regent's Canal
CAMDEN TOWN
Avenue Rd.
Prince Albert Rd.
London Zoo
Regent's Canal
Albany St.
Mornington Crescent
KILBURN
Abbey Road
NW8
St. John's Wood
Wellington Rd.
ST. JOHN'S WOOD
REGENT'S PARK
NW1
St. Pancras Station
British Library
Eversholt St.
Maida Vale Rd.
BAKERLOO
Maida Vale
Lord's Cricket Ground
St. John's Wood Rd.
Park Rd.
METROPOLITAN, JUBILEE
Boating Lake
QUEEN MARY'S GARDENS
Albany St.
Hampstead Rd.
Euston Station
Euston
EUSTON
MAIDA VALE
Maida Vale Rd.
Euston Sq.
Woburn Pl.
PICCADILLY
W9
Warwick Avenue
Church St.
Marylebone Station
CIRCLE, METRO., HAMMERSMITH
Euston Rd.
Great Portland St.
Gower St.
WC1
Russell Sq.
BAKERLOO
ST. MARY'S CHURCHYARD
Edgware Rd.
Marylebone
Baker St.
Marylebone Rd.
Regent's Park
Tottenham Court Rd.
BLOOMSBURY
Goodge St.
Edgware Rd.
Marylebone Rd.
MARYLEBONE
FITZROVIA
Portland Pl.
BAKERLOO
Harrow Rd.
Edgware Rd.
Gloucester Pl.
Baker St.
Marylebone High St.
Gt. Portland St.
NORTHERN
British Museum
Royal Oak
HAMMERSMITH & CITY
Paddington
Paddington Station
PADDINGTON
WESTMINSTER
W1
Regent St.
Goodge St.
Tottenham Court Rd.
New Oxford St.
Bishop's Bridge Rd.
Westbourne Terr.
Praed St.
Wigmore St.
CENTRAL
Oxford St.
Charing Cross Rd.
Monmouth St.
Paddington
Seymour St.
Orchard St.
Bond St.
Oxford Circus
W2
Spring St.
Edgware Rd.
Oxford St.
Marble Arch
SOHO
BAYSWATER
CIRCLE, DISTRICT
CENTRAL
Bayswater Rd.
JUBILEE
VICTORIA
Regent St.
BAKERLOO
Shaftesbury Ave.
Bayswater
Lancaster Gate
Piccadilly Circus
Leicester Sq.
Bayswater Rd.
WC2
Queensway
National Gallery
Charing Cross
KENSINGTON GARDENS
The Long Water
HYDE PARK
MAYFAIR
Piccadilly
Regent St.
Trafalgar Square
Park Ln.
Green Park
ST. JAMES'S
Pall Mall
Round Pond
The Serpentine
PICCADILLY
Piccadilly
The Mall
Whitehall
Kensington Palace
GREEN PARK
St. James's Palace
ST. JAMES'S PARK
W8
Hyde Park Corner
10 Downing Street
Albert Memorial
Constitution Hill
Queen Victoria Memorial
Knightsbridge
Kensington Gore Rd.
Knightsbridge
Hyde Park Corner
Buckingham Palace
Birdcage Walk
Westminster
Royal Albert Hall
Exhibition Rd.
KNIGHTS-BRIDGE
PALACE GARDENS
St. James's Park
KENSINGTON
Brompton Rd.
Harrods
Belgrave Pl.
Buckingham Palace Rd.
CIRCLE, DISTRICT
Westminster Abbey
Science Museum
Imperial College
Gloucester Rd.
PICCADILLY
Pont Street
Eaton Sq.
WESTMINSTER
Natural History Museum
Victoria & Albert Museum
Sloane St.
Victoria
Westminster Cathedral
Cromwell Rd.
BROMPTON
BELGRAVIA
Cromwell Rd.
South Kensington
Gloucester Rd.
Old Brompton Rd.
Victoria Station
VICTORIA
SW1
DISTRICT, PICCADILLY
SW7
CIRCLE, DISTRICT
Fulham Rd.
Sloane Sq.
Ebury St.
Victoria Coach Station
Vauxhall Bridge Rd.
SOUTH KENSINGTON
Tate Britain
King's Rd.
Pimlico Rd.
Warwick Way
Belgrave Rd.
VICTORIA
Old Brompton Rd.
SW5
KENSINGTON & CHELSEA
CHELSEA
Chelsea Bridge Rd.
Sutherland St.
PIMLICO
Pimlico
Redcliffe Gardens
EARL'S COURT
Royal Hospital Rd.
Lupus St.
SW3
Vauxhall Bridge
Beaufort St.
King's Rd.
Oakley St.
Grosvenor Rd.
Fulham Road
Chelsea Embankment
Chelsea Bridge
BROMPTON CEMETERY
Edith Grove
River Thames
Nine Elms Lane
Cheyne Walk
Albert Bridge
Queenstown Rd.
SW10
BATTERSEA PARK
Battersea Bridge
Battersea Bridge Rd.
Albert Bridge Rd.
Wandsworth Rd.
Stamford Bridge Stadium (Chelsea Football Club)
SW11
Boating Lake
SW8
Battersea Park
SW6

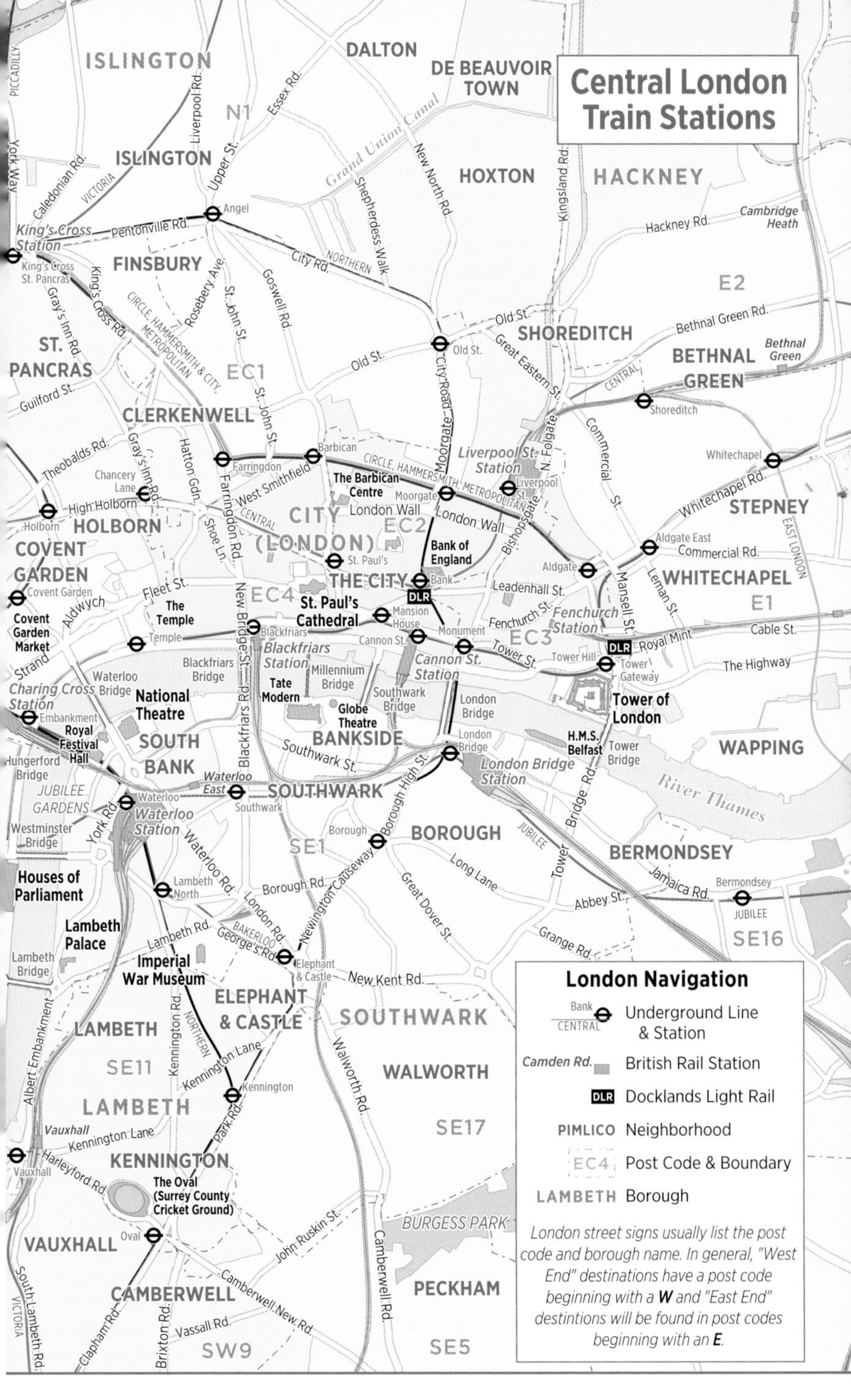

Central London Train Stations
ISLINGTON
DALTON
DE BEAUVOIR TOWN
N1
HOXTON
HACKNEY
FINSBURY
E2
SHOREDITCH
BETHNAL GREEN
ST. PANCRAS
EC1
CLERKENWELL
King's Cross Station
King's Cross St. Pancras
Angel
Old St.
Shoreditch
Whitechapel
Bethnal Green
Cambridge Heath
Barbican
Farringdon
Chancery Lane
Moorgate
Liverpool St. Station
Liverpool St.
Holborn
HOLBORN
CITY (LONDON)
EC2
STEPNEY
COVENT GARDEN
Covent Garden
Covent Garden Market
St. Paul's
THE CITY
Bank of England
Bank
DLR
Aldgate
Aldgate East
WHITECHAPEL
E1
EC4
The Temple
St. Paul's Cathedral
Mansion House
Blackfriars
Temple
Cannon St.
Monument
EC3
Fenchurch Station
Royal Mint
Tower Hill
Tower Gateway
Blackfriars Station
Cannon St. Station
Charing Cross Station
Embankment
Waterloo Bridge
Blackfriars Bridge
Millennium Bridge
Tate Modern
Southwark Bridge
London Bridge
Tower of London
National Theatre
Globe Theatre
Royal Festival Hall
SOUTH BANK
BANKSIDE
H.M.S. Belfast
Tower Bridge
WAPPING
Hungerford Bridge
Waterloo East
SOUTHWARK
London Bridge Station
JUBILEE GARDENS
Waterloo
Waterloo Station
Southwark
River Thames
Westminster Bridge
Borough
SE1
BOROUGH
BERMONDSEY
Houses of Parliament
Lambeth North
Bermondsey
Lambeth Palace
SE16
Lambeth Bridge
Imperial War Museum
Elephant & Castle
ELEPHANT & CASTLE
SOUTHWARK
LAMBETH
SE11
Kennington
WALWORTH
LAMBETH
SE17
Vauxhall
KENNINGTON
The Oval (Surrey County Cricket Ground)
BURGESS PARK
VAUXHALL
Oval
CAMBERWELL
PECKHAM
SW9
SE5
Pentonville Rd.
City Rd.
Goswell Rd.
Old St.
Great Eastern St.
Bethnal Green Rd.
Hackney Rd.
Kingsland Rd.
New North Rd.
Shepherdess Walk
Grand Union Canal
Essex Rd.
Upper St.
Liverpool Rd.
Caledonian Rd.
York Way
Gray's Inn Rd.
King's Cross Rd.
Rosebery Ave.
St. John St.
Guilford St.
Theobalds Rd.
High Holborn
Hatton Gdn.
Farringdon Rd.
West Smithfield
Shoe Ln.
New Bridge St.
London Wall
Moorgate
City Road
Commercial St.
N. Folgate
Bishopsgate
Whitechapel Rd.
Commercial Rd.
Leman St.
Mansell St.
Leadenhall St.
Fenchurch St.
Tower St.
Cable St.
The Highway
Fleet St.
Aldwych
Strand
Blackfriars Rd.
Southwark St.
Borough High St.
Tower Bridge Rd.
Long Lane
Great Dover St.
Jamaica Rd.
Abbey St.
Grange Rd.
York Rd.
Waterloo Rd.
Borough Rd.
Newington Causeway
London Rd.
St. George's Rd.
Lambeth Rd.
New Kent Rd.
Kennington Rd.
Kennington Lane
Albert Embankment
Walworth Rd.
Park Rd.
Harleyford Rd.
John Ruskin St.
Camberwell New Rd.
Camberwell Rd.
South Lambeth Rd.
Clapham Rd.
Brixton Rd.
Vassall Rd.
PICCADILLY
VICTORIA
NORTHERN
CIRCLE, HAMMERSMITH & CITY, METROPOLITAN
CENTRAL
JUBILEE
BAKERLOO
EAST LONDON
London Navigation
Bank
CENTRAL
Underground Line & Station
Camden Rd.
British Rail Station
DLR
Docklands Light Rail
PIMLICO
Neighborhood
EC4
Post Code & Boundary
LAMBETH
Borough
London street signs usually list the post code and borough name. In general, "West End" destinations have a post code beginning with a W and "East End" destintions will be found in post codes beginning with an E.

**BRITRAIL FLEXIPASS** This pass allows you to travel any 3, 4, 8, or 15 days within a 2-month time period. Savings-wise, it makes sense only if every one of your day-trip destinations is to a place some distance from London, such as Stratford-upon-Avon, Bath, or York. The Flexipass allows you to visit Wales and Scotland, in addition to every place we list in this guide.

### LONDON'S TRAIN STATIONS

London has 11 major train stations, all served by the Underground. (Throughout this book, we always tell you which London train station serves the particular destination we're describing.) In every station, a large overhead display, usually near the platforms, lists the departing trains and platforms.

It's sometimes possible to use more than one station, and services may change depending on day of the week, track work, and other considerations. It's always a good idea to check with **National Rail Enquiries** (✆ **08457/484-950**) before setting off.

If you're day-tripping from London, you'll depart from one of the following stations (you can locate each station on the "Central London Train Stations" map on p. 216):

**LONDON BRIDGE STATION** Use this station for Hever.

**CHARING CROSS STATION** Trains from here travel southeast to Canterbury, Dover, Rye, Sevenoaks (for Knole), Staplehurst (for Sissinghurst), and Tunbridge Wells.

**FENCHURCH STREET STATION** For Leigh-on-Sea.

**KING'S CROSS STATION** Head here for trains to Cambridge, York, and Kings Lynn (for Sandringham).

**LIVERPOOL ST. STATION** Use this station in East London for East Bergholt and Dedham Vale, Ipswich (for Woodbridge), Norwich, and for Sudbury (for Lavenham).

**MARYLEBONE STATION** Use this small station for trains to Stratford-upon-Avon.

**PADDINGTON STATION** This station is for trains to Windsor, Bath, and Oxford.

**ST. PANCRAS STATION** Use this grand station near King's Cross for trains to Ashford (for Rye).

**VICTORIA STATION** Head here for trains traveling to the south and southeast of England, including Bearsted (for Leeds Castle), Brighton, Canterbury, Chichester, Lewes, Sevenoaks (for Knole), and Whitstable.

**WATERLOO STATION** Use this station for trains going to the south of England, including Hampton Court, Portsmouth and Southsea, Salisbury, Winchester, and Windsor.

## Tripping by Bus

The main, long-distance bus company is **National Express** (✆ **08717/818-178;** www.nationalexpress.com). Their comfortable buses are equipped with reclining seats and a toilet. Tickets usually cost around half of what the train fare costs but the journey often takes twice as long.

If you travel by bus from London, you'll depart from **Victoria bus station,** Buckingham Palace Road (✆ **020/7730-3466;** Underground: Victoria), two blocks from Victoria train station—signs point you to it. On your way back, the bus normally picks you up near each town's train station.

National Express offers several **Brit Xplorer passes** for unlimited travel on their extensive network, which covers all of England. A 7-day pass costs £79, a 14-day pass costs £139, and a 28-day pass costs £219.

# DAY-TRIPPING BY CAR

Although not impossible without a car, if you want to visit castles (including Leeds Castle, Hever and Sandringham) and smaller villages, such as those in Dedham Vale, you'll find it much easier if you have your own wheels—local bus service is sporadic and taxis can get pricey.

## Before You Rent a Car

If you're visiting England from another country, remember that you must drive on the left and pass on the right.

## Renting a Car

If you rent a car in London, bear in mind that if you drive in the center of the city you must pay a daily £8 "congestion charge," although the rental company will explain how they handle this. If you want a car to explore the countryside for just a day, it might be easiest to rent it at Heathrow or Gatwick airports so you don't have to navigate London's traffic.

Americans, Canadians, Australians, and New Zealanders renting a car in England need a valid driving license from their home country that they've had for at least 1 year. In most cases, depending on the agency, you must be at least 23 years old (21 in some instances, 25 in others).

## Rental Car Costs

Prices of cars in England are fairly reasonable—expect to pay £29 to £40 a day, including insurance, but you can get a better deal if you book in advance online.

## Insurance for Car Rentals

Standard insurance is usually included in the prices quoted on car rental company websites. The **Collision Damage Waiver (CDW),** which limits your liability for damages caused by a collision, is covered in many cases if you pay with a credit card. Check with your credit card company before you go so you can avoid paying this fee unnecessarily (it can be as much as US$15 per day).

## Car Rentals on the Internet

Here are a list of car rental agency websites:

- **Alamo** www.alamo.com
- **Auto Europe** www.autoeurope.com
- **Avis** www.avis.com
- **Budget** www.budget.com
- **Dollar** www.dollar.com
- **Enterprise** www.enterprise.com
- **Europcar** www.europcar.com
- **Hertz** www.hertz.com

- **Kemwel (KHA)** www.kenwel.com
- **National** www.nationalcar.com
- **Thrifty** www.thrifty.com

## Where to Rent a Car

***Note:*** For contact details on major car rental agencies operating in Britain, see p. 219.

You'll save yourself time, bother, and expense if you rent a car at one of London's two major airports, Heathrow or Gatwick. Both are connected to the city by excellent public transportation: You can reach Heathrow on the Underground or via the **Heathrow Express,** which makes the trip from Paddington Station in just 15 minutes. The **Gatwick Express** connects Victoria station with Gatwick Airport in 30 minutes. A regular train service runs from Gatwick to Victoria station about every 20 minutes and takes a bit longer, 44 minutes, but costs a bit less.

From both airports, you can easily get onto the M25, the ring road that encircles London; and from it you can reach the major roads out of the city.



## Motorways, Dual Carriageways & Roundabouts

The biggest roadways are called **motorways** (indicated as "M" plus a number on maps). A two-way road is a **single carriageway,** and a four-lane divided highway (two lanes in each direction) is a **dual carriageway.** Country roads, some of them paved-over tracks, are full of twists and turns and some are barely wide enough for two cars to pass.

One element of British roads that invariably throws non-native drivers is the **roundabout**—a traffic junction where several roads meet at one traffic circle. On a roundabout, the cars to your right (that is, those already on the roundabout) always have the right of way.

Reading a map and navigating all of this can be a bit difficult, but most rental companies will rent you a GPS to do the map-reading for you. This is highly recommended.

## Rules of the Road

- All distances and speed limits are shown on signs in miles and miles per hour (mph).
- Speed limits are usually:

  30 mph (48kmph) in towns

  40 mph (65kmph) on some town roads where posted

  60 mph (97kmph) on most single carriageway (two-way) roads

  70 mph (113kmph) on dual carriageways and motorways
- The law requires you to wear a seat belt. If you have children, ask the car rental agency about seat belts or car seats.
- You can pass other vehicles only on the right.
- Parking in the centers of some towns is hard to come by. Read all posted restrictions or park in a carpark.
- You must stop for pedestrians in crosswalks marked by striped lines (called **zebra crossings**) on the road. Pedestrians have the right of way.

## Emergencies on the Road

If you break down or have an accident and need help, your rental company will provide you with information about who to call for recovery. In a severe emergency, dial the police, fire, and ambulance services on ✆ **999.**

## Filling the Tank

**Petrol** (gasoline) stations are self-service. Prices vary wildly, but petrol is usually more expensive farther from large conurbations, and so it pays to fill up before you hit the road. You purchase petrol by the liter (3.78 liters equals 1 US gallon). Expect to pay about £1.35 per liter (around US$7 per gallon) for unleaded fuel.

# TRAVELING LOCALLY FROM YOUR DESTINATION

## Using Local Buses

In some day trips we list major attractions several miles outside of towns or cities. To reach these places—Jane Austen's House in Chawton, for instance, which is 17 miles (28km) from Winchester—your cheapest option if you don't have a car is to take a local bus. The local bus information we provide is current as this book is being written, but double-check times and services—either on the bus company websites or at the local tourist information office (in Winchester, for example, if you're going to Chawton). Local bus services are reliable, but timetables change frequently.

If your train station is a little way from the town center and you don't want to walk, there will almost always be a local bus that travels between the station and the center of town. Have some small change with you because drivers usually don't take bank notes.

## Taking a Taxi

If you don't mind paying a little extra, an alternative to grappling with local bus systems is to take a local taxi. Usually taxis wait outside train stations, but in some small towns you'll need to reserve one in advance. In the "Getting Around" section in every day trip, we provide the numbers for local taxi companies. The amount you pay obviously depends upon the length of the journey, but for journeys under 10 miles (16km), expect to pay £10 to £15.

## Escorted Tours

Maybe you only have time for a trip or two outside of London and don't want to bother with train schedules, admission hours, and other details. If so, traveling by tour bus is a good option. Prices usually include admission fees as well as pickup in central London and at some central London hotels:

- **Premium Tours** (✆ **0207/713-1311;** www.premiumtours.co.uk) offers day trips from London to Stonehenge, Leeds Castle, Canterbury, and Dover, among others. Prices start at £19.
- **Evan Evans Tours** (✆ **0207/950-1777;** www.evanevanstours.co.uk) offers similar trips, including to Stonehenge and Bath, Windsor Castle, Leeds Castle, and Canterbury. Prices start at £25.

## TRAVELER'S checklist

When setting out on a day trip, be sure you have:

- Your passport (and driving license if you're renting a car).
- A credit card other than those issued by American Express; many establishments outside London don't accept Amex.
- An extra set of camera batteries, and enough memory card space.
- AAA and AARP cards, student IDs, and other cards that might entitle you to discounted admissions.
- Called ahead or checked websites to verify the place you plan to visit will be open.
- Checked with National Rail Enquiries (or the bus company) to make sure there are no delays or cancellations.



- **First Festival Travel** (✆ **0208/896-6070;** www.firstfestivaltravel.com) offers similar trips, usually combining destinations—Windsor, Eton and Oxford, for example, or Stonehenge and Bath. Prices start at £40.
- **Great Expectations Tour Co.** (✆ **0870/225-5303;** www.welcome2britain.com) offers busy-day tours that pack a lot in—like Salisbury, Old Sarum, Stonehenge and Avebury for £85. These usually include a pub lunch and all entrance fees.
- **Best Value Tours** (✆ **0208/133-8378;** www.bestvaluetours.co.uk) offers unique tours such as a trip to Stonehenge that gets you past the ropes and up among the stones. This trip also includes time in Bath and nearby Lacock. Prices around £90.

# SAVING MONEY ON ADMISSIONS

If you plan to make several day trips and visit a number of historic properties, consider arming yourself with the **Great British Heritage Pass** (www.britishheritagepass.com). The pass gives you free entry to hundreds of National Trust and English Heritage properties, including many listed in this book. Included are Blenheim Palace, Dover Castle, Hampton Court, Hever Castle, Knole, the Roman Baths and Pump Room in Bath, Shakespeare's Birthplace in Avon, Sissinghurst Castle Garden, Stonehenge, and Windsor Castle.

A 3-day pass costs £39 and a 7-day pass £69.

Before you jump in and purchase the pass, check admission fees for the properties you might want to visit and do the math. Fees vary but usually run between £9 and £18 per property. If you plan to visit only one or two properties, the pass might not be for you. If, however, you plan to make several trips out of London and visit four or more properties, the pass could save you a bit of money.

# Index

## C

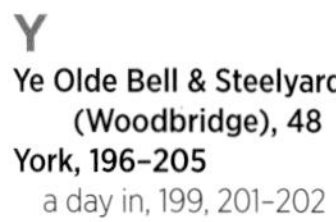

# PHOTO

Front cover, top: © Chris ottom: © World Pictures / Alamy Images.

Back cover: © Kumar Sriskandan / Alamy Images.

Title page: King's College Chapel, Cambridge © Andy Milne / Frommers.com Community.

Contents pages: South Foreland Lighthouse © Elizabeth Blanchet; Shrine of St. Thomas Becket, Canterbury Cathedral © Jenny Hardy.

Interior images

© Elizabeth Blanchet: p2, p6, p7, p8, p10, p11 right, p12, p13 right, p14-p22, p25-31, p34, p35, p39 left, p40 right, p41, p42, p43, p44 top right, p46, p79-85, p93, p100-104, p134, p135, p137, p142-151, p155-164 left, p169, p170-179, p191-196.

© Jenny Hardy: p1, p11 left, p38, p39, p40, p52, p98, p105-111, p206.

© Jill Emeny / Frommers: p44 bottom, p164 right, p165.

© katiepay / Frommers.com Community: p120.

© Naomi Kraus / Frommers.com Community: p121.

© neilbeer.com: p9, p23, p50, p60, p61, p62, p74, p76, p77, p123-131, p138, p153, p168, p169 top and bottom left, p180-188.

© Norman Emeny: p47, p48.

© NTPL / Andreas von Einsiedel: p89.

© NTPL / Rod Edwards: p97.

© Paul Harris: p54, p57, p67-71, p112-115.

© Sandringham Estate: p92.

© Tim Smith / Panos: p13 top, p199-205.